In Pictures and In Words

In Pictures and In Words

Teaching the Qualities of Good Writing Through Illustration Study

KATIE WOOD RAY

HEINEMANN
Portsmouth, NH

Heinemann
361 Hanover Street
Portsmouth, NH 03801–3912
www.heinemann.com

Offices and agents throughout the world

The author and publisher wish to thank those who have generously given permission to reprint borrowed material:

"Winter Dark" from *Mural on Second Avenue and Other City Poems* by Lilian Moore. Originally published in *I Thought I Heard the City* by Lilian Moore. Text copyright © 1971 by Lilian Moore. Illustrations copyright © 2004 by Roma Karas. Published by Candlewick Press, Somerville, MA. Reprinted by permission of the publisher.

Excerpt from *"Let's Get a Pup," Said Kate* by Bob Graham. Copyright © 2001 by Bob Graham. Reprinted by permission of Candlewick Press, Somerville, MA, on behalf of Walker Books Ltd., London.

Excerpt from *"The Trouble With Dogs . . ." Said Dad* by Bob Graham. Text and illustrations copyright © 2007 by Blackbird Design Pty Ltd. Reprinted by permission of Candlewick Press, Somerville, MA, on behalf of Walker Books Ltd., London.

Excerpt from *Up, Down, and Around* by Katherine Ayres. Text copyright © 2007 by Katherine Ayres. Illustrations copyright © 2007 by Nadine Bernard Westcott. Published by Candlewick Press, Somerville, MA. Reprinted by permission of the publisher.

Excerpt from *Full, Full, Full of Love* by Trish Cooke. Text copyright © 2003 by Trish Cooke. Illustrations copyright © 2003 by Paul Howard. Reprinted by permission of Candlewick Press, Somerville, MA, on behalf of Walker Books Ltd., London.

Library of Congress Cataloging-in-Publication Data
Ray, Katie Wood.
    In pictures and in words : teaching the qualities of good writing through illustration study / Katie Wood Ray.
        p.   cm.
    Includes bibliographical references.
    ISBN-13: 978-0-325-02855-2
    ISBN-10: 0-325-02855-9
    1. Children's literature—Authorship.   2. Illustration of books.   3. Illustrated children's books.   I. Title.
    PN147.5.R39 2010
    372.62'3—dc22   2010005847

Editor: Kate Montgomery
Production: Elizabeth Valway
Cover and interior designs: Lisa Fowler
Title on cover written by Kathryn Day
Composition: Cape Cod Compositors, Inc.
Manufacturing: Steve Bernier

Printed in the United States of America on acid-free paper
17 16   ML   5 6

For Lisa Cleaveland

Contents

Acknowledgments *xi*

SECTION ONE **Illustration Study as a Foundation for Strong Writing 1**

CHAPTER ONE *Why Illustration Study Matters to the Development of Young Writers 2*

CHAPTER TWO *Building Stamina for Writing by Supporting Children's Work as Illustrators 19*

CHAPTER THREE *Writing and Illustrating as Parallel Composing Processes 36*

CHAPTER FOUR *Teaching an Essential Habit of Mind: Reading Like Writers in the Context of Illustration Study 57*

CHAPTER FIVE *Learning Qualities of Good Writing from Illustration Techniques 67*

CHAPTER SIX *The Writing Workshop: Planning and Implementing a Unit of Study in Illustrations 77*

SECTION TWO **Fifty Illustration Techniques and the Qualities of Good Writing They Suggest: A Predictable Framework 89**

CHAPTER SEVEN *Ideas and Content, In Pictures and In Words 95*

TECHNIQUE 1 Crafting with distance perspective *99*

TECHNIQUE 2 Crafting with positioning perspective *102*

TECHNIQUE 3 Crafting the background *105*

TECHNIQUE 4 Showing two sides of a physical space *108*

TECHNIQUE 5 Using scenes to show different actions *110*

TECHNIQUE 6 Using scenes to capture the passage of time *113*

TECHNIQUE 7 Using scenes to show movement through different places *116*

TECHNIQUE 8 Using scenes as a list *119*

TECHNIQUE 9 Showing, not telling *121*

TECHNIQUE 10 Crafting a "backstory" *123*

TECHNIQUE 11 Manipulating point of view for effect *125*

TECHNIQUE 12 Seeing through the eyes of a narrator *128*

CHAPTER EIGHT   *Precision and Detail, In Pictures and In Words*   **131**

TECHNIQUE 13   Crafting details of expression and gesture   *137*

TECHNIQUE 14   Crafting physical details of characters   *140*

TECHNIQUE 15   Revealing character with background details   *143*

TECHNIQUE 16   Crafting details from the world of nature   *146*

TECHNIQUE 17   Showing the effects of weather on a scene   *149*

TECHNIQUE 18   Crafting details from the world of people   *152*

TECHNIQUE 19   Using authentic, object-specific details   *155*

TECHNIQUE 20   Creating the illusion of motion with detail   *157*

TECHNIQUE 21   Creating the illusion of sound with details   *160*

TECHNIQUE 22   Using details as an element of surprise   *163*

CHAPTER NINE   *Wholeness of Text, In Pictures and In Words*   **165**

TECHNIQUE 23   Keeping static details consistent   *170*

TECHNIQUE 24   Making seemingly insignificant details reappear   *173*

TECHNIQUE 25   Building meaning from one idea to the next   *176*

TECHNIQUE 26   Crafting an ending that returns to the lead   *179*

TECHNIQUE 27   Crafting artful repetition   *182*

TECHNIQUE 28   Crafting an ending that pulls multiple text elements together   *185*

TECHNIQUE 29   Repeating details of landscape   *187*

TECHNIQUE 30   Using details of light to show the passage of time   *190*

TECHNIQUE 31   Using details of weather to show the passage of time   *192*

CHAPTER TEN   *Tone, In Pictures and In Words*   **195**

TECHNIQUE 32   Crafting tone with color   *201*

TECHNIQUE 33   Shifting tone by shifting color   *204*

TECHNIQUE 34   Crafting tone with background color   *207*

TECHNIQUE 35   Crafting tone with size   *210*

TECHNIQUE 36   Crafting tone with physical space   *212*

TECHNIQUE 37   Crafting tone with shape and texture   *216*

TECHNIQUE 38   Accentuating or exaggerating features to impact tone   *220*

TECHNIQUE 39   Using whimsical detail to lighten the tone   *223*

CHAPTER ELEVEN *Layout and Design, In Pictures and In Words* *226*

TECHNIQUE 40   Designing the placement of words and pictures *231*

TECHNIQUE 41   Using word layout to convey meaning *233*

TECHNIQUE 42   Using size and color to convey meaning *235*

TECHNIQUE 43   Designing print to convey meaning *237*

TECHNIQUE 44   Designing a cover *239*

TECHNIQUE 45   Designing end pages to convey meaning *242*

TECHNIQUE 46   Using borders *244*

TECHNIQUE 47   Using the space implied outside a picture *246*

TECHNIQUE 48   Using visual elements in the white space around words and pictures *249*

TECHNIQUE 49   Using paper artifacts as visual elements *251*

TECHNIQUE 50   Using graphic features to show information *253*

Bibliography *255*

Picture Book Bibliography *259*

Acknowledgments

First, I'd like to thank Lisa Cleaveland, to whom this book is dedicated. For more than ten years now she has graciously welcomed me into her classroom and let me live and learn alongside her and her students. I would not be the teacher I am today if it weren't for the opportunity I have had to learn from this amazing teacher. I discovered the wonderful promise of illustration study in her classroom.

Matt Glover and Gaby Layden read drafts of this manuscript and gave me incredibly helpful feedback and encouragement along the way. Thank you Gaby, especially, for helping me get point-of-view and perspective straight. You are always so smart about words. Thank you Matt, especially, for sending me great stories of children and their illustration decisions, and for always telling me how helpful these ideas have been to your teaching.

Thank you to Sandra Hardee, artist *extraordinaire*, who has been thinking and sharing about the connections between art and writing for years. Sandra read portions of the illustration possibilities and helped me believe I was on the right track with them.

In the early stages of planning this book, I tried out the big ideas behind it with some teachers at Kamehameha School in Honolulu. Their enthusiasm was just what I needed to push me forward at the time. Thank you to them all: Kehau Akiona, Jackie Eppling, Chelsea Keehne, Joelle Lee, Anna Lee Lum, Loke Melchor, and Kathy Wurdeman.

Without a doubt, this book would not be the book it is if it weren't for my editor Kate Montgomery. In a long conversation on a snowy morning last winter, Kate helped me see so much more potential in my ideas than I would have ever seen on my own. I can't believe how much I have grown as a teacher and a writer simply from following Kate's suggestion to make the craft connections between illustrating and writing more clear. Every writer should be so lucky to have an editor as extraordinary as Kate.

While it is perhaps not customary to thank nonhumans in your acknowledgments, I would be remiss if I didn't at least mention how wonderful it has been to have the happy company (and sometimes happy chaos) of my four dogs around me as I write. So thank you Montana, Journey, Ivy, and Dallas Ray for making all this writing time so much less lonely.

My family, the Rays and the Woods, are such a source of encouragement and support, and I thank you for all you do that makes the work I love to do possible. And finally, once again, thank you to my husband Jim Ray. Eight books ago I thanked you for balancing everything out. Now I thank you for remaining so steady alongside me in this work and in this life.

SECTION ONE

Illustration Study as a Foundation for Strong Writing

"What if we could support children as they make meaning both visually and verbally and know that in doing so, neither ability or competency is diminished; instead, both are strengthened?"

1

CHAPTER

1

Why Illustration Study Matters to the Development of Young Writers

> *We have a particular interest in the place of the visual in the lives of children, and we hope to show that children very early on, and with very little help (despite all the encouragement), develop a surprising ability to use elements of the "visual grammar"—an ability which, we feel, should be understood better and developed further, rather than being cut off prematurely as is, too often, the case at present.*
>
> —GUNTHER KRESS AND THEO VAN LEEUWEN, *Reading Images: The Grammar of Visual Design*

SIX-YEAR-OLD CLAY'S MOTHER knew he was becoming invested in his work as a writer when requests like this began making their way into his nightly prayers: *Dear Lord, please help me have good ideas for my bat book in writing workshop tomorrow.* In his kindergarten class, Clay and his classmates were studying informational books, and making this kind of picture book clearly appealed to him as a beginning writer. He was always thinking ahead. At any given time, Clay would be working on a book, but he could also tell you the topic of the next book he was planning to write. Planets. Spiders. Skeletons. Clay truly seemed to relish thinking about ways he could engage and inform his readers as he made books about topics he knew a lot about.

Figures 1.1, 1.2, and 1.3 show three books Clay wrote during this study. Each is filled with interesting decisions he made as he crafted them, but three stand out in particular. In the bat book, Clay carefully constructed a page where the reader can lift the flaps to see the bat hanging upside down in a sleeping position during the day and in flight (notice the sideways position) during the night. In the book about watches, Clay was very intentional as he thought ahead about how he could trace his hand to show a close-up of the watch on the wrist. And in the book about spiders, Clay included something he had seen other writers of nonfiction include in their books: a graph showing the relative danger of the black widow—five red x's of danger! He also used a clever sequence of three drawings on the last page to show the reader how to draw a spider, the spidery font topping it all off.

Too often, I'm afraid, it's easy to look at what Clay has done in these books, exclaim, "How cute is that!" and then not think much more about it. It is cute, but it is so much more than cute, and understanding all the ways in which it is so much more than cute is a big part of how this book came to be.

Consider, if you will, the sophistication of Clay's composition process. He wasn't just making picture books about bats and watches and spiders; he was *designing* them (Kress 2000) with readers in mind. As a maker of books, Clay was able to move seamlessly between content and design as he composed, and the decisions he made about how he might best represent his meaning were purposeful and deliberate. Clay thought about his writing even when he wasn't working on it, both in his planning ahead for content and design, and in reading like a writer—getting ideas from his reading to use in his own work. In daily reflection times at the end of writing workshop, Clay was able to explain his process and decision making to other students in his class who were eager to learn from him. And finally, Clay would spend days on a single book, exhibiting a strong will for the stamina of creative work.

I think most teachers of writing would agree that their primary, long-range goal is for children like Clay to become competent, effective communicators who can use text to accomplish their meaningful goals in the world. Yes, it's a long-range goal, but when I look at Clay's work now, when he's *six*, I can't help but see all the ways in which he's already well on his way to being just this kind of communicator. I also see into his future, and I know that when he is sixteen or twenty-six, or however far I want to look, being an effective communicator will involve getting words down on paper, but it will involve *so much more than that*—just as it involves more than that for him now, when he's six.

Seeing all this, I can't help but wonder, "What if there is a way to teach some of the *so much more than that* through the illustration work Clay and

Figure 1.1   Clay's book about bats. (1) Bats. (2) 1. Bats are nocturnal. 2. Bats can climb. 3. Bats hang down. 4. Boo! Bats can fly. 5. Cool! (3) Bats are nocturnal. (4) Bats are nocturnal.

Figure 1.1 *continued* (5) Bats can climb. (6) Bats hang down. (7) Boo! Bats can fly. (8) Cool.

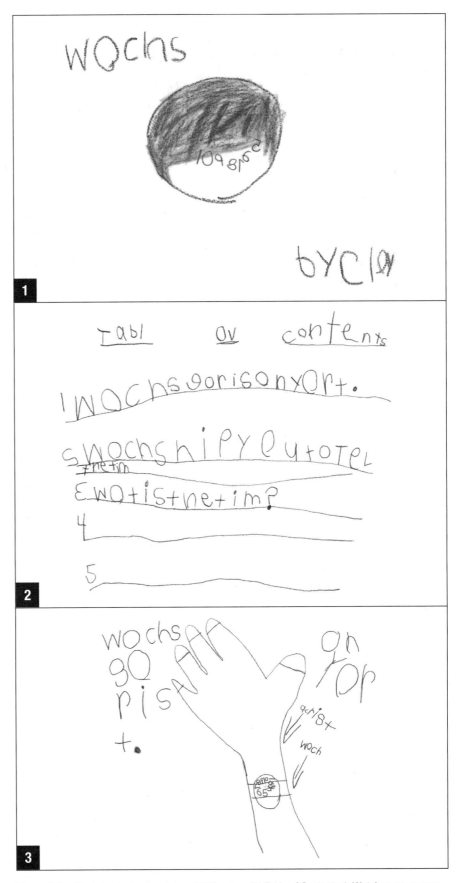

Figure 1.2   Clay's book about watches. (1) Watches. (2) Table of Contents 1. Watches go on your wrist. 2. Watches help you to tell the time. 3. What is the time? (3) Watches go on your wrist (labels: wrist, watch).

Figure 1.2   *continued*   (4) Watches help you to tell the time (label: spots). (5) Some watches look like robots. (6) What is the time?

Figure 1.3   Clay's book about spiders. (1) Spider. (2) 1. Web 2. All kinds of spiders 3. Black widows have hour glass. 4. How to draw a spider. (3) Spiders spin a web! (Labels: web!, heart). (4) There are all kinds of spiders (labels: Black Widow, Tarantula, Wolf Spider, eye).

Figure 1.3 *continued* (5) What do black widows do? (6) Black widows have an hour glass. (7) How to draw a spider.

other children are doing as they make picture books? What if we can support children as they make meaning both visually and verbally and know that in doing so, neither ability or competency is diminished; instead, both are strengthened? What if children are introduced to key qualities of good writing in the context of illustrations? What if children gain lots and lots of experience planning, drafting, revising, and editing content in the process of composing illustrations for their books?" These are the ideas that drive this book.

To imagine how all this rich teaching might be possible, it's first helpful to understand some of the context in which Clay is becoming an effective communicator in his kindergarten classroom. The most important understanding, no doubt, is the fact that he works at making picture books each day in a writing workshop. The nature of this work is critical to his development as an effective communicator.

Picture Book Making as a Template for Playful Exploration

In many primary writing workshops, children like Clay use a combination of words and illustrations across a series of pages to make picture books about topics of interest to them. The developmentally appropriate nature of this template for writing is well documented in professional literature on the teaching of writing (Calkins 2003; Corgill 2008; Horn and Giacobbe 2007; Ray and Cleaveland 2004; Ray and Glover 2008; Rowe 1994). Making picture books is developmentally appropriate because, when supported to do so, children bring to book making the same exploratory spirit they bring to all sorts of other play. As they make books, most children (again, with support) are willing to approximate and try on the roles of writers and illustrators, much as they would try on roles in other kinds of play. And as the NAEYC *Position Statement: Developmentally Appropriate Practice* (2009) makes clear, the spirit of play matters because "Play is an important vehicle for developing self-regulation as well as for promoting language, cognition, and social competence" (14).

Making picture books is important for beginning writers for other reasons as well. Because it takes some time for children to become fluent and proficient with transcription (getting words down on paper), being able to represent meaning in illustrations makes so much more possible for beginning writers. Alea's book about fruits you'd never see, for instance (Figure 1.4), involved some very clever thinking—thinking that wouldn't have happened if Alea weren't comfortable using illustrations to make meaning.

A picture book is the perfect "container" for the composition of beginning writers like Alea. Children understand that when they make books, they're not drawing *instead* of writing, and they haven't been asked to make

Figure 1.4   Alea's fruit book. (1) You've never seen a grape nose. (2) You've never seen a blueberry rain. (3) You've never seen an apple face. (4) You've never seen a banana mustache.

Figure 1.4   *continued*   (5) OH NO! (6) The thing is we eat fruits. (7) End page with pieces of orange on it.

picture books because they don't yet know how to write. They've been asked to draw pictures to make meaning—along with words—because that's what makers of picture books *do*. The most experienced authors and illustrators use a combination of pictures and words to make picture books, just as beginning writers like Alea and Clay do. Related to this, because young children are surrounded by picture books at school, it makes sense that their writing should match the kind of texts they know best. And when they see themselves as people who make picture books, people just like Mo Willems and Emily Gravett, for example, young children notice and pick up ideas for writing and illustrating from the books adults read to them.

When they are rendered with specific detail, illustrations can also help children read their approximated spellings much more easily, serving as important picture cues for the written text. When Starr wrote a book about school, everyone at her school knew exactly what the picture represented on the page you see in Figure 1.5. Because of the meticulously drawn colored flags, it was easy for Starr's classmates to see that the illustration was of the gym, and this assisted her classmates as they read what she'd written on this page: "At PE, Mr. Sebastyn teaches us."

Using illustrations in picture books to make meaning is also essential for children who enter school as English language learners. Image is, in a way, a universal language, and as Danling Fu points out in *An Island of English: Teaching ESL in Chinatown*, "Drawing is a good way for English language beginners to tell their stories" (2003, 89). Making picture books and learning to

Figure 1.5 Starr's illustration of the gym

connect illustrations in meaningful ways makes much more possible in the expression of ideas for English language learners. And because they see picture books all around them, and they see other children making them as well, the picture-book-making context helps ELLs feel very much included—and on more equal footing—in the literate life of the community.

Finally, when young children make books, they can't help but engage in a process of constant decision making. *What will I write about? What should come first? How should I draw it? Does this look the way I want it to look? What should come next? And next? Etc.* These process decisions are given over to children as they build ideas across the pages of books, and the experience of making so many decisions over time nurtures their development in important ways.

Different Stances to Illustrations

In writing workshops where children make picture books, it seems there are two different stances one might take to the illustration part of composing. The different stances suggest different teaching practices and, as a result, different composition experiences for children.

Teaching Out of Illustrations

One stance is that the goal of teaching should be to teach children *out* of illustrations and *into* words as quickly as possible. When this is the stance, children may be encouraged to spend less time on their illustrations and to forego the use of color and other materials like the tape and sticky notes Clay used to make the flaps in his bat book. When the goal is to get away from illustrating as quickly as possible, children may be taught just to sketch an idea that they can then put into words—the sketch serving simply to hold the meaning rather than expand it the way illustrations do in picture books.

The countywide rubric used to assess writers like Clay takes this basic stance to the illustration part of his development. The rubric says that a Level 2 writer "uses drawings to express meaning," while a Level 3 writer "uses drawings to plan a story." By Level 4, writers should "use drawings to plan and describe an experience." The shift in language certainly suggests that teaching should help children move away from drawing as expressive meaning making to drawing essentially as prewriting.

Looking at Clay's work from this stance, one truly appreciates the thoughtful way he planned ahead for and captured meaning in his illustrations, but ultimately the hope would be that Clay would learn to write this meaning instead of illustrate it: *Bats are nocturnal. During the day when the sun is out, they hang upside down in dark places and sleep. At night, when the moon and stars come out, they fly about and go hunting for food.*

Teaching Into Illustrations

The other possible stance when children are making picture books is to teach *into* the illustration part of the composing process. When teaching from this stance, children are encouraged to linger longer with illustrations, to use color and other media to make meaning, and to expand what the words say by intentionally composing with illustrations. Teachers who take this stance are also supporting children to move toward more fluent transcription, but they don't necessarily privilege word making over image making. They value them equally. Their hope is that Clay will someday be able to write this meaning instead of illustrate it, but only if he chooses to do so.

Looking at Clay's work from this stance, one also truly appreciates the thoughtful way he planned ahead for and captured meaning in his illustrations, but the appreciation goes an important step further. This teaching stance recognizes that Clay is doing with pictures exactly what he might be doing with words, were he more fluent in his transcription or, simply, if he *chose* to make this meaning with words instead of pictures. He might just as efficiently use a combination of text and other media to get his meaning across effectively, even when he is fully proficient at the writing part. It depends on what kind of text he is creating. In this case, of course, he is making a picture book, and in this form of writing it is absolutely appropriate, even expected, to make lots of meaning in the illustrations.

As I've presented them here, teaching *out* of illustrations and teaching *into* illustrations may seem like oppositional stances, but I don't believe they have to be—just as they clearly weren't in Clay's writing workshop. There is a bridge between the two, and that bridge is understanding how both writing and drawing are acts of meaning making—they are simply generated with different compositional tools. Composers of words share many of the same understandings about meaning making with composers of pictures, so choosing to teach into illustrations doesn't necessarily mean that time for teaching writing is sacrificed. If teachers are willing to make a composing connection and show children how an illustrator's decisions about pictures are a lot like a writer's decisions about words, she forms a bridge of understanding that nurtures children as both illustrators and writers.

A Forward-Looking Stance to Teaching

Teaching into children's illustration work is not a laissez-faire stance to teaching, a "just let them draw—they're children" kind of stance. Instead, it is an incredibly intentional, forward-looking stance. It requires teachers to hold deeply grounded understandings about composing all sorts of texts in effective ways, both in terms of process and product. It requires a double sort of vision, if you will, where teachers can see how children learning a certain illustration technique are also learning a way of representing meaning that they could just as well do with words, in a different sort of text. Clay's page showing bats in contrasting diurnal and nocturnal settings, for example, shows he has a beginning understanding of what it means to compare and contrast. His illustrated steps for how to draw a spider show he clearly understands what it means to render something procedurally, as writers do when they write steps about how to do something. The understandings Clay is using to compose his illustrations are operationally the same understandings he'll need to compose well-written text.

Teaching into illustrations asks teachers to understand that when children illustrate, they prewrite (or predraw, perhaps), draft, revise, and edit just as they do when they write, and to value this process equally in this parallel context. As pointed out earlier, Clay spent lots of time thinking ahead about how he would show important information in these books. He may very well grow to be the kind of writer who does a lot of prewriting in his head, planning carefully before he sets out to draft. He's developing a fairly sophisticated process of working that way now in his illustrations. And if you look closely at the traces left by an eraser, you can also see he's engaged in revising both pictures and words. He knows what it means to go back over something he's made and reconsider the making of it (the essence of revision and editing).

Finally, the forward-looking nature of teaching into illustrations asks teachers to understand that the world these children live in—and will ultimately grow to be effective communicators in—is a world where the definition of text will be greatly expanded: what it means to compose a text will go far beyond composition with words only. Can you imagine, for example, going to find information on bats or watches or spiders and finding even a single resource that was only written in text, with no images at all to help convey the meaning? That's just not what consumers of informational text find when they go looking for information, not in books or magazines or newspapers or websites. It would be exceptional to find a unimodal, text-only, resource in the world of information we live in. And so this fact begs the question, "Why would children like Clay be asked to write informational text and not be supported—with intentional teaching—to use their illustrations thoughtfully to carry important meaning in their books?"

In a recent reformatting of *Newsweek* magazine, the back-page essay written for years alternately by George Will and Anna Quindlen, was ditched. In its place: a graphic feature titled Back Story, "a visual dissection or explanation of an important issue or phenomenon that will satisfy one's curiosity or pique one's interest." Personally, I've been fine dissecting important issues verbally with Will and Quindlen for years now, but I suppose the move to combine the visual and the verbal was inevitable as consumers have come to expect communication to be delivered in multimodal ways. And we cannot imagine the evolving meanings of text that might exist in the world where Clay and his classmates will grow to be effective communicators.

The National Council of Teachers of English *Position Statement: The NCTE Definition of 21st Century Literacies* speaks so clearly to the need for an expanded view of text when considering effective communication. "As society and technology change, so does literacy. Because technology has increased the intensity and complexity of literate environments, the twenty-first century demands that a literate person possess a wide range of abilities and competencies, many literacies. These literacies—from reading online newspapers to participating in virtual classrooms—are multiple, dynamic, and malleable" (NCTE 2008).

A Hope for Future Practice

What very young children are doing with pictures and words when they are five and six and seven, they will no doubt one day be doing with interactive audio, video, simulated environments, and other technologies we can't even imagine at the moment. Words will no doubt be a part of these texts, but composing these texts will involve a lot more than just words. I love to think of Clay as an adult one day, creating a text to inform and engage readers about the marvelous world of bats, and having at his disposal all the many tools of technology. He'll need more than just prayers to help him work his way through all the possibilities before he composes a text!

Because of the rich, professional conversations around the teaching of writing, many, many children now go to school and find themselves in writing workshops where they make picture books. And because of the excellent unit-of-study work that has grown out of this same professional conversation, many of these children also find themselves learning to use their picture books to do all kinds of meaningful composition. Inside these books, children compose stories about their lives. They craft texts that engage and inform and teach readers how to do things. They write poetry.

In classrooms where children compose meaningfully inside picture books, teachers have created an amazing context in which to teach composition—and at a much deeper level than perhaps anyone ever imagined possible with children so young. But to get at the really deep work, teachers must look at children's illustrating not as an afterthought or simply the means to another, more important end. To get at the really deep composition work, teachers must understand illustrating in this way—as composition. And teachers must believe that if they teach into this work, they are helping children become the kinds of effective communicators the twenty-first century demands, "possessing a wide range of abilities and competencies, many literacies."

How This Book Works

In Pictures and In Words is about bringing the fullness of illustration study into the writing workshop. The book is divided into two sections. The first six chapters (including this one) work in consort to build a case for why teaching into children's illustration work matters so much to their overall development as effective communicators. My professional mantra has always been, *Don't talk about how to teach without first building a case for why it matters to teach.* So in the true sense of building, my intention is that not one of these chapters should be considered on its own, but always in conjunction with the others. The case for teaching into illustration work is multifaceted and doesn't come into true focus until all the pieces are in place.

Chapter Two explores the idea of building stamina for creative work and the role that illustrating plays in the development of stamina in young writers. Chapter Three makes the case that creative work is always process work, and how supporting understandings about process in children's illustration work makes sound curricular sense for them as writers. Chapter Four explores an important habit of mind all writers possess—the ability to read like a writer—and how children may be taught this habit of mind in the context of illustration study.

Chapter Five explains how illustrators make many decisions about pictures for the same reasons writers make decisions about words. Understanding how these decisions are the same can help teachers be much more intentional in how they talk about illustrations with children, supporting meaning-making possibilities in pictures and words at the same time. And finally, Chapter Six describes what a unit of study in illustrations might look like in a primary writing workshop.

Following these chapters is Section Two of the book, and it's all about looking at illustrations with new eyes. These new eyes will help you and your students see more in illustrations, think about the decisions illustrators have made behind what you see, find new possibilities for your own illustration work, and also grow in your understanding of many qualities of good writing.

Fifty different illustration techniques are grouped into five clusters based on the qualities of good writing to which they correspond: ideas and content; precision and detail; wholeness of text; tone; and layout and design. Each cluster of techniques begins with an introduction explaining their connection to a general quality of good writing. These explanations are critical as they fuel the forward thinking teachers need in order to see how talking about illustration decisions can also help children understand important qualities of good writing. Because the content in Section Two is so different from what you'll read in the first six chapters of the book, it has its own introduction explaining how it works and how it might be used to support your teaching.

CHAPTER

2

Building Stamina for Writing by Supporting Children's Work as Illustrators

I have found that with the intense focus on literacy development, promoted by testing, even very young writers are often given paper that is almost all lines, with perhaps a small space at the top of the paper for a cramped illustration, as if the writing-plus-drawing model is only an early "stage" of development that needs to be bypassed as soon as possible. "Real writing" is the unimodal production of print text—there are, after all, no points for drawing on most standardized tests. Yet a more accepting and supportive attitude toward drawing can keep some reluctant writers engaged with literacy, connected to the visual models they love.

—TOM NEWKIRK, *Holding on to Good Ideas in a Time of Bad Ones*

AS I SIT AND WRITE THIS, it's a Friday morning in April. Beautiful spring is springing here in the mountains of North Carolina. The clock in the upper right hand of my computer screen says 10:22 A.M. I've been here since about 8:15. For the past two hours, I've been rereading and revising two other chapters for this book that are already drafted. I spent as long as I could revising because I couldn't bring myself to pull down the tab and let go on "New Blank Document" and start this chapter. It's the *blank* part of *new blank document*

I've been avoiding. As long as I've been at this business of writing, I still have that moment of dread when the screen is completely blank and I've got to get something started. This is why so many writers say they love revision—at least you're working with something that's already written.

Okay. Now the clock says 10:27 A.M. It took me five minutes to draft that last paragraph, and now I'm on my way. The screen isn't blank anymore. At 11:45, I'll stop and go downstairs to eat lunch. I need to be back here by 12:15, and today I'm planning to stop around 2:00 and walk the dogs with my husband. That's calling it an early day for me. Usually, I work until around 4:00, but it's Friday, and it's beautiful. . . .

That little riff is more than just a way to avoid writer's block (write about how time is passing). I was trying, in a small way, to represent what it is like for me to work as a writer. When I'm writing, I think a lot about what time it is and how much longer I have to go. I think a lot about how much I've written in that time and how much more I need to write. The central reality of my work life when I'm writing is facing down blank pages and a ticking clock. It takes a certain measure of discipline, and—it occurs to me, *faith*—to sit so long in a chair and work at writing.

In this chapter, I'd like to consider the role that children's illustrating can play in helping them learn to sit in chairs and face down blank pages and ticking clocks. To become proficient, writers have to develop some serious stamina, and it's critical that teachers understand what writing work is like so they understand the kind of stamina writers need. And I do think of it as writing *work*—in the sense of purposeful effort—not in an onerous way much of the time, sometimes writing is quite joyous, but it is work nonetheless.

Understanding the Work of Writing

Writing work, or indeed any creative endeavor, is just not like other kinds of work in the world. Writing work asks you to go from *nothing* to *something*, all on your own (unless you're coauthoring and sharing the responsibility), over and over for long stretches of time. I often think that the fact that I spend so much of my time writing explains why I love to do all sorts of other mundane chores. I actually like to wash and fold clothes, do dishes by hand, and vacuum. I love to iron. I don't even mind scooping up the yard after my dogs. And with four large dogs running in and out, there's a lot to vacuum and plenty to scoop.

What these chores have in common, and what I think attracts me so about them, is that the work I need to do is so clearly there in front of me to do. I can see the work, and I can so easily see when it's finished. I can accomplish so much in just an hour with this kind of work. I get my bucket and my scooper, I work the yard in quadrants, empty the bucket, put it away, wash my hands, and then go walk around a bit with my eyes looking out instead of down just to enjoy the work I've accomplished.

An hour of writing work, on the other hand, is nothing like this. When I go up to my office to work at writing, all I have in front of me is a blank screen, a word count, and a deadline. I sit down with a vision in mind of what I want to write—an article, a chapter of a book, a community newsletter. I know my topic and my key ideas, but I don't really have a sense of how it will take shape until I start writing it. It's up to me to figure out how to work my way through time and accomplish what I've set out to do. Knowing when it's finished can be very difficult, too: meeting the word count doesn't mean it's finished. Usually my guideline is, "It's finished when it's due," but even then there is the question of whether it's good enough yet to make its way out in the world. Just because it's due doesn't mean it's finished either. Top all this off with the fact that writing anything of substance takes not just one hour, but hour upon hour, day after day; add the fact that I only finish something every year or so, and you get a feeling for why I don't mind scooping poop. At least it gives me a sense of accomplishment.

The Curriculum of Time

Understanding the rather dramatic difference in these kinds of work in my life leads me to believe that as teachers, we need to talk about the *curriculum of time* in our conversations about the teaching of writing. Time is not just when writing instruction happens in school; time must be part of the curriculum, part of what students are learning about as they develop as writers. You see, it really doesn't matter how many craft lessons or genre studies a teacher plans for students if she doesn't first teach them how to sit down in chairs, stay there for a long time, and make some work for themselves that leads to writing. With blank paper in front of them, students have to learn how to make *something* out of *nothing*, and they must learn to come back the next day and do it again. The curriculum of time is fairly simple: Sit. Stay. Put something on the paper.

In her book *The Writer's Life*, Julia Cameron says,

> *Writing is the act of motion. Writing is the commitment to move forward, not to stew in our juices, to become whatever it is we are becoming. Writing is both the boat and the wind in the sails. Even on the days when the winds of inspiration seem slight, there is some forward motion, some progress made. The ability to show up brings with it the ability to grow up. (2001, 96)*

For children to grow up as writers under the care of teachers, those teachers must teach them how to show up and move forward, how to be both the boat and the wind for their forward motion as writers.

When children regularly fill time with work they've made for themselves, they will come to understand what it means to do the creative work that writing demands. On the other hand, children who spend their school days completing work that is laid out in front of them to do, work they can *see*—a puzzle for math, a worksheet on colors, a match-the-animals game sheet—are doing scooping-poop work all day long. Something is already on the paper for them to do, they do it, and they finish. They're vacuuming and folding clothes and ironing with this kind of work. And this doesn't mean this work may not have value; it just means students aren't learning anything about the curriculum of time when they're doing it. Someone else has determined their forward motion by putting work in front of them to do.

If the goal of writing instruction is for students to become proficient communicators, then teachers must first help them understand and build stamina for creative kinds of work. And I do mean *first*, before any other curriculum or instruction is even considered. To do creative work, students will need both the stamina to sit for a long time and the stamina to work on something over time, returning to the same project day after day.

This is the first reason that I believe teachers should support children's illustration work in primary writing workshops—because that work helps children understand the curriculum of time. When children are first getting started as writers, some of them haven't been exposed much to how letters make sounds, or even how to *make* letters for that matter. So composing with illustrations is the only logical entry point for them to begin developing stamina for creative work. And even for children who have enough information to generate logical spellings for key words, the intellectual demands of this are taxing when they're first getting started. Adults can hardly relate to how demanding this might be for children because spelling has become so automatic for us and requires so little thought. If these children can move between writing some words and working on illustrations, then staying with the work for long stretches of time becomes much more possible for them, and the expectation for them to build stamina becomes much more developmentally appropriate.

To understand what stamina looks like in beginning writers, and how illustrations support its development, I'd like to introduce you to three writers in kindergarten—Daniel, Reilly, and Thomas. Their stories all unfolded in the first few months of kindergarten as their teacher intentionally supported them in coming to understand how to work their way through time in her writing workshop.

Daniel's Story

On a Tuesday morning in early October, Daniel came over and whispered to me as children were gathering for writing workshop. He said, "I'm going to finish my dinosaur book today (Figure 2.1). I've got to write *swimming* on the 'dinosaur swimming page' and then put the title and the picture on the cover." He told me this because he knew I was interested in this book—we'd had a conference about it the week before.

During our conference, Daniel was trying to think of an ending for the book. After looking at the pages he already had with their bold, almost scary use of color (especially on the eating page), we talked about ways he could sum it all up. I said, "They look pretty ferocious to me, so maybe you could say something like, 'Dinosaurs are ferocious.'" As a class, we were talking a lot at that time about endings for list books that "sum it all up," and many of the children were just beginning to understand what that meant. But Daniel didn't like my idea, saying instead he wanted the ending to be happy. And that's just how he made it, with the two dinosaurs going off to play together on the last page.

Thinking about the ending required Daniel to think about his book as a *whole* text, not a series of isolated illustrations. He hadn't just been drawing pictures of dinosaurs as he worked on this book; he'd been composing a text. He thought about how he wanted the pages to work together in the end and the feeling he wanted to leave for readers of his book. The sort of thinking he was doing, in kind and substance, is the same kind of thinking a writer does when composing only with words. This is an idea I'll examine more fully in the next chapter.

I watched Daniel as he went off to get his dinosaur book out of his folder that day he whispered his plans to me. I thought about the significance of what he'd said. Daniel had been working on this book, *What Do Dinosaurs Do?* for more than two weeks. That's a very long time to stay with something when you're five or six years old. On that particular morning, a Monday, he'd been away from his book for three whole days over a long weekend. The book had been out of Daniel's sight but not out of his mind. Clearly he'd been thinking about it while he was away from it. He knew where he was in the process of making it, and he could name the work he still needed to do to finish it. Children who only know the kind of schoolwork that is finished quickly several times each day never get the experience of thinking about a project that is ongoing in the way Daniel thought about his dinosaur book, because nothing ever lasts longer than a day.

What is so significant about Daniel's story is that it shows he was fully engaged in the real, creative work of writers in *October*. In *kindergarten*. And it was his work. He *owned* this work; no one walked him through it. For thirty to forty minutes a day, Daniel returned to the pages of this one book for more than two weeks. He chose his topic, clearly one of great interest to him. He spent lots of time making the illustrations dazzlingly vivid. He spent more time carefully generating spellings for a few

Figure 2.1 Daniel's book: *What Do Dinosaurs Do?* (1) What Do Dinosaurs Do? (2) Dinosaurs swim. (3) (no caption).
(4) Dinosaurs eating.

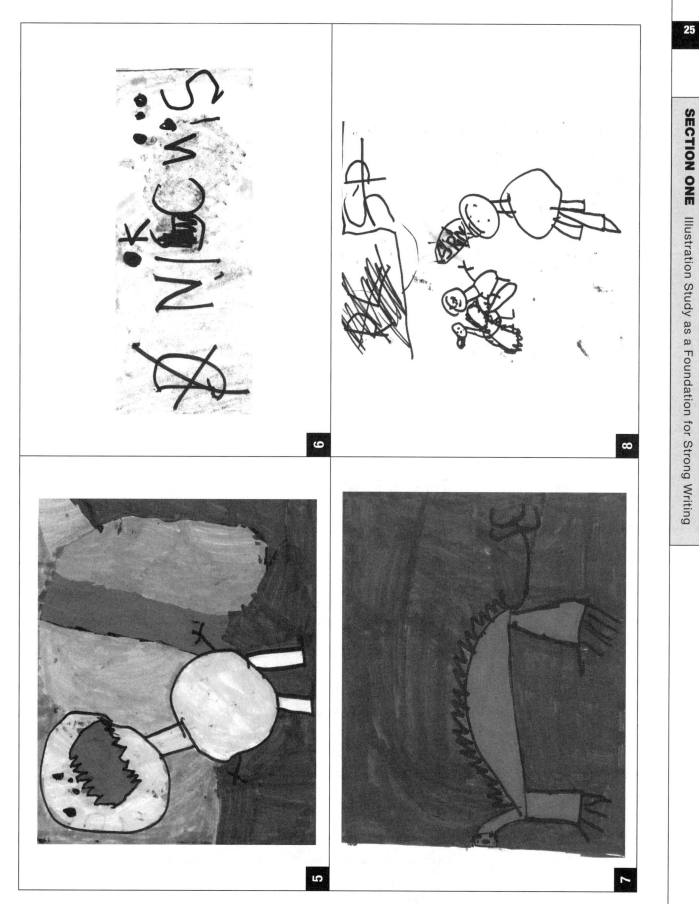

Figure 2.1 *continued* (5) (no caption). (6) Spikey dinosaur. (7) (no caption). (8) Dinosaurs playing.

key words on each page. The once blank pages filled up because Daniel faced them down.

When I think about the work this young writer did in his book, it doesn't even matter to me much what that work was, exactly. What matters to me is that he did so much of it for such a long time. I can value all that red and green and blue ink precisely because it took Daniel so long to get it all on that paper. As a writer myself, I admire his stamina.

Daniel's story of stamina would not have been possible if his teacher didn't value the time he spent on his illustrations and the role they played in helping him stay with his book for a long time. You can see in this book that Daniel came to kindergarten with enough sound–symbol knowledge to generate logical spellings for words he needed to express his ideas, but developmentally, spelling was still a very demanding intellectual task for him. If he'd been asked to spend most of his time generating text, instead of balancing text with illustrations, it is likely this expectation would have raised his frustration level, worn him out, and made him unwilling to spend the time he did on this book. And if that were the case, Daniel would not have learned what he did about what it means to spend most of two weeks on a single writing project. In October. In kindergarten.

Reilly's Story

Like Daniel, Reilly began work on a book in early September and stayed with the book for several weeks. The book is about CAT® machines—bulldozers, excavators, cranes, demolition rigs. The topic was clearly engaging to Reilly, and he spent lots of time illustrating with very specific detail. From his illustrations, it's easy to see that Reilly, like Daniel, was very knowledgeable about his topic. The level of detail shows that he knows about the machines themselves and also how they go about their work. Not yet very confident to generate text on his own, his teacher nudged and supported him to add text to the book during a series of writing conferences.

Looking at the pages of this book, it is so clear how slowly and carefully they were rendered. Like his classmate Daniel, imagine how much Reilly must have learned from working on this book, specifically about spending a very long time on a single project. But Reilly's story takes a different twist when, in October, a peek over his shoulder showed that Reilly had begun a new book. A new *CAT® machines* book. Oh, what to do?

I can imagine all sorts of heady debate about what the best teaching decision would be in this case. Should Reilly be supported to continue working on another book about CAT® machines? Or should he be encouraged to move on to something new and different? In Reilly's writing workshop, children are allowed to start new books without the okay of the teacher, so

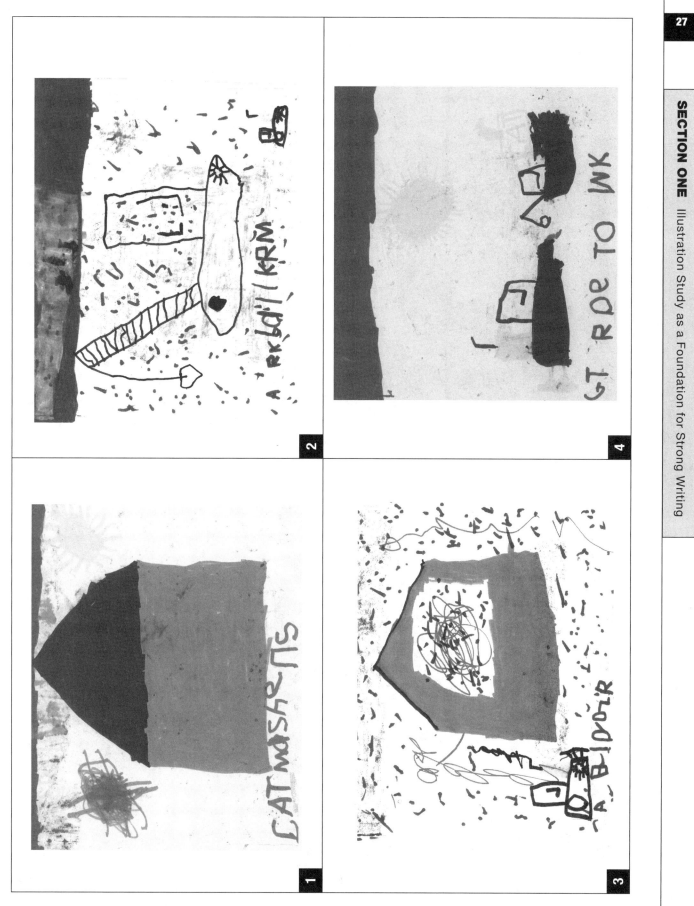

Figure 2.2 Reilly's first book about CAT® machines

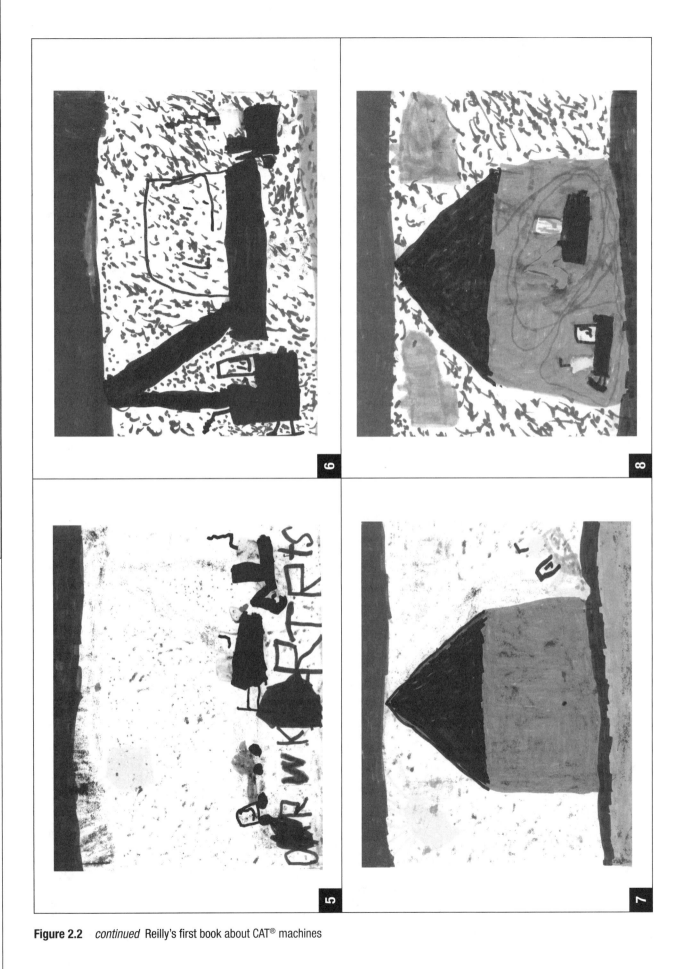

Figure 2.2 *continued* Reilly's first book about CAT® machines

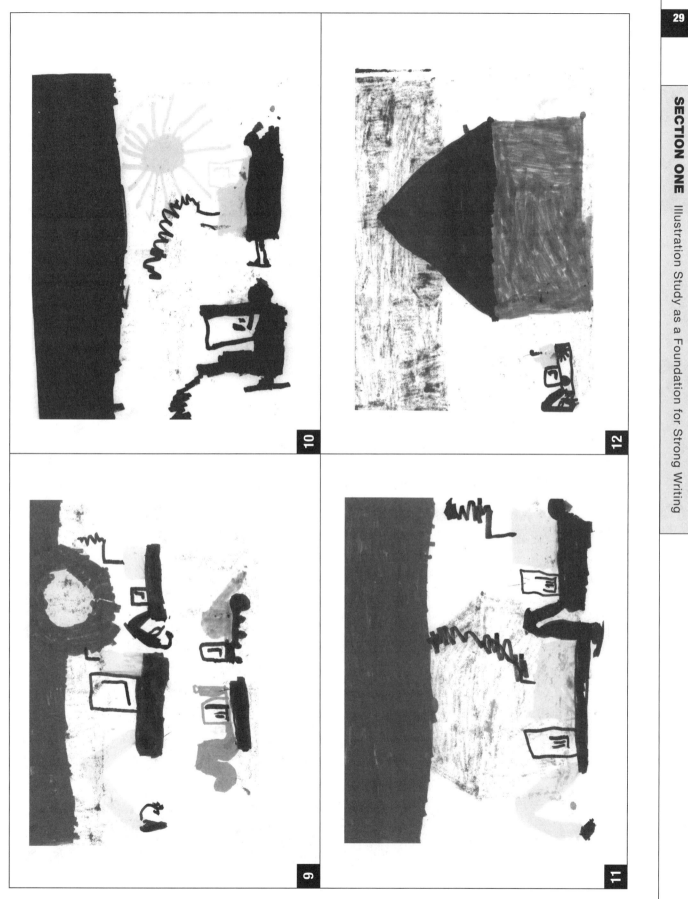

Figure 2.2 *continued* Reilly's first book about CAT® machines

Reilly already had a good start on the second book by the time his teacher knew about it. A decision had to be made, and Reilly's teacher decided to let him stay with it. After all, lots of writers write about the same topic more than once, and this might give Reilly a chance to experience what it's like to find new meaning in a familiar topic. There was a chance, of course, that he would not find new meaning and instead would sort of do the same thing all over again, but if he did it again for a very long time, there would be value in that.

As it turns out, the second book is not a copy of the first, though some of the text does appear to be duplicated. But it's extended, as well, and in it you also see some beginning experimentation with punctuation that was not evident in the first book. The illustrations carry clearly different meaning, though themes reappear (the focus on the weather, the delineation of grass and dirt, etc.). The idea of CAT® machines held Reilly's interest for a significant amount of time as he composed the second book; he spent not quite as long on it as he did on the first book, but close.

As I thought about the teaching decision that supported Reilly's long work on very similar books, I was reminded of the wise advice I got when I read Tom Newkirk's book *Misreading Masculinity: Boys, Literacy and Popular Culture*. Tom gives several pieces of advice for supporting boys in better ways, but one of them is to make room for obsession:

> *Some degree of obsessiveness, even narrowness, is essential for literacy development . . . The central characteristic of an obsession is repetition that to*

Figure 2.3 The cover of Reilly's second CAT® machines book

*an outsider seems extreme, even nonproductive. The obsessive student seems
to persist in an activity beyond the point of mastery, and we regularly talk
about the student being "in a rut." (2002, 183–84)*

Reilly's teacher didn't see him as being in a rut. She understood the curriculum of time, so she could see that Reilly was developing in very important ways as a writer, learning all about the process of creative work, and she chose to support him in that development. She recognized what Newkirk so aptly explains when he says, "what seems like excessive repetition to the outsider does not seem that way to the child absorbed . . ." (185). Reilly's story of stamina would not have been possible if his teacher hadn't valued the time he spent on his illustrations, and also made room for his wonderful obsession for all things CAT®.

Thomas' Story

Thomas' story is a little different, but no less compelling as a story of stamina. During his kindergarten year, Thomas was very into the Bakugan characters and created elaborate story lines for them both in his play and in the books he made from time to time. He wrote about other things too—his pet bird, Gaby, amazing sea monsters, his family—but Bakugan was a topic he was clearly drawn to as a writer.

I had a writing conference one morning with Thomas as he was working on a Bakugan book. Well, it was supposed to be a writing conference. It sounded more like a comedy routine as I proved woefully unable to say back the names of the Bakugan characters he was trying to discuss with me, and Thomas would politely correct me every time. I finally gave up and just pointed and referred to characters as "this one" and "that one."

When we looked at the date stamp to see how long he'd been working on this book (a common practice in writing conferences), I was a little surprised that he wasn't further along in it. But then I looked more closely at the cover. "How long did you work on this page?" I asked him. He replied, "A couple days."

It wasn't surprising to me to see children work for multiple days on a single illustration, but Thomas' work was a little different. While writers like Daniel and Reilly would spend long stretches of time coloring things in so they looked like the illustrations they saw in picture books, what struck me was the very busy nature of the illustration work Thomas had done. There were so many creatures represented on the cover, and each one looked different. I wondered if, in fact, each one held different meaning for him. So I asked, and they did.

For many more minutes than I would normally spend in a conference, Thomas began to tell me about each of the creatures he'd drawn on the

Figure 2.4 The cover of Thomas' Bakugan book

page—what their special powers were, and how some of them were interacting on the page (hence the connecting lines). I continued to listen because, quite frankly, I was awed. For this young writer, there was an intensity of meaning on this paper that was rare in the illustration work many children do—an intensity that would have been impossible for him to achieve with written text at this point in his development.

As I listened, it was sobering for me to think how easily I might have dismissed this page as just a bunch of color and drawings, and in doing so missed the incredibly intentional rendering—through illustration—of this young writer. What I experienced wasn't the same thing as when children go on and on about a topic they love as long as someone will listen. Thomas was going on and on, but it was about things he had actually represented in this picture. He was talking and pointing the whole time. The focus Thomas showed to stay with this page and to fill it up so thoroughly with such meaning would not have been possible if his teacher didn't value him as a lover of Bakugan and value the time he spent illustrating.

Picture Books Invite Stamina

While lots of good teaching is nurturing Daniel, Reilly, Thomas, and their classmates as writers, a single, simple instructional decision probably makes more difference than anything else in helping these children build stamina for creative work. When their teacher launched them into the work of writing workshop in August, she gathered together several pieces of blank paper, stapled them down the side, and then invited children to "make books" with the paper. Blank paper invites children to work for a very long time at filling it up, and the verb *make* suggests that they might do all sorts of things as they fill it up (in a way that the verb *write* would not suggest). The classroom library is filled with published picture books and books written by other children, and this gives children a vision that they can work toward over time. They can see the kind of thing they are making all around them.

My point in this chapter has been to suggest that when young children make books, teachers may value the time children spend illustrating as much as they value the time children spend writing, not because they privilege one over the other, but simply because they value children *spending time*. While this may sound like a bold suggestion, it is perfectly aligned with one of the twelve NAEYC core principles of developmentally appropriate practice (2009). The twelfth principle states: "Children's experiences shape their motivation and approaches to learning, such as persistence, initiative, and flexibility; in turn, these dispositions and behaviors affect their learning and environment" (15). In the discussion of this principle, the document cites research that has shown: "Children with more positive learning behaviors, such as initiative, attention, and persistence, later develop stronger language skills" (15). The four named behaviors in these two statements—persistence, initiative, flexibility, and attention—could be cited as clear themes in the stories of the three writers in this chapter.

Even so, I know that the suggestion that teachers value students simply spending time raises practical questions. When should we expect the stamina to manifest itself in writing instead of illustrating? Is there a transfer of stamina from one context to another? Is there a fine (or not so fine) line between *spending* time and *wasting* time? What about children who rush through everything, words and illustrations? How do we help them build stamina?

I don't have answers to all these questions. I only know that my ability to sit in a chair and stay focused and go from nothing to something day after day is the most important ability I possess as a proficient writer. It's the truest thing I know about writing—the time spent in my chair in front of a computer. I use my own good measure of persistence, initiative, flexibility, and attention to get my work done. I can't imagine teaching writers, whether they're five or fifty-five, without making the development of stamina a prominent goal of that teaching. Because illustration work so clearly supports the development of stamina in young writers, I support illustration work.

I have talked throughout this chapter about the curriculum of time, and I would be remiss not to note that it was Randy Bomer who really first got me thinking about the importance of understanding time in literacy work with children and adolescents. His book *Time for Meaning* is an intensely practical and theoretical book about teaching reading and writing, but in between its chapters there is also an extended meditation about time and its immense power in our lives. One of my favorite passages is this:

> *To live in time successfully, we have to learn to manage our own deliberate being in time. That is, we have to learn to embody in time our best intentions, to do what we mean to be doing, to live on purpose. It takes most of us our entire lives to do this, and some of us never do. That's partly because, until we are adults, people in authority so vigorously control our schedules that we never learn to intend our own acts. (1995, 41)*

More than once in this chapter, I made the statement that "this story of stamina would not have been possible if the teacher had not valued the time spent illustrating." But as I read Randy's reflection, I realize that what teachers must really value is not illustrating itself, but that children like Daniel and Reilly and Thomas learn to intend their own acts. Children, or adults for that matter, can't do what they mean to be doing if they're always doing what someone else tells them to do. They can't live on purpose if they aren't ever allowed to follow their purposes. If children are to become proficient writers, teachers first must give them a ticking clock, some blank paper, and a big vote of confidence that they will be the kinds of writers who can face it down.

❋ Instructional Tips for Helping Children Build Stamina in Illustration Work

- Teach children to date-stamp their books when they begin working on them and when they move on to a new book.

- In writing conferences, make it a habit to ask children how long they've been working on the book you are conferring about. Over time, the familiar question will teach them that you expect them to think about the process of their work over time.

- Explain to children that it is fine for them to sometimes put a book away for a while and then decide to come back and work more on it later. Writers do some of their best work when they've been away from something for a time. If children do this, encourage them to put a new date stamp on the book to show the day they picked it up again.

- Go public when you see evidence of children exhibiting good stamina in their work. During share and reflection times, have these children talk about their process and how they've managed to stay with their work for so long. Let good stamina be a badge of honor in the room.

- Save books from year to year that are good examples of work that took a long time to do. Early in the launching of the writing workshop, look at these books together and have the children help you name things they see in the books that must have taken a long time to do.

- In writing conferences, help individual children imagine ways they might stay longer with a book. Help them imagine possibilities for how they might fill up the white space with images and words.

- Consider a demonstration lesson where you model your own thinking about how to spend a long time on a book you're making.

- Encourage children to talk with people at home about their (the children's) ongoing books. Set aside time for the children to report on their conversations from home. Children may come to class with great ideas they got from talking about their books with family members. And all of this talk helps them to think of themselves as "in the midst" of something, even when they're away from the actual work of it.

- If you have access to professional writers or folks who write a lot as part of their professions, invite them to visit the class and share about their work—how long it takes them to work on a project and how they manage their work over time.

- When looking up information (in books and on websites) about illustrators to share with children, be on the lookout for any mention of stamina and time. Share what you learn with children.

 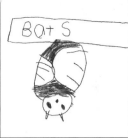  

3

Writing and Illustrating as Parallel Composing Processes

*A*rtists at work have a lot to teach us about the composing process. I
think there is probably more to be learned by teachers of writing from time
spent backstage and in practice rooms and studios than from time spent at
conferences or in the study of rhetorical theory. We need to see the
imagination in action in order to understand it as the forming power.

—ANNE E. BERTHOFF, *Reclaiming the Imagination:*
Philosophical Perspectives for Writers and Teachers of Writing

SOME NOISE OUTSIDE WOKE ME UP about 3:00 A.M. last night. I looked at the clock, adjusted
my pillows and my covers, and then—oh no—I started thinking about this book (the
one you're reading now). I hate when that happens because I know it will be a while
before I'll be able to go back to sleep. And it always happens when I'm working on a
big project like a book, especially when I know I'll spend the next day writing. The
writing is just there on the edge of my consciousness all the time.

As I lay in bed, I was thinking that the first thing I needed to do when I got to my
desk was to read everything I'd written so far—everything that would come before the
chapter I'd be working on. I had been away from the book for a few days, and I needed
to get the momentum from the earlier writing to push me into new territory. I work this

way a lot, first reading everything that comes before the starting point. I always do a good bit of word work and revision when I reread.

I lay there thinking about the chapter on stamina, which I'd worked so hard on my last day writing. I was pleased with the boys' stories I'd included to illustrate what stamina looks like, and I looked forward to reading it through start to finish after several days away. Then a thought came to me: "Didn't Tom Newkirk write something about boys and obsessions in *Misreading Masculinity*?" I was almost certain he did, and the thought of that excited me so much I wanted to get up right then and go look for it. If I could find that part, I was sure I could use it to shed some light on the CAT® machines books. What a great idea. . . . but it was pushing on toward 3:30 A.M. by this time, so I willed myself back to sleep with a new plan about how to start in the morning.

As you know, if you're reading the chapters of this book in order, I found the Newkirk quote and wove it into my discussion of Reilly's story of stamina. Of course, you would never have known it wasn't in the first draft if I hadn't told you, because readers don't see the process behind what they read. They only see the end result of that process. Readers never know the things they see in texts that woke the writers in the night.

You can't see process. This same line of thinking is just as true of the picture books children make. So often we see the illustration work and the word work children have done in their books, but we don't know the story of process that led to what we see. For example, if you only saw six-year-old Lucas' finished book about eagles, you would look at the page in Figure 3.1

Figure 3.1 Lucas' revised page

and never know that originally that page looked very different, as you see in Figure 3.2. The page in the finished book was actually the result of a very intentional revision decision Lucas made after a writing conference. When one of his classmates asked Lucas how he knew eagles had sensitive eyes, he said that he'd seen a picture in a book of an eagle hunting at night. "I just figured, if they can hunt in the dark, they must have sensitive eyes," he explained. He then decided he should revise the illustration to make it look like nighttime and extend the words to make this meaning clear. Knowing the story of Lucas' revision decision, you understand something of his development as a writer, and all that nighttime color in the background really matters in a way you'd never realize if you didn't know the story of how it came to be.

Because process is invisible in finished texts, the only way a person comes to really understand writing as process is to engage in the act itself, to go from nothing to something and see how that happens. Teachers of writing, in particular, need to understand lots about how writing comes to be if they are to support children in this work. And without a doubt, teachers of writing also need to understand the creative process children use as they illustrate to be a valuable parallel process to the one children use as they write.

Understanding Process as Engagement

A question I am often asked as I think with other teachers about writing workshops is, "Don't you need to teach students the writing process before they get started so they'll know what to do?" What drives this question, I be-

Figure 3.2   Lucas' original page

lieve, is partly a fear of management problems: "What will they do if they don't know what to do?" Partly, though, the question represents a misconception that process can be presented as explicit curriculum, process as *procedure* if you will. "First you do this, then you do this, next this. . . ."

Though never the intention, some early descriptive research into the writing process led to misunderstandings about process as procedure. And these misunderstandings have been cultivated over time as process became packaged. This doesn't mean there is a problem with understanding writing as process; it means there is a problem with understanding process as procedure, as it is so often presented in packaged curriculum materials and school textbooks.

Anyone who writes knows that at some point, you think ahead about what you are going to write. You may capture this thinking in great detail with outlines and the like, or you may capture it with just a little detail or with no detail at all, preferring just to sit down and see what happens after all your thinking. And at some other point, you have to start putting words on paper, and invariably when you do, you'll want to change some of those words or add to them or take some of them away. Also invariably, you'll find things that aren't quite right—misspelled words, punctuation out of place, typos. You'll fix those when you see them. Finally, depending on your plans for the writing, you'll do something with it when you feel it's finished.

In other words, anyone who writes knows that she will prewrite, draft, revise, edit, and publish along the way. But the thing is, these aren't steps writers follow, they're just names for kinds of things (sometimes lots of kinds of things) that happen along the way when writers write. Revision, for instance, encompasses a whole range of things a writer might do for a whole range of reasons, all in the name of revision: add something, move something, take something out, change something. And with the advent of word processing, these kinds of things happen in increasingly recursive, seamless ways, much more so than they did when the original research into writing as process was first undertaken.

Teachers don't need to teach children "the writing process" before they begin a writing workshop. Writers like Daniel and Reilly and Thomas, whom you met in the last chapter, can't make books like the ones you saw without going through some sort of process. Think about it. It's impossible for a person to go from *nothing* to *something* without a process. And it's equally impossible for a person to go from nothing to something the same way each time he writes. All the dynamics of words and meanings and genres and formats and audiences—all the things that impact what is being written—make duplicating a process time after time impossible, even for a single writer. This is why the article *the* is very problematic when it modifies *writing process*. There's not just one process, as that article might imply.

The process a less experienced writer uses may not be as efficient as the process of a more experienced writer, but that's what teaching and experience are for.

Writing and Illustrating as Parallel Composing Processes

What's important to understand about writing as process in the context of this book, then, is how much the process of illustrating is just like the process of writing, and how forward-thinking teachers can support children's growth as writers by simultaneously nurturing the process of illustrating. Several paragraphs back I briefly described the kinds of things that happen as writers go from nothing to something—I described writing as process. Now I'm going to use almost those exact same words, changing them just enough to use them in the context of creating illustrations:

> *Anyone who* ~~writes~~ *illustrates knows that at some point, you think ahead about what you are going to* ~~write~~ *draw or picture somehow. You may capture this thinking in great detail with sketches and the like, or you may capture it with just a little detail or with no detail at all, preferring just to sit down and see what happens after all your thinking. And at some other point, you have to start putting* ~~words~~ *lines and shapes and colors on paper, and invariably when you do, you'll want to change some of those* ~~words~~ *lines and shapes and colors. Also invariably, you'll find things that aren't quite right—* ~~misspelled words, punctuation out of place, typos~~ *a line that's a little too heavy or a color that's not quite the right shade. You'll fix those when you see them. Finally, depending on your plans for the* ~~writing~~ *illustration, you'll do something with it when you feel it's finished.*

Just as different writers describe different processes for working their way to a finished piece of writing, so do illustrators. For example, consider the contrast in these two process statements by two different illustrators. Marla Frazee says, "I like to impose a structure on my books early in the process. I do this with thumbnail sketches; determining where the page turns will be, how the words and pictures will relate to each other on the page, where the drama will build, and what the overall design of the book will be" (www.marlafrazee.com). Of her picture-making process for a book, Nikki McClure says, "I'm not one to storyboard my own work. I usually just let the story evolve" (www.cwdesigner.blogspot.com). If encouraged, children too will find different ways of working through the process of both writing and of illustrating. There is no one right way.

Process and Composition Development

In our study of the writing development of preschoolers (2008), Matt Glover and I took a long time to settle on the word *composition* as the best word to describe the dimensions of development that interested us in the writing of very young children. We chose the word *composition* because we felt the simple definitions our computer dictionary gave for the verb *compose* best captured the parallel processes of writing and illustrating:

> *compose* (v)   1. to make something by combining together *2.* to put things together to form a whole

Writers make something by combining together words; illustrators make something by combining together images. Writers put words together to form a whole; illustrators put images together to form a whole. The symbols themselves are different—words and images—but in the *making* and *combining* and *putting* and *forming*—in the verb sense of composing—writers and illustrators really do quite the same kinds of thinking and decision making.

As I recounted earlier, Lucas added the darkness of night to his illustration for one simple reason: to make his meaning clearer. This is the same reason I added the first two sentences in the last paragraph after the definitions of *compose*. I wanted to make my meaning clearer. I considered just leaving the definitions to stand alone and let readers make the connection on their own, but I decided not to risk that; the idea is too important. Similarly, Lucas could have stopped after adding the words, "Eagles can see at night," but instead went one step further to an illustration revision that made his meaning even clearer.

When I woke in the night with the idea to find the Tom Newkirk quote and add it to my book, I woke because—well, process really never sleeps. As long as I am working on something I am engaged in working on it, even when I'm not at my desk. I know so many stories of children who come to school with great ideas for the books they are engaged in writing over time. Daniel, who once brought in a torn out section of a sales circular so he could get the word *Bionicle*® right for a book he was making, and so he could look closely at the picture as he drew his own. Or Clay, whom you met in Chapter One, who came to school with a great idea to have a combination lift-the-flap/cutaway in his book about skeletons (Figure 3.3). Thinking of great ideas for an ongoing project is one of the hallmarks of creative work, and both writers and illustrators understand the energy a great idea can bring to the evolving process of that work.

Figure 3.3   A page from Clay's skeleton book. (1 and 2) Will you see the skeleton? (labels: skeleton).

New Possibilities, Deeper Engagement with Process

As writers plan and draft and revise and edit, as writers compose, they engage in an endless series of decisions. Really, every move a writer makes is the result of a decision made. Some of them are made almost the instant they're enacted on paper and the writer isn't even aware he's made a decision. Other decisions are deliberated over for minutes, hours, or even days. *What should come next? Does that sound right? How can I say this? Does this fit with what I said earlier? Is it all coming together? This is awkward. How could I fix it?* Moving forward with writing requires endlessly decisive action.

When children first start out composing and making books, they can only decide to do what they can imagine is possible to do, either with words or with illustrations. With their limited experiences, possibilities are limited. Teaching children about the process of composing, then, is really about showing them new ways they might *decide* to do things, because the more decisions a child makes, the more involved his process becomes. Processes and their resulting products become more sophisticated as children are introduced to new possibilities and begin to try these possibilities out as they compose.

In the last chapter, I explained the value of children developing the stamina to work their way through time—no matter what that work might be. But now I'm adding an important idea to that one. Supporting children in their illustration work can help them work their way through time *purposefully*, teaching them to "intend their own acts" (Bomer 1995) in the fullest sense of intention. All the experience children gain as they fashion their pictures in particular ways for particular reasons is just the experience they need to gain control and ownership over the process of composing.

Text—whether it's composed with words or pictures or both—doesn't just happen by accident. Text happens because someone makes it happen and decides it should be that way, and all the making and deciding is the essence of process.

Children Making Interesting Illustration Decisions

Helping children to focus on the decisions illustrators have made in picture books can greatly expand their potential for decisive, purposeful action when they do their own composing—and this also helps them become more fully engaged in their process. To understand what it looks like when children compose with a greater sense of possibility, let's look at a few interesting decisions children in kindergarten made after studying illustration possibilities.

In Figures 3.4 and 3.5, you can see that Sammi learned to divide an illustration into boxes to show contrast or differences in meaning. In *Seasons*, Sammi attended to very fine detail in each of the boxes. Note the falling snow in the first frame, the newly green tree not quite covered in leaves in spring, the heat radiating from the sun in summer, and the rake at the ready for the swirling colored leaves in autumn.

In the book about seashells, Sammi divided the page to show the ocean and the beach separately, an interesting decision because she might just as easily have shown them together in a single illustration as they are closely connected. My theory about the decision Sammi made is this: Learning a technique to show differences in illustrations, and recognizing that her words suggested two different places where shells are found, she chose the divided illustration to most closely match this meaning.

Sammi was also learning in the illustration study to attend closely to details that would make her meaning clear in her illustrations. On the cover of

Figure 3.4   From Sammi's book *Seasons*

Figure 3.5 Sammi's divided seashell page. Shells are on the beach and ocean.

her book *Me and Katie Go to the Waterfall* (Figure 3.6), you can see she took this lesson to heart. The Katie in the book is me, and there is no doubt which one is me and which one is Sammi. She gave me wonderfully wild and curly hair, which I have, and she carefully drew her own glasses sitting just so above her smile, which she has too.

Blake and Nate coauthored a book about basketball during a study of illustrations. They played recreational basketball together, and so they enjoyed collaborating on a book about it and particularly enjoyed trying things they were learning in their study. In Figure 3.7, you can see they have shown both the inside and outside of the gym in a single illustration. By composing it in this way, the illustration adds meaning to the words, showing that practice happens in the afternoon. The tiny lines around the basketball are meant to show the motion of the ball, another technique they learned through the study.

Figure 3.6 Me and Katie go to the waterfall.

Figure 3.7 Nate and Blake practice basketball.

Another student, Katie Faye, made a book called *I Can Paint the World* (Figure 3.8). In this book, Katie Faye used an interesting cumulative technique as she added something to the beginning illustration across a series of four pages. The words match what is added each time, of course, and she carefully recreated the essential visual elements as she added a new detail on each page. In making a book like this, Katie had to keep the whole of it in mind during the entire process, making all the elements work together toward a satisfying conclusion. When composing, keeping the whole in mind is perhaps the biggest challenge for writers and illustrators alike, and this kindergartener was able to meet that challenge with her use of a sophisticated illustration technique. Just imagine her carrying what she learned about the wholeness of texts from this experience throughout her life as a writer.

And finally, Ella's wonderful *Book About Dresses and Weddings* (Figure 3.9) is filled with interesting decisions she made, both as a writer and an illustrator. Rather than pointing them all out, I'd like to focus only on the importance of color to Ella's decision making. Color is one of the most important tools an illustrator uses to compose, and certainly it was a very important tool for Ella in this book. The meticulous color in all the dresses is simply stunning, and the book would lose so much of its meaning and appeal if it didn't have its visual meaning and appeal, rendered with the tool of color.

If teachers are to understand and *teach into illustration* as a composing process, then understanding the role that color plays in children's decision making is paramount. Children need to explore a wide range of color options as they make decisions about their texts. When their efforts are purposeful, teachers can embrace the time it takes children to get the color right in a picture—the time spent capturing intensity or refining detail. The teaching response can shift from, *She's just coloring*, to understanding, *She's making that dress particularly interesting for her reader to see*. Rather than taking markers and crayons away from children during writing workshop, teachers can embrace these fine, fine tools for drafting, revising, and editing.

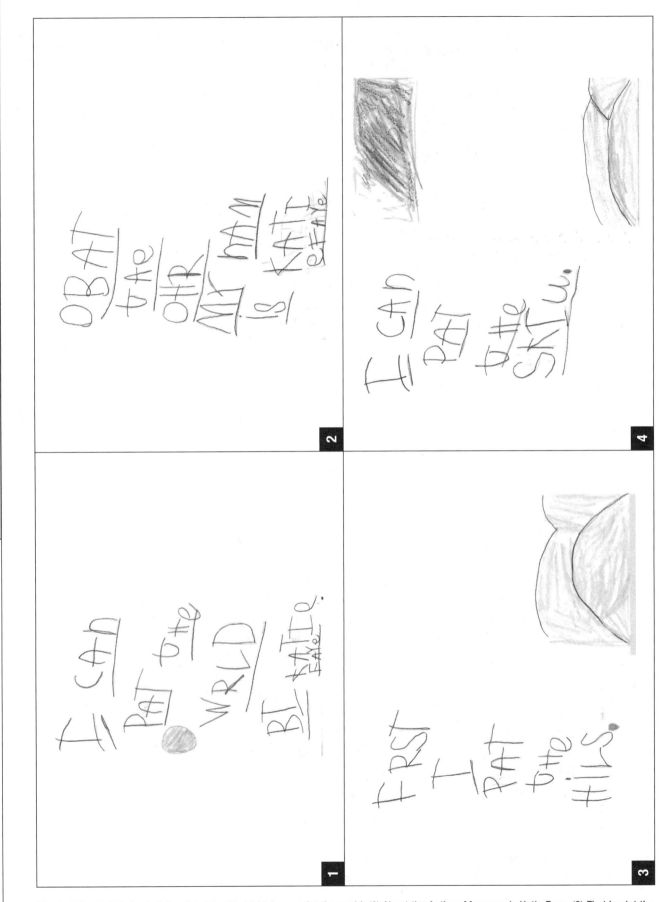

Figure 3.8   Katie's book: *I Can Paint the World*. (1) I can paint the world. (2) About the Author: My name is Katie Faye. (3) First I paint the hills. (4) I can paint the sky.

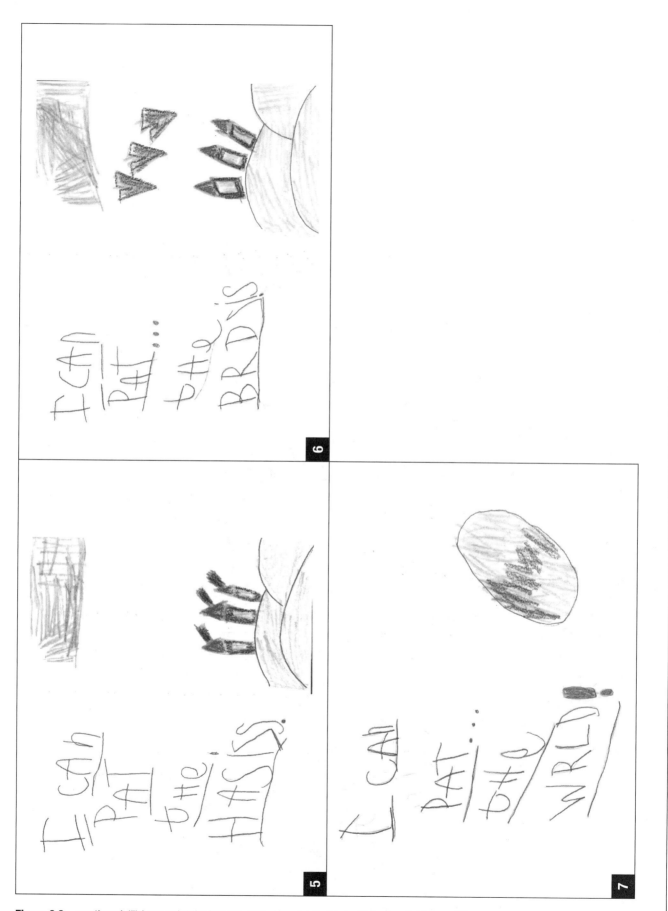

Figure 3.8 *continued* (5) I can paint the houses. (6) I can paint the birds. (7) I can paint the world!

Figure 3.9   Ella's *Book About Dresses and Weddings*

Figure 3.9 *continued* Ella's *Book About Dresses and Weddings*

The illustration techniques themselves are not what matters in these examples; what matters is children learning to be decisive as they compose texts about ideas that interest them. The more possibilities children know and understand, the more decisions they can make about how their books might go and the more complex their composing process will become. And as you no doubt have noticed from all the examples in the last three chapters, teachers clearly embrace children's artistic approximations as they try out different illustration possibilities, just as teachers embrace linguistic approximations in children's writing. Creating a climate of fearlessness (Ray and Cleaveland 2004) about both writing and illustrating in the workshop is key to children growing as meaning-makers. Children need to know that if they can imagine it, they can try it—and trying is what will be celebrated.

The Difference That Time, Teaching, and Experience Make

In the last chapter, you met Daniel and learned about the book he spent more than two weeks making early in his kindergarten year, *What Do Dinosaurs Do?* As the weeks and months of the school year went by, Daniel continued to make books about topics of interest to him, and he continued with his class to study the process of making books. A look at a book Daniel wrote in late winter of that year during a study of informational nonfiction shows just how much Daniel learned from experience—and how much more intentional he became in his composing process, especially in his illustrations. It's a book about snakes, and in it we see that Daniel acquired a clearly expanded repertoire of illustration possibilities.

Looking at Daniel's book through an assessment lens, here are some of the things it's clear he knows as he composes:

- *An illustration can show just a part of something.* A man is stepping on a snake, but only the foot is pictured on page 1. On page 3, a person can be seen at the very top of the illustration shown from the waist down in the water. And on page 6, the broken shell from which the two-headed snake has hatched is partly off the page to the side.

- *Text can be incorporated into the illustration.* (pages 1, 4, and 6)

- *A series of illustrations can show something happening across time.* An egg is being swallowed on page 2 and is hatching on page 6.

- *Boxes around illustrations make them distinct from the main illustration.* (pages 2 and 6)

Invite children into that magical moment when they first put markers to paper

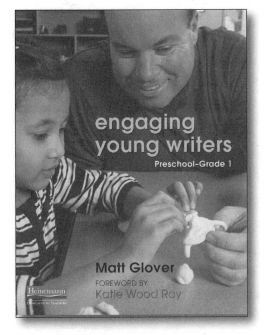

...with resources for every developmental step

Help young children take their first step toward a lifetime of writing

Katie Wood Ray and **Matt Glover** show how to gently nudge the youngest writers forward once they've put markers to paper. They guide you through fundamental concepts of early writing with helpful student examples—complete with transcriptions—and suggestions for:

▶ **making sense of children's writing**

▶ **seeing important developmental signs**

▶ **recognizing young children's thinking.**

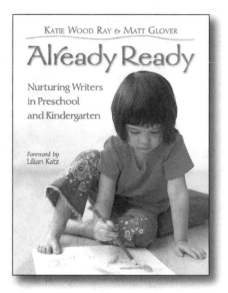

978-0-325-01073-1 / 240pp

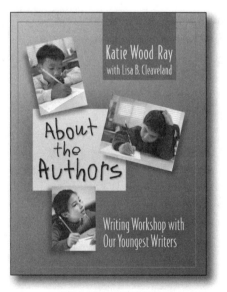

978-0-325-00511-9 / 256pp

Show young writers their next step with writing workshop

About the Authors explains how to set up and maintain a primary writing workshop, with eleven units of study that cover idea generation, text structures, different genres, and illustrations for text. **Katie Wood Ray** draws on the language of first-grade teacher Lisa Cleaveland so we can "listen in" as Lisa helps young students learn from professional writers, work with intention, and think about their own process.

CALL **800.225.5800**   FAX **877.231.6980**   VISIT **Heinemann.com**

DEDICATED TO TEACHERS

Trust Katie Wood Ray
and bring out the writer in young children

If you found *In Pictures and In Words* powerful, explore Katie's other resources for early writing. She turns research into teaching techniques that help you lead children step-by-step toward a lifetime of joyful writing. Katie's passion for helping young writers develop is both inspiring to teachers and the foundation of her research, her writing, and her suggestions for instruction.

"I want to say here that I am not concerned at all about children's development as writers. Nothing about how I work with young children has grown from concern about their development as writers. I believe that curriculum that grows from concern has the potential to be curriculum that is shoved down on students who may not be ready for it.

My work has grown, instead, from a **fascination** with their development as writers. I have seen again and again that when we get those markers and that paper in their hands, worlds of possibilities simply open up for all kinds of interesting developments that feel natural and joyful and absolutely appropriate. I believe that the curriculum that follows these possibilities is a "shoved-up" curriculum, pushed upon us as teachers when young children show us what they are capable of doing. I hope that my fascination, and the respect I have for the young children who instill it, will shine through in every chapter of my books."

—Katie Wood Ray

Heinemann

DEDICATED TO TEACHERS

Technique 11

Manipulating Point of View for Effect

Something to Notice

The content of an illustration may directly contradict what the words say, usually for humorous effect.

An Illustration Example

In a number of different illustrations in Marla Frazee's book *A Couple of Boys Have the Best Week Ever* (2008), the author/illustrator chose to picture something that is the exact opposite of what the words say, to great humorous effect. In one of the illustrations, one of the two main characters, a young boy named Eamon, chats on the couch with his grandparents and waits for his friend James (who'll be spending the week with him) to arrive. The words say, "Eamon thought this chat was fascinating. But he hoped James would arrive soon. And finally, James did . . ." When you turn the page, you see James standing with two oversized pillows in one arm, a bag in his other hand, and behind him there is a huge mound of overstuffed boxes and bags towering above him, twice his size. The words, a continuation of the sentence from the previous page, say, "with just a couple of his belongings."

On her website, Frazee says, "The text and illustrations of a picture book combine to create a larger and more expansive meaning than the sum of its parts. The words tell part of the story, the pictures tell part of the story, and sometimes they may tell different stories" (www.marlafrazee.com). In this illustration and quite a few others in *A Couple of Boys Have the Best Week Ever*, her pictures and words tell very different stories. Frazee developed her ideas and content with irony to great comedic effect.

An Understanding for Young Writers and Illustrators

Irony—something humorous based on a contradiction—is a sophisticated sort of humor that may be unfamiliar to many young children, so first you'll want to help students understand irony itself a little bit better. To do this, give children other examples of this sort of humor, perhaps based in your classroom life together. Then, reread parts of the text without the illustrations. Think about how the story makes perfect sense that way, but it's a totally different story than the one told by the pictures.

Next, you'll need to help children understand why an illustrator would decide to picture the exact opposite of what the words suggest should be pictured. Because it's funny, of course, but make sure you emphasize this

decision making in your talk around this illustration possibility. You might consider talking with children about how writers learn to connect with their audience—for example, writers who understand the fine art of humor have the power to make their readers laugh or chuckle.

You'll definitely want to introduce the word *narrator* in your talk about illustrations like this. By choosing to illustrate in this way, the narrator, the voice that's telling the story, is shown to be unreliable or as if she or he doesn't really get what's actually happening. You will almost certainly see that the illustrator employs this illustration technique several times in a book because using it only once would seem odd. Using it multiple times, however, tells the reader something about the narrator.

In a Teacher's Voice: An Idea for Trying It Out

If I were making a humorous book about our class trip to the museum when nothing seemed to go quite right, I might try this illustration technique. On the opening page my words could say, "I knew it was going to be a great day for a field trip when I first got out of bed that morning. The weather was perfect." My illustration would then show me from the back, looking out my bedroom window as I watch rain pouring down from a dark sky. For this kind of humor to work, I'll have to be consistent and make my illustrations contradict my words off and on throughout the book. That way my readers will know that I'm deliberately delivering a funny account of the class trip where nothing went quite right.

A Writing Connection

In many ways, this illustration possibility is about the concept of narration and point of view in story. Most stories are told either in the first-person voice (*I*) of one the characters, or in the third-person voice (*he*, *she*, *it*) of a narrator who is not a character at all. The third-person narrator may be omniscient and know everything that's happening both in the action and in the thoughts and feelings of all the characters, or the third-person narrator may be more limited in viewpoint, able to access the mind of only one or a very limited number of characters.

Marla Frazee decided to use a third-person narrator in *A Couple of Boys Have the Best Week Ever*, but because of this repeated illustration technique, her narrator is not only *not* omniscient, he or she is sort of clueless about what is really happening. The narrator is telling the story, but because of the illustrations, readers know that he or she is not necessarily telling it the way it actually happened.

In the sixth edition of *Writing Fiction: A Guide to Narrative Craft* (2003), Janet Burroway wrote, "Apart from the significant use of detail, there is no more important skill for a writer of fiction to grasp than this, the control of point of view" (256). Consistency is key to this control, Burroway says, and "a writer signals amateurism in the failure to make a point-of-view contract and

stick to it." If Frazee's narrator had only gotten the details wrong once in the book, as she did in this early illustration, then it might have been humorous but it also would have been a little weird. Readers would just be left wondering why the narrator didn't get it right in that particular case. But the fact that the illustrations belie the words *repeatedly* proves the narrator is quite unreliable, actually, and creates a consistent point of view throughout the story.

Technique 12

Seeing Through the Eyes of a Narrator

Something to Notice

Illustrations may show the perspective of the narrator, so we actually see things through his or her eyes.

An Illustration Example

In the introduction to *Loki & Alex* (2001), author/photographer Charles R. Smith, Jr., lets one of his characters, Alex, explain how the book will be narrated:

> *My name is Alex. I'm going to tell you about my dog, Loki, and Loki is going to tell you about me . . . I learned that dogs see the world a little differently than humans do. Dogs can't see colors quite the same way as humans. So everything Loki sees in the story is in black and white, and everything I see is in color.*

As the boy and his dog go for a walk, the book alternates between their two voices and perspectives on everything from digging in the trash to tummy rubs. Each time the boy speaks, the photo illustration is in color and the reader looks through his eyes and sees what the dog is doing. Each time the dog speaks, the photo illustration is in black and white and the reader looks through his eyes and sees what the boy is doing. The illustrations and words together help the reader understand that the boy and his dog sometimes are experiencing things very differently. For example, when Alex wants Loki to fetch, Loki responds, "No treat, no fetch" and wonders why the boy doesn't throw him a treat instead of a "stupid ball."

An Understanding for Young Writers and Illustrators

If children are to use this rather sophisticated illustration possibility in their own work, they'll need a strong sense of perspective and how a narrator brings perspective to both pictures and words. Knowing this, you'll want to linger with the talk around "seeing it through the eyes" of the narrator. Talk about what you see and *why* you see it that way—because that's what the narrator is seeing and it's also *how* he's seeing it. Be sure to think about how the narrator feels about what he or she is seeing. How might the narrator see the exact same scene if he or she was feeling very differently about it (e.g., frightened, excited, shy).

In a Teacher's Voice: An Idea for Trying It Out

If someone were to make a book about our classroom and let the pet hamster narrate the book, everything would need to be pictured as if the hamster were seeing it. Since he sees what happens most often through the thin bars of his cage, many of the illustrations would need to be framed by the cage itself and have little lines running through them so readers feel they are looking through the bars of the cage to the outside.

A Writing Connection

As with the previous illustration possibility, this possibility has everything to do with understanding narration. The entire text, of course, is "in voice" (it's not really dialogue because they're not exchanges), alternating between the two voices of the boy and his dog. What's significant, though, is how the illustrations help us see things through the eyes of each narrator, a crafting skill that is important for good writers to understand and one that I've written about before.

In one of the "Craft Pauses" in my book *Study Driven* (2006), I show how Cynthia Rylant helps the reader see things clearly through the eyes of her narrator, Summer, in *Missing May* (1992), a book that won the Newbery Medal award. Here's the excerpt:

> . . . *May turned me to the kitchen, where she pulled open all the cabinet doors, plus the refrigerator, and she said, "Summer, whatever you like you can have and whatever you like that isn't here Uncle Ob will go down to Ellet's grocery store and get you. We want you to eat. . . .*
>
> *My eyes went over May's wildly colorful cabinets and I was free again. I saw Oreos and Ruffles and big bags of Snickers. Those little cardboard boxes of juice that I had always, just once, wanted to try. I saw fat bags of marshmallows and cans of SpaghettiOs and a little plastic bear full of honey. There were real glass bottle of Coke looking cold as ice in the refrigerator and a great big half of a watermelon taking up space. And, best of all, a carton of real chocolate milk that said Hershey's. (7–8)*

In *Study Driven*, I explain the crafting in this excerpt like this:

> *[The] writer helps us see the scene through the character's eyes. Good description is not about including every possible detail; it's about selecting details that help the reader take in the scene with the same feelings the character is experiencing. Just before this scene when the little girl (and narrator), Summer, walked into May and Ob's trailer for the first time, she said she felt like "Alice who had fallen into Wonderland." What we see in the kitchen helps us capture this feeling. Surely there was salt and pepper out somewhere, a tub of Crisco shortening, perhaps a jar of Tums on the counter,*

but these aren't included. Only the things a six-year-old—who felt like Alice in Wonderland—would see are included. (106)

Seeing this crafting technique used in illustrations (as it is in *Loki & Alex*) can help children understand what it means to craft a scene so the reader experiences it through the eyes and feelings of the narrator.

8

Precision and Detail, In Pictures and In Words

ONCE WHEN I WAS CHATTING WITH SOME TEACHERS about books, I asked if they knew Bob Graham's *"Let's Get a Pup!" Said Kate*. Almost immediately someone said, "Isn't that the book where the mom has the great nose ring and tattoo?"

"Let's Get a Pup!" Said Kate (2001) is the wonderful story of a family who goes to an animal rescue center to adopt a dog and ends up adopting not just one, but two lovely canine companions. The story is compelling, especially for dog lovers, but it's also a wonderfully crafted text, with lines like these about the dogs they see at the center: *They found . . . big dogs, small dogs, sniffers and sleepers, wire-haireds, short-haireds, scratchers and leapers. They found fighters and biters, growlers and snarlers, short dogs, dogs long and thin, and dogs with their cheeks sucked in.* And yes, by the way, it's also the book where the mom has the great nose ring and tattoo.

What struck me about the teacher recalling the book in this particular way, of course, was that these small illustration details clearly left quite an impression on her as a reader. The nose ring and tattoo don't play any part in the story line; they are simply two details that lend a huge amount of character—very hip, very cool character—to Kate's mom. I was reminded of Ralph Fletcher's words about details from *Breathing In, Breathing Out: Keeping a Writer's Notebook*:

> *Details matter. In a poem, essay or story, a powerful detail allows the reader to understand the emotional drama. And it gives the reader plenty of space to enter the world of the text.*

*When we read a piece of writing it is often the apparently irrelevant detail
we remember, even more than brilliant argument or lyrical language.
(1996, 20)*

The nose ring and the tattoo were such powerful details—though ar-
guably irrelevant—they stuck with this reader and became, in many ways,
what the book was about for her.

Details Matter

Details do matter. As an illustrator, Bob Graham is a master of details. In all
his many wonderful books, he develops powerfully distinct personalities
for his characters by including small but telling details in his illustrations.
Similarly, his settings come to life as real places because of his keen eye for
the significant detail in the backdrops of scenes. When crafting pictures,
Graham and other illustrators use the same basic understandings about the
power of detail that good writers use when they craft written texts.

Consider what a few writers have to say about details. John Gardner
wrote in *The Art of Fiction*, "In all the major genres, vivid detail is the life
blood" (1983, 26). Janet Burroway echoed this in *Writing Fiction: A Guide to
Narrative Craft*: "Specific, concrete, particular details—these are the life of
fiction" (2003, 76). And what about nonfiction? Details matter there just as
well. Lee Gutkind wrote in *The Art of Creative Nonfiction*, "To make scenes
seem authentic . . . writers attempt to include memorable small or unusual
details that readers would not necessarily know or even imagine" (1997, 47).

Life blood. Life. Authenticity. When it comes to details, the illustrator and
the writer have the same important work to do. One uses pictures, the other
uses words, but each must select and incorporate details that will bring a
work to life for readers.

Details as Description

While illustrators incorporate details using visual elements, writers may incorporate details in a variety of ways. For example, sometimes writers seem
to be almost painting a picture with words, rendering a character or a scene
with such detail that the reader experiences them visually, as if seeing them
through the narrator's eyes. In this case, the selected details form a passage
of description. This is the sort of detail work Gary Paulsen did in this passage from *Lawn Boy* as the character Arnold is introduced for the first time.

I had plenty of time to study him as I mowed toward him.

*Very short. I'm pretty short and he wasn't much taller than me and kind of
round. Not fat, not heavy, just round. Everything about him was round.*

Rounded shoulders, hips, arms, legs—even his head was a ball. And his hair-cut looked like somebody had put a large bowl on his head and cut around it with scissors.

Wild clothes. I saw a seventies show on television once and everybody had shirts with impossibly long collars and colored patterns that looked like maybe somebody had taken a bucket of flowers dipped in paint and thrown it at the actors.

That was Arnold's style.

And he had a wide, wild tie and a kind of sport coat that looked suede but was cut with wide lapels and shoulders and a narrow waist that didn't look too good on his round body. He looked like somebody who had flunked clown school. It was hard not to smile. (2007, 16–17)

Paulsen selected details that help us picture Arnold in a very visual sense. Some of the details are quite direct and specific—the sport coat that looked suede, the impossibly long collars, the wide, wild tie. Significantly, he doesn't tell us every single little thing, either. He chooses. This is where precision is important—in the selection. A detailed description is not about the quantity of detail, but rather the quality. Paulsen gives a few important details, then, through the voice of the narrator, he uses a more indirect method of detailing: "He looked like somebody who had flunked clown school." Figurative language like this can do great visual work for writers, especially when it is supported by specific detail.

The Telling Detail

While the passage above is clearly descriptive in mode, detail and description are not synonymous. Consider, for example, a very different sort of detail work Paulsen uses so artfully later in *Lawn Boy* when a fight that's been brewing is about to break out.

The first three trucks I recognized. The fourth one was a red pickup angled into the curb, not parked parallel like the others. A man was sitting behind the wheel with the driver's-side window open and two men were leaning against the end of the truck. One of them was pretending to clean his finger-nails with a knife. Several of Pasqual's family members were standing around by the door of the house. They seemed a little afraid, maybe, but mostly confused.

"The one in the truck is Rock," Pasqual said, stopping.

Joseph opened the door and slid out. The truck rose visibly when his weight was gone. (57)

The precision of detail in this passage conveys so much. Without ever saying words like *menacing* or *threatening*, we know that's just what the guys in the red truck are trying to be. The details suggest a driver making a show of his disrespect for rules and order, uncaring as he not only parks against the grain but runs the truck right into the curb. The guy *pretending* to clean his fingernails would be far less threatening if he was actually cleaning them. The fact that he's *pretending* suggests manipulation and dark cunning (especially because he's using a knife). And finally, the truck rising visibly tells us all we need to know about Joseph, a guy who will soon throw another full-grown man headfirst through the window of the truck.

When crafting narrative, writers of nonfiction will use details in the same ways you've seen them used in these examples from fiction. But details are important to non-narrative writing as well. In a recent *Newsweek* article (May 25, 2009) about former Treasury Secretary Hank Paulson, writers Evan Thomas and Michael Hirsch included some interesting details to shed light on Paulson's character.

> *He is not a Wallstreet smoothie: no trophy wife (he remains married to his college sweetheart), and at Goldman he was known for wearing penny loafers, not handmade Italian shoes. He's an avid birdwatcher. A nonsmoking, nondrinking Christian Scientist, he did not head for the Hamptons on the weekend but visited his mother in Barrington, Ill. (53)*

The particular details the writers chose to include in this list are meant to shed a different, softer light on Paulson, a man whose career has been distinguished, the authors say, by tenacity and drive. And the details do their work. Think about the significance of including *Barrington, Ill.*, in the already telling detail that Paulson spends his weekends visiting his mother. My apologies to the town of Barrington and all its inhabitants, but it sounds like such an ordinary place (especially in contrast to the Hamptons) that its value as a detail in this passage is simply priceless.

Details do matter. In her book *Reading Like a Writer: A Guide for People Who Love Books and for Those Who Want to Write Them*, Francine Prose said this about the importance of detail in writing:

> *Great writers painstakingly construct their fictions with small but significant details that, brushstroke by brushstroke, paint the pictures the artists hope to portray, the strange or familiar realities of which they hope to convince us: details of landscape and nature, of weather, of fashion, of home decoration, of food, of botany, of music, of sports, art, of all the things with*

which we humans express our complex individuality. Often, a well-chosen
detail can tell us more about a character—his social and economic status, his
hopes and dreams, his vision of himself—than a long explanatory passage.
(2006, 198)

I love that Prose used the metaphor of writers painting pictures with words, because it makes the composing connection relevant to this book so clear. Writers paint pictures with words, and illustrators paint pictures with pictures, but they are both trying to help readers experience and understand, and precise detail is certainly one means to that end for both word artists and picture artists.

An Eye for Detail: The Importance of Observation

Developing the power of observation is important for children in so many ways. James Dickey was quoted in Donald M. Murray's *Shoptalk: Learning to Write with Writers* as saying, "That could almost be cited as the definition of a poet: Someone who notices and is enormously taken by things that somebody else would walk by" (1990, 17). Think about how many words could be substituted for *poet* in that statement: *mathematician, scientist, historian, musician*—and certainly *writer* and *illustrator*. A habit of noticing and paying attention is essential to good writing and good illustrating, especially when it comes to noticing detail.

Young children, of course, are already very adept at noticing. A study of illustrations will make them aware of this habit of mind and how vital it is to their work as writers and illustrators. They'll be called on to notice at two levels: first as they study the details in illustrations, and second as they study details in the world, looking closely at the people, places, and objects they want to represent in their pictures. The study will encourage them to do the sort of noticing Elizabeth Berg wrote about in *Escaping into the Open: The Art of Writing True*:

> *It is not enough to give a passing glance at something if you want to really*
> *see it. Whether you are talking about the colors of an island sunset or the*
> *grime in a down-and-outer's flophouse bathroom, you have to look deeply.*
> *You have to give yourself enough time to transcend the impulse we usually*
> *have of naming or classifying something—thereby often dismissing it. To re-*
> *ally see something is to let yourself move beyond the narrow place of words and*
> *into a 360-degree kind of noticing, an act which, if done correctly, temporarily*
> *takes up all of a person, and utilizes much more than the eyes—utilizes, for ex-*
> *ample, the heart and the soul. (1999, 88–89)*

The possibilities you will find in this section are all about using the "360-degree kind of noticing" to study the specific detail decisions illustrators make. Studying decisions about detail will help children compose far more meaningful illustrations, and at the same time help them develop very important understandings that will serve them well as writers long into the future.

Technique 13

Crafting Details of Expression and Gesture

Something to Notice   Facial expressions and gestures are meaningful details.

An Illustration Example   Trish Cooke's *Full, Full, Full of Love* (2003) is a wonderful celebration of Sunday dinner at Grandma's house, and the details in Paul Howard's illustrations bring the family to life, particularly in the facial expressions and gestures found on page after page. In one illustration, the family is sitting around the table having dessert and coffee and after-dinner talk. One of the aunties is leaning back in her chair and her arms are crossed high across her middle, just above her stomach. The expression on her face is one of skeptical amusement, as if she might be thinking, "Girrrlll, what are you talking about?" Everyone pictured at the table has equally telling, though different, expressions and gestures. Later, in the last illustration in the book, Howard shows four different people waving good-bye, and every wave is a little different, particularly the specifically hip, back-of-the-hand, thumb-extended wave of a young cousin.

An Understanding for Young Writers and Illustrators   Perhaps because they're still so close to that time when they read faces and gestures to understand, that time before they understood words, children seem especially keen at noticing the expressions and gestures of the people pictured in illustrations. "Why is that man so mad?" they ask, when they see an angry face or a furious gesture. This natural keenness will serve them well in understanding how important details of this kind are to both good writing and good illustrating.

To understand how key facial expressions and gestures are to meaning making, imagine watching a couple having coffee through the front window of a diner. You can't hear a word they're saying, but just by watching them you can probably tell whether they are happy and in love and glad to be together, or bored out of their minds with one another, seriously discussing some matter of great import, or mad as hell and holding nothing back. You can tell all this because of gesture and expression. For a writer or an illustrator to truly bring a scene to life, attending to the details of gesture and expression is critical.

The key for teaching is to bring the natural noticing children do as they people-watch in books to a very conscious level. As you notice the looks on characters' faces and the gestures suggested by their postures, stress the fact that showing them in this way is a result of the illustrator's decision making. Wonder with children about those decisions. A person's facial expressions and gestures happen in direct response to what's happening around him, so how does it seem the character is experiencing the moment in time captured by the illustration? Based on what you see, what does the illustrator want you to believe this character is thinking or feeling? What other expressions or gestures might have been appropriate? These lines of thinking and discussing will help you build in your students a very important understanding: that details of expression and gesture always communicate something important about a character's experience, both in illustrating and in writing.

Interestingly enough, while children notice facial expressions and gestures as they read, they don't normally use this level of detail in their own illustrations of people unless nudged to do so. Be sure to demonstrate for the whole class the kind of thinking that leads to adding such details to an illustration. You'll also want to help children include this sort of detail as you work with them one-on-one in writing conferences. If a child has pictured a person as part of a scene, help that child imagine the person's response to the scene and then craft the facial expression and gesture to match that response.

In a Teacher's Voice: An Idea for Trying It Out

If I were making a book about my nephew's birthday party, I might have an illustration where he has opened a present and looked inside the box, but the reader can't see what's inside. Instead, the reader sees my nephew with his head thrown back, his eyes shut tightly, his mouth spread wide in what appears to be a big "yeeesss," and his arms raised triumphantly in the air, fists balled with the feel of victory. In other words, he likes the Wii he sees in the box.

A Writing Connection

Natalie Goldberg wrote the following advice in her book *Thunder and Lightening: Cracking Open the Writer's Craft*:

[I]magine a scene as a photograph—the moment a husband tells his wife he's just been fired from his job—and describe what you see. You cannot say, "She was shocked and furious." You cannot say, "She was sympathetic." These are not pictures. We are trying to bring the scene vividly alive in the reader's mind. Instead, focus on the face of the woman in the photo; her lower lip is curled, ringed hand stretched out toward the man across the couch, eyes narrowed in slits. What does he look like? What are they wearing? And the room? Flowered carpet? Black-and-white linoleum? Fern in the corner?

Window open? Ceiling fan? Probably that photo will not reveal whether it's in Illinois or Florida—unless there's a palm tree out the window. We cannot know what the photo does not directly impart. No past or future is in a picture, only the revelation of the moment. Don't let wild mind travel off into introspection—what could have happened?—or imagine how he is feeling or how she is feeling. Stay with what is given. The reader will glimpse the feelings far more immediately in the gesture—the curled lip, the outstretched arm—than in any abstract statement. Here we are developing writing as visual art, using our eyes as the primary way into a scene. (2000, 165–66)

Writing as visual art. The revelation of the moment. The connection between the use of detail in writing and its use in illustration could not be clearer. The mediums are different—words and pictures—but the understanding about crafting is exactly the same: both authors and illustrators know that readers "will glimpse the feelings far more immediately in the gesture."

Crafting Physical Details of Characters

Something to Notice

The physical detail of characters—clothing, hairstyles, adornments—are revealing.

An Illustration Example

Poppa, a character in Phyllis Root's *Rattletrap Car* (2001), is dressed in my own personal, very-favorite outfit in the whole world: overalls. I'm wearing a pair right now as I write this, as a matter of fact.

In choosing overalls with no shirt underneath for Poppa, illustrator Jill Barton seems to have captured the good father's personality perfectly. He matches his rattletrap car, a car that falls apart, piece by piece, as the family travels to the lake on a hot day. Poppa ably fixes it along the way, however, and of course he does, he's wearing overalls. Barton also gives Poppa spiky red hair (not hair gel spiky, but naturally, messy spiky), rosy cheeks, kind eyes, and prickly stubble on his arms and legs. He's barefoot, and the overalls are rolled up about four inches above his skinny ankles. The only adornment Poppa wears is what appears to be a pair of glasses or maybe a pen sticking out of one of his pockets, visible in some of the illustrations but not all. The illustrator has crafted the physical appearance of Poppa with great intention, lending great appeal to him as a character.

An Understanding for Young Writers and Illustrators

Just as in life, appearances matter in writing and illustrating. It's human nature to respond to appearance—inwardly at least, if not outwardly—and form opinions about others based on their appearance. And while in our everyday interactions with real people we may work to keep our judgments in check, for the writer and the illustrator trying to convey character, appearance is a powerful tool.

For any picture book with people in it, at some point the illustrator must decide how to dress his characters. He may be trying to achieve veracity, whimsy, absurdity, or any of a whole range of portrayals, but the details of the character's appearance will communicate much to the reader, so the decision is a major one. As you study illustrations with children, help them think about why an illustrator has portrayed a character in a particular way. Why those clothes? Why that hairstyle? Why that huge peace-sign necklace

around his neck? What assumptions do we think the illustrator wants us to make about this character based on his or her appearance?

Without a doubt, these particular lines of thinking are going to raise critical reading questions about how children "read" people in the world, and this is a good thing. You'll want to follow these questions where they lead because they are important questions for children as citizens of the world. These conversations will also help children realize how, using the tool of detail, an illustrator has powerful control over a reader's response to a character.

In the end, you want the talk about this kind of detail to help children become much more intentional as they dress their own characters and style their hair and give them tattoos and watches and rings for their toes. Also make sure that children notice that characters stay dressed the same way across pages, unless time has brought about a change of clothes. This is a small thing that children sometimes don't think about in their own illustrations.

In a Teacher's Voice: An Idea for Trying It Out

If you were making a book about our principal, Ms. Crawford, it would be just plain weird to draw her in a dress, don't you think? She never wears dresses. She always wears great pantsuits with funny little pins on her lapels. Her hair is almost always pulled back in a plain brown headband, and her glasses hang around her neck, when she's not wearing them. These are details that would be really important to include when you draw her.

A Writing Connection

When it comes to the details of physical appearance, the big difference between writing and illustrating is that writers select the details readers "see" and illustrators generally must select details showing the entire person, especially for a character who will appear across a book. Writers might give a lot of details all at once, forming a description, or they might spread physical details out, letting readers form a picture of a character bit by bit over time.

Gordon Korman's novel, *Schooled*, has alternating narrators across its thirty-one chapters. The first chapter is narrated by the main character, Capricorn, so we don't have any physical details of him in that chapter. But the second chapter is narrated by the school guidance counselor, Mrs. Donnelly, and the opening sentences capture her first glimpse of Capricorn:

The instant I saw him standing there with all that hair and all those beads, I just knew.

Garland Farm. It had to be. Nobody else looked like that. Nobody had looked like that since 1970. Except at Garland. (2007, 10)

Garland farm is a hippie commune where Capricorn has lived his whole life. The third chapter is narrated by the "big man" on the middle school campus, Zach Powers, and Korman gives us a much more detailed look at Capricorn through Zach's eyes when he first sees the strange new kid at school:

> *I was on my way to homeroom when Mr. Kasigi, the assistant principal, flagged me down. Standing beside him was the strangest-looking kid I'd ever seen. He was tall and skinny as a rake. I swear he'd never been anywhere near a barbershop in his life. His long blond flyaway hair stretched all the way down to the middle of his back. His clothes looked like pajamas—home-made pajamas. And his shoes were something out of a social studies project on the pioneer days. They were sandals woven out of cornhusks, and rustled when he moved. (15)*

The writer does with words what the illustrator does with pictures, and of course, the wonderful sound detail—the sandals that rustle when Capricorn moves—is much more easily achieved with words than pictures. But what both artists understand is the importance of physical detail to character development.

Technique 15

Revealing Character with Background Details

Something to Notice

Life and character are revealed through details in the background of a scene.

An Illustration Example

Told through a series of narrative poems, Nikki Grimes' *Oh, Brother!* (2008) is the story of two young boys whose parents marry and make them stepbrothers. Grimes used the voice of one of the brothers to capture the natural, sometimes difficult adjustments that come with blended families. In one of the poems late in the book, the brother who is narrating says, "I want to play like A-Rod." A-Rod being, of course, Yankees infielder Alex Rodriguez. But before readers ever get to this poem, they know Xavier loves baseball because illustrator Mike Benny has incorporated background details into several scenes in the boys' bedroom that make this love of the game clear. In one bedroom scene, two action pictures of baseball players can be seen on the wall just above the bed, and a baseball cap hangs from the bedpost. In another scene, a different ball cap hangs from a shelf. There's also a trophy on that shelf leading readers to wonder, "Could that be a baseball trophy?" And on the bedside table sits a lamp whose base is the shape of a large mitt with a baseball tucked snugly inside.

An Understanding for Young Writers and Illustrators

The background of our lives is very telling. If you could see me right now, for example, sitting in my office where I'm writing, you could learn so much about me just by looking at what surrounds me here. You'd know I'm a tea drinker because an empty cup sits on a saucer with a soggy, limp tea bag beside it. You'd know I love the University of North Carolina Tar Heels because the 2005 and 2009 basketball championship bumper stickers are plastered above one window. You'd know I need glasses to read (I can see at least three pairs left about), I probably love dogs (an empty dog bed sits right next to my chair and my mouse pad has doggie faces on it), and that I once earned a PhD (my computer monitor sits atop my doctoral dissertation so the screen is at eye level). I could go on and on, but I think the point is clear: what folks surround themselves with tells us a lot about who they are as people.

Both writers and illustrators know that one way to reveal character is to include details about what surrounds a scene, details that help readers understand various aspects of a character's life. When you see details like this included in the background of illustrated scenes, ask children to think about what the details tell you about the life of the character(s) in the scene. How much can you learn just from looking at what's on the walls, placed on the shelves, strewn about the yard or taped to the refrigerator? You'll see a real range of how much small detail is included in the background of scenes; often there is very little. But when there is a lot of detail, it's almost always purposeful and revealing. Help children understand that the illustrator included the details so readers would know more about the life behind the scene.

Imagine with children how much they can reveal in their illustrations by including background details in the environment of their pictures. To deepen this thinking, you might lead your students in selecting which background details you would include in a drawing of your classroom. Which details would reveal important things about who you are as a class? Also, as you work with children one-on-one in conferences, help them imagine including details like this in the books they are making (when it makes sense to do so, of course).

In a Teacher's Voice: An Idea for Trying It Out

If I imagine a page in a book about my father, I can easily picture him on the sofa in his living room, and I can imagine several background details that would reveal a lot about him. If I angled my picture so you could see the TV, it would show a shot of *Jeopardy!* on the screen. My dad loves game shows. There would also be a crossword puzzle book lying on the coffee table next to a bowl of pistachios. I would have to move the "picture wall" to include it in this scene, but I could do that, and it would show multiple framed pictures of his children and grandchildren.

A Writing Connection

Writers, just like illustrators, understand the power of the well-chosen background detail. In *Writing Magic: Creating Stories That Fly*, Gail Carson Levine wrote, "In general, you want to put in details that reveal character, or move the story along, or establish the setting or the atmosphere. The best details do more than one at the same time" (2006, 108–9).

Consider the double-duty one small background detail does in this passage from an essay in Naomi Shihab Nye's collection, *I'll Ask You Three Times, Are You OK?*

In a small Michigan village the young taxi driver who picked me up before dawn to drive me eighty miles to a town with an airport was driving a car

that didn't look like a taxi at all. It looked like an old beat-up car a kid would drive. There was no meter or sign.

I said, "Are you really the taxi?"

He said, "No, I'm really a guy trying to make enough money to go to college and stay tanned, but they call me a taxi."

I threw my bags into the backseat with a bit of suspicion and climbed in, closing the dented door behind me. There were empty Gatorade bottles on the floor.

"Stay tanned?" (2007, 109–10)

Those empty Gatorade bottles in the back of a beat-up "taxi" certainly reveal character and establish atmosphere in a very powerful way. As someone who often rides in taxis, I responded immediately to that detail, thinking, "I'd probably have gotten right back out with my bags and called for a different car."

The detail does something else for me as a reader, too. Those Gatorade bottles help me trust the writer and believe her story of what happened. They make it seem like she was paying attention. In this case, Nye was writing from a true personal experience, but details work the same way to build a sense of truthfulness in fiction where they are fabricated. John Gardner wrote in *The Art of Fiction: Notes on Craft for Young Writers*, "The reader is regularly presented with proofs—in the form of closely observed details— that what is said to be happening is really happening" (1983, 26).

Crafting Details from the World of Nature

Something to Notice   Using details from the natural world brings authenticity to a setting.

An Illustration Example   Anyone who's ever spent any time in a garden in summer knows that it literally hums and crawls with life. The vegetables don't make any noise or movements, of course, but the creatures living in and around them do. Nadine Bernard Westcott was mindful of this truth from nature when she crafted the illustrations for Katherine Ayers' book *Up, Down, and Around* (2007). The whimsical illustrations of life in a garden feature all manner of worms, ants, grasshoppers, centipedes, flying insects, and just bugs in general crawling and flying around the vegetables. Their colors aren't necessarily lifelike and their faces have funny human expressions on them (adding to the whimsical feel), but their presence as a significant, recurring detail in the book is a cue straight from nature itself. After all, why would anyone draw a garden up close without bugs?

Barry Root took a similar cue from nature in his illustrations for Mary Lyn Ray's book *Christmas Farm* (2008). In one illustration, the reader is looking down on a landscape covered in snow. In the distance there are mountains and forests and fields, and in the foreground you can see the two houses of the main characters, Wilma and Parker. They are next-door neighbors, and there are footprints in the snow between their houses. What a fine, fine detail. Of course there are footprints. Wilma and Parker are best friends, and there is snow on the ground.

An Understanding for Young Writers and Illustrators   The world of nature is rich with detail. Just looking out my window right now I notice the varied texture and color of the bark on the trees. I can see tiny gnats flying around, seemingly going nowhere but in every different direction at once. I see shadows spreading out behind bushes and big rocks. I see weeds (too many of them) growing in the cracks by the front walkway.

If an illustrator decides to show the natural world, either as a landscape or as the backdrop to a scene, capturing some of the detail of nature lends authenticity to the scene. When you study an illustration that has interesting natural detail in it, talk about the specifics of what you see. Name each detail separately so that children understand the layers of detail crafting required to

make, for example, a creek, seem authentic. Rendering an authentic creek would involve way more than simply drawing blue water cutting through green grass.

One of the most significant details from nature that you see in both indoor scenes and outdoor scenes is the effect of light on objects. Be sure that children notice the use of shadow in illustrations and that they understand how shadows come to be. One of my favorite books for studying the effect of shadows and light is *Baseball Hour* (2008), written by Carol Nevius and illustrated by Bill Thomson.

As with so many other details, using the detail of nature to bring illustrations to life requires close observation. You might consider having your students go outside and sketch or write exactly what they see in a small space of nature, capturing as much detail as possible. And certainly as you confer with children, help them realize the potential for natural detail in their own drawings based in nature.

In a Teacher's Voice: An Idea for Trying It Out   If I were to make a book about running on the beach in the early morning, I'd need to really think about what details to include that would make it seem like a real beach scene. I'd need sand, of course, but I'd also need seashells in all different shapes and sizes and colors strewn about. I'd need some washed-up jellyfish, and footprints behind me but not in front of me. And I'd definitely need that line the waves make between the darker wet sand and the lighter dry sand.

A Writing Connection   In many ways, both writers and illustrators must ask themselves the same question, "What details must I include in this natural setting if it is to seem authentic to the reader?" When this question is answered, an illustrator can't possibly just draw a vegetable garden; she must fill it with bugs. He can't just draw a snowy landscape; he must cross it with footprints. And I can't just draw the beach; I must also draw the seashells and the washed-up jellyfish and that fine line between wet sand and dry.

Barbara Kingsolver's painting with words of a forest in Africa is, in my opinion, one of the greatest renderings of a natural setting in all of literature. It's in the opening paragraph of *The Poisonwood Bible*:

Imagine a ruin so strange it must have never happened.

First, picture the forest. I want you to be its conscience, the eyes in the trees. The trees are columns of slick, brindled bark like muscular animals over-grown beyond all reason. Every space is filled with life: delicate, poisonous frogs war-painted like skeletons, clutched in copulation, secreting their precious

eggs onto dripping leaves. Vines strangling their own kin in the everlasting wrestle for sunlight. The breathing of monkeys. A glide of snake belly on branch. A single-file army of ants biting a mammoth tree into uniform grains and hauling it down to the dark for their ravenous queen. And, in reply, a choir of seedlings arching their necks out of rotted tree stumps, sucking life out of death. This forest eats itself and lives forever. (1998, 5)

While I might write a whole book on just what can be learned about writing from this single amazing passage, just consider if you will the *choir* of seedlings. At first I thought seedlings might be some sort of animal I didn't know because I thought *choir* referred to sound. But then I realized *choir* refers to posture and I could perfectly picture the new green plants sticking up out of tree stumps like a choir, a gospel choir in my mind's eye—swaying a little bit and not stuck in their places. The perfect metaphor doing the perfect illustration work for a great writer.

Technique 17

Showing the Effects of Weather on a Scene

Something to Notice   Details can show the effect of weather on a scene.

An Illustration Example   Martin Jenkins' book, *The Emperor's Egg* (1999), is all about emperor penguins. These magnificent creatures live in Antarctica, so as you might imagine, the illustrations by Jane Chapman picture a snowy landscape throughout. One illustration, however, stands out from the others because it appears so exceptionally cold and windy. The text on this page reads, "And when it gets really cold and windy, they all snuggle up together and shuffle over the ice in a great big huddle" (18). The penguins are huddled together tightly in the center of the illustration. From the top left side of the spread, white snow streams down over them in a curving swirl, as if it's riding down on a strong wind. The whiteness is also much more concentrated in this area, furthering the impression that the wind is blowing down and across the huddled penguins from this direction.

An Understanding for Young Writers and Illustrators   So many days are sunny days in young children's books, and often they are sunny days with rainbows! Because many young writers don't think a lot about the details of weather in their writing and illustrating, studying these details will open up an important new line of decision making for many children.

The first aspect of weather detail to help children understand is the effect of seasonal weather on any landscape. A book about emperor penguins in Antarctica would be very inauthentic without snow in the background. As you look at books with illustrated landscapes, talk about the kind of place the illustrator has pictured and what season it likely is in the picture. What details help you know this? In the mountains of western North Carolina where I live, for example, we are surrounded by deciduous trees. Because of the trees, the landscape looks dramatically different in different seasons of the year. In other locations, such as the Arctic or the desert or the tropics, seasonal weather changes the landscape very subtly or not at all. Following this angle of your study, help children think about their own landscapes in the books they write and illustrate.

Illustrators also use details to represent a specific weather event in a landscape, just as Jane Chapman did when she showed the strong gust of

wind blowing snow at the huddled penguins. As you study illustrations, you'll see all sorts of weather events pictured: rain, snow, wind, lightening, hail, fog. You'll also see the impact of weather events on landscapes: puddles after downpours, white caps on a windy body of water, sometimes even a rainbow in a clearing sky after a passing storm.

You'll also want to talk about how details of weather often go a long way in setting a particular mood or feeling in a text (just as weather affects mood in real life). As you think about how weather details affect the mood of a picture, be careful not to oversimplify: sunny doesn't always mean happy and rainy is not always sad. For example, if an illustration shows a person wrapped in a warm blanket, drinking cocoa and reading, but through the window you see pouring rain, the illustration may convey a very warm, safe, cozy feeling. What feeling does it look like the illustrator was trying to achieve? What meaning does the weather event bring to the unfolding meaning of the book?

The goal of these weather-related lines of thinking, of course, is to help children use details of weather more purposefully in their own composing. When children are drawing landscapes, encourage them to think about representing weather and its effects with specific detail.

In a Teacher's Voice: An Idea for Trying It Out

If we were to make a book about the day we got out of school early for snow last week, we'd definitely want to include some weather detail. Remember when we were standing outside waiting for the buses and it just kept snowing harder and harder? The ground wasn't white when we first went out, but it was completely covered by the time the last bus came. Maybe we could show that over a series of pictures—the ground getting more and more covered in white.

A Writing Connection

Writers often include detail about the weather as a way of setting mood or foreshadowing something that will happen. Look at how meticulously E. B. White detailed the rain and set the right mood in the opening of the fourth chapter of *Charlotte's Web*, a chapter titled "Loneliness":

> *The next day was rainy and dark. Rain fell on the roof of the barn and dripped steadily from the eaves. Rain fell in the barnyard and ran in crooked courses down into the lane where thistles and pigweed grew. Rain spattered against Mr. Zuckerman's kitchen windows and came gushing out of the downspouts. Rain fell on the backs of sheep as they grazed in the meadow. When the sheep tired of standing in the rain, they walked slowly up the lane and into the fold.*
>
> *Rain upset Wilbur's plans. (1952, 25)*

What's interesting about the crafting here is that White could have stopped after saying the day was rainy and dark, but he didn't. The series of images he included to show the rain are purely visual in nature; after all, they don't add any new meaning. The sentences all mean exactly the same thing: it was raining. It's almost as if White stopped moving his narrative forward for a moment and became an illustrator, giving a clear and vivid picture of just how the rain looked on that wet dark day. A great writer, painting the weather with words, just as an illustrator would with pictures.

Technique 18

Crafting Details from the World of People

Something to Notice   Using details from the world of people brings authenticity to a setting.

An Illustration Example   The street scenes created by Lauren Castillo for Emily Jenkins' book *What Happens on Wednesday* (2007) are alive with the detail of city streets. There are antennas and chimneys on the roofs of row houses, fire escapes and front stoops, cars and bicycles parked along the curbs, awnings over doors and windows, bare-leaved trees stretching across the street, fire hydrants, signs on storefronts with real names in them—Brooklyn Bridge Reality, Ltd., and Hidden Bean (a coffee shop) and Florist and Barbershop and Luncheonette and Delicatessen—and all sorts of people carrying all manners of things out and about on the busy street.

An Understanding for Young Writers and Illustrators   Just as close detail is important when crafting scenes in the natural world, so it is when crafting scenes in human-made settings. Writers and illustrators must be close observers and recorders of the details of all sorts of settings. When studying illustrations set heavily in the world of people (nature is always there, too, of course), be sure to innumerate all the different details you see the illustrator has included. Naming them specifically will help children understand both the quantity and quality of details that help bring a scene like this to life. Notice, particularly, the use of environmental print as it is such a situating detail in the world of people.

Consider with children how the details of setting *outside* a character's home reveal differently than the details of setting *inside* the home. Readers assume that the details of setting inside someone's home reflect the life of the person who lives there (as we discussed in an earlier detail possibility). What you see in that home setting was placed there by someone who lives there. But once characters move out into the world—to a ball game, a county fair, a movie theater, for example—the details of setting belong to that place and not to the character anymore. The only thing we can assume about the character from the details in settings outside the home is that this is where the character is at the moment frozen in time by the picture; this is where he finds himself. And this moment in this setting may actually tell us a lot about

the character, even the quality of his life, but in a different way than the details of home tell us about him. This distinction is an important one for children to understand about the illustration details of settings.

Finally, just as you might have done with details in natural settings, you might want to take children somewhere (or even stay in your classroom) and have them really look at a setting and capture as much detail as possible about it. Teach them to see that setting through the eyes of an illustrator and become faithful recorders of detail.

In a Teacher's Voice: An Idea for Trying It Out

If Thea were to illustrate scenes of her grandmother shopping in Walmart, she could bring that scene to life with real attention to details. Just imagine what she might include: food products lining the shelves with labels you can read, the lobster tank with fresh lobsters swimming around in it, the floor tiles in the same pattern as the one at the store, the store greeter with a name tag that says "Sylvia," people waiting in line at the self-checkout, and big signs hanging from the ceiling that say things like "Pharmacy" and "Women's Underwear." (Okay. I don't think there's really a sign that says "women's underwear," but it would be worth a good laugh as long as we're imagining.)

A Writing Connection

I have collected the columns from the *Miami Herald* written by Pulitzer Prize winning writer Leonard Pitts, Jr., for years now. As I wrote about capturing details from the world of people, I remembered this column from several years ago (August 2, 2004). Pitts wrote it in response to a life-changing visit to Sierra Leon and Niger. While I hadn't read the essay in a long time, I remembered the detail of the roof with the rocks on top to hold it down. That detail has stuck with me. Here's the passage in which it's embedded:

> *Around us, Kroo Bay goes about its business. A mangy dog with open sores sleeps on a sidewalk. Gray water trickles in a stream filled with garbage. The air is pungent with the smoke from cook fires. An old man sits in front of his home smoking his pipe. He lives in a shanty with a roof made from corrugated metal. There are rocks on it to keep it from blowing away in a high wind.*

> *It occurs to me that this is the worst place I have ever been.*

That's a powerful summation he makes, but he earns it with the details you see here and several more that follow in the column. As Natalie Goldberg says said in *Wild Mind: Living the Writer's Life*, "You have to earn the right to make an abstract statement. You earn this right by using the concrete bricks of detail" (1990, 208). The weight and importance of the

work Pitts is doing here as a writer reminds me of another thing Natalie Goldberg said, this time in *Writing Down the Bones*:

> *We are important and our lives are important, magnificent really, and their details are worthy to be recorded. This is how writers must think, this is how we must sit down with pen in hand. We were here; we are human beings; this is how we lived. Let it be known, the earth passed before us. Our details are important. Otherwise, if they are not, we can drop a bomb and it doesn't matter. (1986, 43)*

Because Leonard Pitts, Jr., wrote about those rocks holding down a man's roof in the wind of Kroo Bay, and because I read that detail and never forgot it, this man's life *does matter* to me. Details matter.

Using Authentic, Object-Specific Details

Something to Notice

Object-specific details bring authenticity to objects, both human-made and natural.

An Illustration Example

Illustrator Diane Goode did a wonderful job of including very specific details on many of the objects pictured in Cynthia Rylant's book *Christmas in the Country* (2002). She chose to show the tiny stitches on the hand-sewn angel tree ornaments and the specific design etched into a Tiffany-style lamp. She included blue stripes on a pair of curtains and red ones on a stick of peppermint. We can see the indentations on a glass that's full of milk and the steam holes cut into the top of a pie. Even the siding on the church has been carefully drawn in, line by line.

Sylvia Long included equally close detail in her illustrations for Dianna Hutts Aston's book *An Egg Is Quiet* (2006). On the page where the baby birds are newly hatched, for example, readers see dark green spots and translucent veins on green leaves, and tiny, prickly nubs on an orange weed. The specific, boxlike pattern of a caterpillar's cocoon is precisely rendered, along with the tiny hairs down the caterpillar's back (living creatures aren't really *objects*, but the detail principal is the same). The soft down covering the baby birds is very clearly drawn, as are the ridges on their skinny legs. And each of the spots covering the cracked eggs is unique.

An Understanding for Young Writers and Illustrators

As the last few illustration possibilities before this one have made clear, deciding which details to include in a scene is the first decision an illustrator makes. Once the decision has been made to include an object, however, other decisions are made about the level of detail to include when drawing that object. Without a doubt, very specific details—like those in the examples above—lend authenticity to objects.

As you study illustrations with very specific object detail in them, name the different decisions the illustrator made about what to include. Talk with children about the effect these details have on you as readers. Such details communicate a feeling that the illustrator *really looked* at an object and recorded it just exactly how he or she saw it. Sometimes such details go beyond the purely visual and lend an added sensation to the visual experience. For example, the down on the backs of the baby birds was so

carefully drawn, you can almost feel it. And that pie with the steam holes in it—let's just say the fresh smell of some good fruit wafts up through them for many readers.

In a Teacher's Voice: An Idea for Trying It Out

If I were making a book about my house, it would be a mistake if I simply drew any old green bushes by the front steps. The bushes planted there are unusual, and people often notice them and ask what they are. They are *Mahonia japonicas*, and if I drew them to look as much like they truly are as I could, my reader would know I had really looked. I'd show the pointy, deep-green leaves that grow perfectly symmetrically along the thick strong branches, and the lovely purple berries that grow in long, full bunches between them.

A Writing Connection

Without a doubt, this sort of detail work is about specificity. Natalie Goldberg speaks to the power of specificity in this quote from *Writing Down the Bones* (1986):

> *Be specific. Don't say "fruit." Tell what kind of fruit—"It is a pomegranate." Give things the dignity of their names . . . It is much better to say "the geranium in the window" than "the flower in the window." Geranium—that one word gives us a much more specific picture. It penetrates more deeply into the beingness of that flower. It immediately gives us the scene by the window— red petals, green circular leaves, all straining toward sunlight. (70)*

With careful, precise detail, an illustrator gives a truck the dignity of being a Ford F-150, a countertop the dignity of granite, a bush by the front steps the dignity of *Mahonia japonica*. The illustrator draws this dignity; the writer writes it.

Creating the Illusion of Motion with Detail

Something to Notice   Details can create the illusion of motion.

An Illustration Example   Marla Frazee's lively *Santa Claus: The World's Number One Toy Expert* (2005) is a book just filled with motion, beginning right up front with Santa bouncing across the cover on a pogo stick. Curved lines of motion trail behind him, showing the path the pogo stick has followed. Inside the book, Santa does a back flip on a trampoline, rides a unicycle and a bicycle, pogos some more, tests a toy by dropping it, erases a chalkboard, shakes his head, and paces and ponders. Using three different techniques, Frazee creates the illusion of motion in each of these actions. One technique is to use motion lines around the action, as if drawing the air that is stirred by the motion. Another is to draw Santa again and again, thirty-three times on the pogo page, to be exact, moving across the page. It's the same Santa all those thirty-three times; he's just moving. The third technique is to draw just the body part that is moving multiple times, still attached to the body, but in different places spatially. She uses this technique to show Santa shaking his head (his head is moving) and erasing a chalkboard (his arm is moving).

An Understanding for Young Writers and Illustrators   Many of the topics children choose to write about—play, in particular—lend themselves naturally to details of motion, and giving the illusion of motion is a very common detail found in picture books. Because of this, children will likely incorporate motion detail purposefully in their own illustrating.

When illustrators make a decision to create the illusion of motion in a picture, it's usually because the meaning being made by the picture clearly suggests motion. Have you ever seen anyone *standing still* on a pogo stick? Children probably won't need lots of time and talk to understand why illustrators show motion because the reasons are fairly obvious. You'll want to focus your teaching attention on the repertoire of techniques you find for creating the illusion of motion. The three used by Marla Frazee and described above are probably the most common techniques you'll see. Another common one is to show the result of impact, which of course suggests motion—a splash, for example, or something flying about because it's been stirred up.

One thing to be on the lookout for is children setting most everything into motion once they get started. Overuse is a natural consequence of learning, but do nudge children to think about showing motion purposefully and selectively.

In a Teacher's Voice: An Idea for Trying It Out

Starr could really use this technique to great effect in her book about gymnastics class. I can imagine all sorts of movement in that book. I especially like the idea of showing how you do flips all the way across the big mat by drawing you over and over, just like Marla Frazee showed Santa on that pogo stick!

A Writing Connection

An illustration represents a moment frozen in time. When illustrators create the illusion of motion in a picture, however, in a sense they are defying the boundaries of time. Motion must happen across some span of time, even if it is only a split second. So the illusion of motion in a picture is also the illusion of time passing.

Photographs are also frozen moments in time, but high-performance cameras can capture motion in a series of those moments. My most recent *Sports Illustrated* (March 8, 2009) contains an amazing sequence of five photographs, each a frozen moment, but combined they show the catch Dewayne Wise made to preserve the perfect game pitched by Mark Buehrle of the Chicago White Sox.

Writers, on the other hand, have no time boundaries. They can take as long as they'd like to follow something in motion. I hadn't read Jerry Spinelli's book *Maniac Magee* in years, but when I went in search of writers showing motion with words, it was the first book I pulled off my shelf. The character Maniac is almost synonymous with motion, and Jerry Spinelli is a master craftsman, so I knew this would be a good place to look.

There's a lot of motion in the book, but I'll just use two examples. If I were to try and illustrate this first example, I would probably use the common technique of motion lines around the ball. It seems to suggest this because the entire action wouldn't have taken more than a couple of seconds in real time. It's from the scene where Maniac gets a hit on a pitcher who's just struck out thirty-five straight batters:

> *McNab fired. The kid swung. The batters in line automatically turned their eyes to the backstop, where the ball should be—but it wasn't there. It was in the air, riding on a beeline right out to McNab's head, the same line it came in on, only faster. McNab froze, then flinched, just in time. The ball missed his head but nipped the bill of his cap and sent it spinning like a flying saucer out to the shortstop. The ball landed in the second-base dust and rolled all the way to the fence in center field. (1990, 24)*

If the book were to be illustrated, the illustrator would have to choose the critical moment in the continuous motion to freeze—probably the nipping at NcNab's hat would be best—and then let the motion lines represent the rest. Those batters in line turning their heads probably need some motion lines around them too.

This second example is from just a few pages later when McNab and his gang are chasing Maniac and throwing stones at him. The motion takes place over much more time, so it suggests an illustration with multiple drawings of the same figure. All of the ellipses are actually part of the text—I haven't added them because I've left parts out.

> *He darted left, skirted the dump, wove through the miniature mountain range of stone piles and into the trees . . . skiing on his heels down the steep bank and into the creek, frogs plopping, no time to look for stepping rocks . . . yells behind him now, war whoops, stones pelting the water, stinging his back . . . ah, the other side, through the trees and picker bushes, past the armory jeeps and out to the park boulevard, past the Italian restaurant on the corner, the bakery, screeching tires, row houses, streets, alleys, cars, porches, windows, faces staring, faces, faces . . . the town whizzing past Maniac, a blur of faces, each face staring from its own window, each face in its own personal frame, its own house, its own address, someplace to be when there was no other place to be, how lucky to be a face staring out from a window . . . (31–32)*

Now that's how a writer shows motion! Spinelli crafts a sentence that, literally, never ends, the construction of the sentence itself matching Maniac's motion. And then, well, just the amazing word work—the verbs, the prepositional phrases, the lists, the punctuation. Without a doubt, the detail of motion can bring writing and illustrating to life, but I think writers have the distinct advantage when it comes to capturing the feeling of motion.

Creating the Illusion of Sound with Details

Something to Notice   Details can create the illusion of sound.

An Illustration Example   Eric Velasquez must have thought a lot about how he could represent sound visually when he agreed to illustrate Carole Boston Weatherford's wonderful book *The Sound That Jazz Makes* (2000). The book is a study in creating the visual illusion of sound. One way Velasquez achieved the effect is to show people with their mouths open wide, shouting or crying or singing. Another way is to show people exuberantly dancing. The reader looks at the dancers and just knows they wouldn't be moving like that if there weren't sound inspiring them. Similarly, many pages show people clearly, physically producing sound from instruments, so while you can't actually hear sound, you sense it is there. And a final way he created the illusion of sound is to show the roiling water spraying up from the wheel on a steamship, the impact of wheel on water clearly making the suggestion of sound.

An Understanding for Young Writers and Illustrators   Children know that books don't have sound in them (except those with built-in sound gadgets) and that sound is not really something they can draw. Your teaching work will be to help them think about how some illustrations suggest sound in powerful ways and others don't. What kinds of details in pictures suggest sound strongly? Velasquez used several common details for this effect: open mouths (not just people's mouths but animals too), showing an action designed to produce sound (musical instruments), showing something that's brought about by sound (dancing), and showing a physical impact that would surely produce sound (the wheel churning the water).

As you study books where illustrations create the illusion of sound, name other ways you see illustrators achieving this effect. You may also want to have children think about illustrations that *don't* suggest sound. How are they different? In *The Sound That Jazz Makes*, for example, one illustration that really doesn't suggest sound is a montage illustration. It shows a close-up of just one side of a man's face, his mouth closed, an excerpt of newsprint announcing a slave auction, and the auction house with the doors

closed and quiet. There just isn't any sound there, but in the very next illustration the sound returns in the wide-open mouth of the slave auctioneer going about his business.

If an illustration suggests sound to a reader, it's because the reader has some experience with what's pictured and knows what it sounds like. A picture of a field full of modern windmills will suggest a lot of sound to folks who've been close to them, and hardly any to those who haven't. While this is a sophisticated understanding, you'll want to talk with children about what readers bring to the text that helps them experience sound in certain illustrations and not in others.

In a Teacher's Voice: An Idea for Trying It Out   If you were making a book about the time you scored a goal in your soccer game, you could certainly show how everyone was cheering by simply drawing lots of folks with their mouths open. You'll probably want their bodies to be in cheering sorts of positions too, but the wide-open mouths will certainly create the feeling of sound.

A Writing Connection   In a forward to his novel *The Winter Room*, Gary Paulsen lamented the fact that books can't have smells and sounds and light. And then, in the very act of lamenting this fact, he wrote words that show they can, if readers are there to smell and hear and see. Here's the part where he pondered the absence of sound:

> *If books could be more and own more and give more, this book would have sound. . . .*
>
> *It would have the high, keening sound of the six-foot bucksaws as the men pull them back and forth through the trees to cut pine for paper pulp; the grunting-gassy sounds of the work teams snorting and slapping as they hit the harness to jerk the stumps out of the ground. It would have the chewing sounds of cows in the barn working at their cuds on a long winter's night; the solid thunking sound of the ax coming down to split stovewood, and the piercing scream of pigs when the knife cuts their throats and they know death is at hand—but they can't.*
>
> *Books can't have sound.*
>
> *If books could have more, give more, be more, show more, they would still need readers, who bring to them sound and smell and light and all the rest that can't be in books.*
>
> *The book needs you. (1989, 2–3)*

Writers trying to capture sound with words clearly have an advantage over illustrators. Imagine, for example, the pigs with the knives at their throats. The illustrator might draw this scene in great detail, but unless readers know what kind of sounds pigs in distress make, they can't really hear the right sound for the picture. They might imagine a deep guttural sound instead of the piercing scream the writer can name with words.

Technique 22

Using Details as an Element of Surprise

Something to Notice A detail may hold an insider's surprise for the reader.

An Illustration Example In the author/illustrator blurb on the back of Donald Crews' book *Night at the Fair* (1998), there is a photograph of Crews taken at the Duchess County Fair. He's wearing a red shirt and a camera hangs around his neck. Savvy readers (aka five-year-olds who notice everything) will notice that Crews painted himself—wearing this same red shirt and a camera around his neck—into one of the crowd scenes at the fair inside the book.

Illustrator Lauren Stringer tucked a similarly surprising detail into Cynthia Rylant's book *Snow* (2008). In this illustration, the grandmother and granddaughter sit at a table sipping coffee and planning their spring garden (we know they're doing this from the telling details, not the words). Again, savvy readers will notice that on the table there are three books. The covers of two of them are visible. One is about gardening, and the other is the cover of the picture book *Scarecrow*, another book written by Cynthia Rylant and illustrated by Lauren Stringer, published in 1998.

An Understanding for Young Writers and Illustrators What a delight to discover this sort of detail in the illustrations of a well-loved book! When readers recognize a detail like this, they feel a sense of intimacy with the illustrator, a sense of being in on the joke, if you will. "I get what you're doing," the reader responds to the illustrator. And the illustrator knows the detail will illicit this sort of response. The crafting of it is quite purposeful in that direction.

When you find insider details like these in your illustration study, don't be surprised if your very observant students discover them first. As you discuss such details with children, help them think about what a pleasure it must have been for the illustrator to include a surprise like this—almost like a gift for the reader. Use the word *surprise* often in your discussion because the idea of surprise is just as important in good writing as it is in good illustrating.

You'll also want to help children understand how these kinds of details work. The surprise and delight come because the reader is able to connect the detail to something outside the book. Lots of humor is crafted in this

same connected way. Something from one context is surprisingly dropped into another, and those who recognize it, get it. I'm a huge fan of Jon Stewart and the *Daily Show* (now that's a revealing detail) and they use this sort of insider's detail to humorous effect all the time. Just last night one of the "senior experts" on the show was using exact language from Sarah Palin's resignation statement as governor, but in a totally different context.

In a Teacher's Voice: An Idea for Trying It Out

Let's see . . . if Thea were making a book about her trip to Florida with her grandparents, maybe one illustration could show their car moving down the interstate and in the background she could draw a Walmart truck. This would be so funny because everyone knows—at least everyone in this class knows because she wrote such a great book about it—that Tara's grandmother loves Walmart more than any place in the world.

A Writing Connection

In his book *Spunk & Bite: A Writer's Guide to Bold, Contemporary Style*, Arthur Plotnik wrote about the role of surprise in good writing. He named a number of different ways a writer might pursue it with words, but he explained that the delight of surprise is what matters:

> *Readers love surprise. They love it when a sentence heads one way and jerks another. They love the boing of a jack-in-the-box word. They love images that trot by like a unicorn in pajamas . . . Everyone knows that good writing stimulates readers with inspired, sneaky surprises. It does so at all levels, from surprises based on twists of plot and character to the smaller but keen surprises of language." (2007, 10)*

Readers do love surprises, and I found one just yesterday as I was reading *Keep It Real: Everything You Need to Know About Researching and Writing Creative Nonfiction*. In a section about forewords and afterwords, Lee Gutkind tucked in a little insider's surprise very similar to the illustrated ones described earlier:

> *In an age when author fabrications have led to firings, forfeited Pulitzer Prizes, and vast reader distrust of a million little memoirs, conscientious writers turn increasingly to forewords and afterwords to bring the reader behind the scenes of the work. (2008, 62)*

"A million little memoirs," of course, is a reference to James Frey's memoir *A Million Little Pieces*, parts of which were exposed as fabrications, causing quite a stir across the literary landscape. Leaving a little surprise like that in a text is quite a pleasure for both writers and illustrators.

9

Wholeness of Text, In Pictures and In Words

$\mathcal{U}$*nity is the anchor of good writing.*

—WILLIAM ZINSSER, *On Writing Well*

ON THE AFTERNOON I BEGIN WRITING this section of text, I do a word count on how much I have drafted so far. As of today, I've written fifty-one thousand, eight hundred, and seventy-nine words. That's a lot of words, and I still have thousands more to go. One of the greatest challenges a writer faces is how to make all fifty-one thousand, eight hundred, and seventy-nine words—plus all the others to come—work together in a way that feels satisfyingly whole for the reader. As Jerome Stern has said, "You start writing the ending when you write the first word" (1991, 130).

I am now writing more than fifty thousand words away from the first word, and yet I must always be thinking about how these words grew from that one and all the others in between. So many words to hold steady in my thinking. So many questions to keep in mind. How does this section do the work that the first chapter promised it would do? Am I writing this section so it fits with the other sections like it—the introductions to the other qualities of good writing? Does it have the same woven feel to it, moving back and forth between writing and illustrating? The thing is, day after day, I can't just write new words; I must also manage an ever-expanding text.

From the first word to the last, whether there are fifty words or fifty thousand, a writer must always keep the text she is crafting in mind as a whole. No part stands alone. Every word must work inside the sentence, every sentence inside the paragraph, every paragraph inside the section, every section inside the chapter, every chapter inside the book. All those words, from the first one to the last, must work to fulfill the purpose that compelled the writer to start in the first place, and they must make someone else want to read it. *All of it.*

Having crafted the text as a whole and believing in the value of every word of it, the writer tries to keep the reader *reading* from the first word to the last. Pulitzer Prize winner Tom French said, "The fundamental purpose of a narrative's first paragraph is to make the reader continue to the second paragraph. And the purpose of that paragraph is to make him read the third paragraph" (2007, 143). I would add to this that by paragraph two thousand, three hundred, and seventy-two, the writer desperately wants the reader still to be reading and to feel like the journey through all those paragraphs has added up somehow.

On the journey from the first word to the last, writers have to think a lot about consistency. In nonfiction, it's consistency of tone and terminology, ideas and theme, layout and design. In fiction, it's consistency of character, setting, and plot detail. Across all those words, writers have to think a lot about content: Does this idea make more sense before that one or after it? Have I already said this somewhere else? Have I used a similar example? Have I quoted this person too many times? Keeping the whole in mind, everything in a text needs not just to work on its own, but also work well with everything around it.

Illustrators face the same challenge to keep the entire text in mind as they draft and revise their illustrations. Notice, for example, how similar illustrator Bryan Collier's point is to the one made by Tom French cited earlier. Collier is talking about his Coretta Scott King honor award book *Uptown* (2000), a beautiful tribute to life in the city of Harlem:

> In Uptown, *the boy wakes up, looks out the window, and sees the red awning. On the next page he is under the red awning in the same building having chicken and waffles. The brownstones are not mentioned in the text, but they appear visually for the first time on the page. One page introduces the next in many ways and that's intentional as visual stories are told.* (2007, 37)

One page introduces the next, just as one paragraph leads the reader to the next paragraph and the next. Illustrators, just like writers, are trying to craft a text that will keep readers with them from the first page to the last.

To create a satisfying journey through a book, illustrators must be mindful of how each illustration is working in relation to all the rest. Illustrators have to think a lot about consistency and content across their texts, just as

writers do. Their tools are different, but many of the issues are the same. The illustrator keeps his tone, technique, layout, design, and details consistent across his text. He asks similar questions about content. Have I overused this sort of picture? Does this illustration make sense in relation to the one just before it? Is the tone in all these pictures consistent? Illustrator Marla Frazee wrote, "By placing image after image, we are creating a visual narrative. We must control this narrative as much as the author who is writing sentence after sentence" (www.marlafrazee.com).

Not only do writers and illustrators share the understanding that a text must work well as a whole, they also employ many of the same techniques to create a feeling of wholeness. For example, in *The Van Gogh Café*, writer Cynthia Rylant used recurring details repeatedly across the span of the short novel. *The Van Gogh Café* is about a café in the middle of Kansas, a café where magic seems to happen quite often. Rylant described the café in the opening chapter:

> *Some say magic comes from heaven, and others say it comes from hell, but anyone who has ever visited the Van Gogh Café knows that magic comes from a building that was once a theater; from a sign above a cash register that reads BLESS ALL DOGS; from a smiling porcelain hen on top of a pie carousel; from purple hydrangeas painted all over a ladies' bathroom; from a small brown phonograph that plays "You'd be so nice to come home to." (1995, 2)*

At least eight times in the fifty-three pages of *The Van Gogh Café*, one or more of the objects in this passage reappear in the text, relating in some subtle new way to the life going on around them. In one passage, for example, it's getting near Christmas, and Rylant writes:

> *Small paper antlers have been glued onto the porcelain hen's head, and over ALL DOGS someone has taped SANTA. BLESS SANTA. The phonograph has changed its tune—the only time of year a different record is played—and Nat King Cole is singing "Silent Night." (30)*

The final appearance is just a mention of the hen—still smiling—on the very last page as the writer is leaving the café, convinced that he will follow his true calling as a writer:

> *When he finally decides to get back on the road to Oregon, he walks up to the register to pay his bill. The hen smiles at him. Marc tells him, "Have a good trip." (53)*

The details reappear not because the reader needs to be reminded of their specifics, but because they have become a part of the unfolding story happening around them.

Author/illustrator Jonathan Bean employed the same understanding when he included a number of recurring details in the illustrations of his wonderful picture book *At Night* (2007). The cat is a particularly compelling, dynamic detail. *At Night* is a simple story about a little girl who can't sleep, so she takes her pillows and a sheet and a blanket and goes up to the rooftop of her home in the city to sleep.

The little girl has a black cat, a detail the reader knows only from the illustrations. The cat is seen in the early illustrations outside the little girl's room as her parents tuck her in. He reappears in later illustrations as the girl starts her journey from her room to the rooftop and he follows her up the steps. In the closing illustration, the cat is snuggled next to the soundly sleeping little girl. His presence there, and off and on in other illustrations, creates a feeling of wholeness across the text for the reader. His reappearance keeps him from being just a static, one-time detail—*The girl has a black cat*—and turns him into a dynamic part of the story unfolding in the illustrations.

One uses words, the other uses pictures, but Cynthia Rylant and Jonathan Bean both seem to understand what Ralph Fletcher explained so well in *What a Writer Needs*: "A detail mentioned early that shows up later can provide a deeply satisfying resolution to any piece of writing . . . The recurring detail works like an echo in which the second mention is nearly always more important than the first"(1993, 52). An echo is always connected back through time to the sound that originally brought it forth. Similarly, a recurring detail is always connected to the text that preceded it, and the reader feels this connection. This is how recurring details help bring a feeling of wholeness to the texts in which they reappear.

The techniques in this section are all about how illustrators make connections between and among illustrations. Through the study, as children learn ways to make illustration connections across the pages of their books, they'll be growing important understandings about the importance of composing a text with a sense of wholeness—understandings that will serve them well throughout their lives as writers.

I would be remiss to end this introduction and not mention that I believe this quality of writing—making a text work well as a whole—is the most important and most challenging aspect of writing well. I have served on editorial review boards for professional journals for years and have read dozens of manuscripts submitted for publication consideration. By far, the most common problem plaguing manuscripts not yet ready for publication is a lack of what Lee Gutkind referred to as "structural integrity" (1997, 127). The authors of these manuscripts often have compelling ideas and compelling ways of presenting them; they just don't know how to make them all come together into something pleasing to read as a *whole text*. Too many adults schooled in the formulaic structure of the

five-paragraph essay are fine if they're writing a five-paragraph essay, but managing longer texts of greater complexity, or managing a text that's not an essay, can be a real challenge.

Because the challenge of managing a whole text is so real for writers, I believe it's critical to help beginning writers think about the wholeness quality of good writing. Illustration study provides a wonderfully developmentally appropriate context in which to do just that.

Technique 23

Keeping Static Details Consistent

Something to Notice   The static details of characters, objects, and places are consistent across a book.

An Illustration Example   In Ralph Fletcher's book *The Sandman* (2008), illustrator Richard Cowdrey included some interesting details in both characters and settings. For example, Cowdrey gave Tor—the Sandman—a deeply pronounced dimple right in the middle of his chin. From any angle on page after page, the dimple is visible. To the dragon, Cowdrey gave a wonderful red goatee, amazingly unsinged despite all his fire breathing. And in Tor's bedroom, Cowdrey helps the reader understand what an inventor Tor is by including all manner of furniture made from everyday objects like pencils and drawers and nuts and bolts. Tor, the dragon, and the bedroom are pictured in multiple illustrations, and in every one, these details are consistent.

An Understanding for Young Writers and Illustrators   You may be wondering whether this illustration technique is even worth the space it takes up to include as a possibility. You may be thinking, "Well of course the dimple is there in every picture. Of course, if the bed is made from a drawer in one scene, it's the same bed in another scene." In general, the physical details of characters, objects, and places are static. They don't change unless something happens to change them: the dragon shaves, for instance. A significant change to a static detail would have to be accounted for in the text, however, or else the change would leave the reader perplexed.

The logic that causes illustrators to keep static details consistent may seem too obvious to be worth considering, but not when you think about this understanding in the context of children's illustrating. Children often make books and have the same people and objects on several pages, but the static details of them are not consistent. A friend will have yellow hair in one illustration and red in another. A house will have four windows early in a book and six by the end, plus a new door and a chimney. An ice-cream cone will change from strawberry to chocolate with just the turn of a page.

To help children quickly gain a greater sense of wholeness in their composing, study the consistency of static detail you see across the illustrations in a book. Quite likely, children are aware of consistency in detail,

they just aren't aware they're aware of it. Certainly, children usually notice if something is suddenly *in*consistent in a book. Your teaching goal is to help children think very specifically about the consistency of detail they see in illustrations. When a child mentions a detail that is striking, like the dragon's goatee, make it a point to notice that it's that way on every page (even though it seems obvious).

As you point out how illustrators have to be so careful to render a character or object the same way each time they're pictured, help children imagine the work it takes to accomplish this. Illustrators must look back often at what's already illustrated in order to keep details consistent as they add new illustrations. This process of looking back to make sure new content fits with old is directly parallel to the process a writer uses to keep wholeness in a text. As writers are drafting and adding new text, they have to stop and reread often to be sure everything is working together as intended.

In a Teacher's Voice: An Idea for Trying It Out   In a book about my dogs playing around outside, there are several details I'll need to keep consistent. First, I'll make sure each of the four dogs has the same color collar on in every illustration. Next, I'll make sure that Montana always looks the biggest, because he is the biggest. And finally, I need to show that tiny black tip on the end of Ivy's tail in every picture, because that's the way we tell her and Dallas apart.

A Writing Connection   Without a doubt, writers of fiction have their work cut out to keep all their details straight. Once a static detail about a character or a setting has been revealed in a text, that detail needs to remain consistent in all the scenes that follow. The thing is, once a bedspread has been labeled pale yellow or a telephone as rotary, those specific details may not be stated again. What the writer must hold onto in subsequent scenes is the truth of yellow, the truth of rotary. The writer cannot say, for instance, that his character didn't see the black cat lying on her bed. *The one with the pale yellow bedspread?* the reader asks. *How could she not see a black cat lying on a pale yellow bedspread?* The writer cannot have his character pick up her phone and punch in her boyfriend's number. *I thought she had an old rotary phone*, the reader thinks. The problem is, of course, that the later details don't fit with the earlier ones. Readers lose faith in a writer when the details don't add up.

Eve Bunting spoke of this issue when she wrote about how she checks for "overwriting" when she's revising. In her essay, "The Power of Words," Bunting said she asks herself the following:

Does the dialogue sound real? I have written, "I know I am well loved." I, the author, might say that. But would my protagonist, the one who is speak-

ing in my book? He's a fourteen-year-old boy. Come on, Eve. Get real! (1996, 224–25).

Getting real with your text and making sure that one detail matches the reality of another is the challenge for the writer.

Presuming the details of their writing are true, nonfiction writers might have to check their notes to remember specific details, but consistency should be embedded in the truth of the subject matter and not something writers have to manage. However, nonfiction writers face a similar, but slightly different challenge because they must check for the consistency of terminology. In a feature article about working people finding health insurance, for example, the writer shouldn't refer to a person who works behind a bar as a *barkeep* in one place in the article and a *bartender* in another. The writer needs to settle on a term and stick with it. Readers want to feel as if they can trust a writer with words, and using words in a consistent manner across a text builds this trust. The idea of consistency across a text is what's important to both illustrators and writers.

Technique 24

Making Seemingly Insignificant Details Reappear

Something to Notice Dynamic details, even seemingly insignificant ones, may reappear in a book.

An Illustration Example Claire Masurel's wonderful book *Two Homes* (2001) is about what it's like for a child to live part of the time with his dad and part of the time with his mom. As the little boy Alex explains, he has two of everything. For example, on one illustrated spread the text says, "I have *two* kitchens. Daddy and I cook here. Mommy and I cook here." On the left page of this spread, illustrator Kady MacDonald Denton shows Alex and his father preparing fresh vegetables in the dad's kitchen, and on the right page, she shows Alex and his mother making gingerbread cookies in the mom's kitchen. Later in the book as Alex explains how he has two telephone numbers, readers see him talking on the phone at his mom's house, and a plate with two gingerbread cookies sits on the table beside him.

An Understanding for Young Writers and Illustrators Recurring details tie illustrations together in powerful ways. Sometimes the details reappear often and seem almost to create their own backstory, as the cat does in Jonathan Bean's *At Night*. But sometimes the detail that reappears is truly small and seemingly insignificant, as the gingerbread cookies are in *Two Homes*. The presence of those cookies there on that plate, however, is anything but insignificant to the illustrator. The decision to include the cookies in the subsequent illustration was a very different kind of decision than the decision to keep the cabinets in the kitchen the same color or to keep Alex's hair the same length. Cabinets and hair length are static details, but the cookies are a dynamic detail. Their reappearance is a reminder that something happened earlier in the text that changed things. There were no cookies; Alex and his mom made some, and now there they are on a table next to him.

Recurring, dynamic details abound in the illustrations of many picture books. The red-striped pail high on a garage shelf in one illustration is pictured later as its used to collect seashells. A girl and her mother leaving a shoe store in one illustration are pictured later at home, the shoe store shopping bag sitting on the couch beside them. A brightly colored dish out on a counter in one illustration is pictured later on a dining room table, filled

with beans. Later, it's there again in another illustration, drying on the dish drain in the kitchen as everyone says good-bye for the evening. Recurring dynamic details such as these are a powerful means of connecting illustrations and bringing a sense of wholeness to a text.

While the difference between static details and dynamic details is subtle, it's worth considering in your conversations with children when they notice a recurring dynamic detail. The reappearance of a dynamic detail requires a different sort of planning and decision making, partly because consistency in static details is expected whereas the reappearance of a dynamic detail is almost always surprising.

Wonder with your students about which illustration with the detail in it came first, because sometimes an illustrator may work backward instead of forward in the process of composing with a recurring detail. Take the red-striped pail, for instance. The illustrator may very well have gone back and placed that pail into the garage illustration *after* he included it in the beach scene as a way of visually connecting the two scenes. Or the pail may have been in that garage right from the start and the illustrator planned to use it in a later scene all along. In one case the detail comes about as a result of revision; in the other it comes about in the process of planning and drafting. This is an incredibly powerful understanding about the process of composing to share with beginning writers: process is inherently recursive and not always a march forward.

As you work with children, help them find ways to use reappearing dynamic details in their own illustrations. You will likely find that adding such details to an existing illustration will be the entry point to this technique for many children, as planning ahead for a detail to reappear requires more sophisticated thinking. As children add these details in revision, however, they will grow in their understanding of how they work and will be more likely to plan ahead for them in future work.

In a Teacher's Voice: An Idea for Trying It Out   In a book about T-ball practice, Mark might have an illustration of him on a bench tying his shoes before practice begins. Beside him sits the bag of oranges his mother sent for all the players. Then at the very end, when he shows the empty practice field, there could be a couple of stray pieces of orange peels around on the ground.

A Writing Connection   Anton Chekhov has been famously quoted many times as saying that if in the first chapter (or scene) the writer says that a gun hangs on the wall, by the end of the third chapter that gun must be fired. Of course, the gun in this case would be quite the dynamic detail.

There is some truth to that old saying that a picture's worth a thousand words. The writer can't always spend a thousand words capturing all the

details an illustrator might in a scene, so selecting details that do lots of work is important. Static details are critical because they help the writer reveal character and setting: "The girl was taller than all her classmates, even the boys"; or, "The house was painted a particularly garish shade of pink, like someone had poured Pepto-Bismol all over it."

Dynamic details like Chekhov's gun, however, do a different sort of work. Dynamic details reappear again because they are changed somehow by the story unfolding around them. They may have a whole lot to do with the action of the story, as a firing gun would have, or they may play just a small, subtle part in what's unfolding. Imagine, for example, that a pack of cigarettes lies on a table in one scene. Several scenes later, two old friends share a smoke from that pack as they talk about their troubled lives. The pack of cigarettes reappears and plays just a small part in the unfolding story. On the other hand, suppose that in the later scene, the old friend comes over for a visit and her teenage son is with her and he *steals* the pack of cigarettes. In this case the cigarettes reappear but with much greater significance to the unfolding story.

Of the recurring detail Ralph Fletcher said, "Freud pointed out that as human beings we hunger for recurrent experience. This helps to explain both the cyclical nature of mythology and a fundamental element of story: The details mentioned early in the story usually recur, often with more significance, toward the end of the story" (1993, 51). Whether the reappearance of the detail is of minor or major consequence really doesn't matter, because either way the detail brings a sense of wholeness to the text. The reader thinks, *Ah, there it is again*, and in remembering he's seen it before, he is reminded of where he's been in the text.

Building Meaning from One Idea to the Next

Something to Notice   Illustrations may be connected so that significant meaning builds across them, the details in one picture suggesting what might be pictured in later illustrations.

An Illustration Example   Marla Frazee's *Roller Coaster* (2003) is a veritable feast of interesting illustration decisions, and of particular delight are all the many ways the illustrations connect across pages. Early in the book it's all about watching the people waiting in line to ride the coaster and seeing which of them later climb aboard and which don't. The two cowboys, for example, don't make it onto the ride, and they are shown just behind the turnstiles as the coaster takes off. One of the three macho guys waiting in line, the one with the "Bad Dogs" tattoo and a muscle shirt, chickens out at the last minute and leaves the line. The family of five dwindles to just the mom and the one child tall enough to ride.

Once the coaster starts, it's all about watching the expressions on the riders' faces as the coaster speeds along the track. The two macho guys whose buddy left the line are probably the funniest to follow. At first the two guys are sitting all nonchalant-like, got their shades on, and they're not even holding on. As the coaster starts down the first hill, however, they are both grabbing the bar with what appears to be uncomfortable intensity. They certainly aren't having as good a time as the two cheerleaders in the seat behind them! By the third curve they've both lost their sunglasses and are bracing against each other for support. Another hill, an upside down curve, and the discomfort on their faces has reached the critical stage. As they disembark, the two macho guys clutch their stomachs and make their way to the closest bench, where they sit with their heads between their knees. Their buddy Bad Dog is waiting for them—oh so cool because he didn't ride.

By the time readers arrive at the disembarking page, they fully expect the two guys to get off a little wobbly and shaken. They've seen it coming for pages, as Frazee has clearly drawn the growing motion sickness into the expressions and gestures of the two grown men. When illustrations cause readers to see things coming, those illustrations are connected and clearly working together in powerful ways.

An Understanding for Young Writers and Illustrators — Understanding this particular illustration possibility is really about understanding what makes a picture book a *true* picture book. Consider the difference between a storybook and a picture book, as explained by Uri Shulevitz, author of *Writing with Pictures: How to Write and Illustrate Picture Books*:

> *A story book tells a story with words. Although the pictures amplify it, the story can be understood without them. The pictures have an auxiliary role, because the words themselves contain images. In contrast, a true picture book tells a story mainly or entirely with pictures. When words are used, they have an auxiliary role. (1985, 15)*

I might amplify this distinction by adding that not all books with pictures and words in them tell stories. Some of them tell about things or explain how to do things. Some of them contain poems and others read more like essays. But whether the book holds a story or not, the point is to understand the difference between words that carry the meaning and pictures that carry the meaning.

Roller Coaster is a picture book in the truest sense because the illustrations do most of the meaning work and the very simple text only amplifies the illustrations in subtle ways. For example, once the coaster starts, the text across five entire illustrated spreads reads, simply, *The train zips. It zooms. It dips and dives. And goes all the way around. Wheee!* That's it. Sixteen words in five turns of the page, and meanwhile the stories of twelve different people riding that coaster are unfolding in the illustrations.

Connections are critical to this sort of illustration work. An illustrator must create for the reader a series of almost continuous scenes, each one unfolding out of the one before it, the illustrations making the connections that aren't made in the words. The illustrator has to be absolutely aware of every single detail in every illustration and how each detail will be affected by what comes next. The illustrator asks, "Based on what's pictured here and what's been pictured so far, what makes sense to come next? How will my next illustration move my idea forward?"

The best way to help children understand how meaning can build across a series of illustrations is to teach them to read the pictures sequentially so they see how one illustration is connected to the next. Look closely at the details the illustrator has included and how they help you predict what might be pictured next in the book. For example, most readers would predict that the macho guys won't be wearing their sunglasses by the time they get off the roller coaster.

When they are first starting out, many young children will be making wordless or almost wordless picture books. Because of this, it makes sense to linger with illustrations like these that are tightly connected and build

meaning across them. Grabbing hold of this idea will help many children compose with far more depth and intention than they otherwise might. And because this illustration possibility can only be understood across a series of illustrations, it probably makes sense to demonstrate your own thinking and composing with a series of illustrations that work in this way, perhaps even carrying the demonstration over several days of teaching.

In a Teacher's Voice: An Idea for Trying It Out   In a book about how Amy's babysitter picks her up from school and the two of them talk the whole way home and the babysitter always brings her a little snack, Amy could show her baby sister in the car seat in the back. On each page, the baby's face could get dirtier and dirtier with the chocolate from her candy bar. In the last illustration she could have the wrapper on her head and big smile on her face, her two teeth showing.

A Writing Connection   In many ways, this single illustration possibility represents the concept of wholeness and connectedness more than any other. The illustrator is almost totally relying on the pictures to do the meaning work (and *is* totally relying on them in a wordless book) just as the writer of an unillustrated text is relying totally on words. But the meaning of a text doesn't lie in individual words or in individual pictures; meaning is in the connections among them.

Consider what Ursula Le Guin said about writing in her book *Steering the Craft*—and consider how this is also true of illustrations:

> *The chief duty of a narrative sentence is to lead to the next sentence. Beyond this basic, invisible job, the narrative sentence can do an infinite number of beautiful, surprising, powerful, audible, visible things. But the basic function of the narrative sentence is to keep the story going and keep the reader going with it. (1998, 39)*

It seems that Le Guin's advice could easily be rewritten, substituting the word *picture* for the word *sentence* each time. *The chief duty of a narrative picture is to lead to the next picture.* The key word here is *lead*. Neither the writer nor the illustrator can simply add on and make a story. One idea has to lead to the next. The young child learning to make close connections from one picture to the next, telling a story or exploring an idea as she goes, is really learning the most basic principle of all writing: Keep the story or idea *going* and keep it *connected*.

Crafting an Ending That Returns to the Lead

Something to Notice

The composition of a beginning illustration may be replicated as a way of ending the book, usually with some changes brought about from the meaning of the text.

An Illustration Example

The last illustration in Elisha Cooper's book *Beach* (2006) pictures exactly the same view of the beach from exactly the same height and distance perspective as the first illustration. The pictures are different, however, because an entire day at the beach has passed between them. In the closing illustration, a few people are about that aren't in the first one, and the clouds and light are different. A few stray beams from the setting sun fan out from behind the clouds, leaving some of them shaded pink.

An Understanding for Young Writers and Illustrators

Replicating an opening illustration is a very effective way to craft an ending in a picture book because it gives the reader the satisfying feeling of having come full circle in the course of the text. When you study books with matching illustrations in the leads and endings, help children think about the illustrator's decision making. Why in this book did it make sense to come back to the first illustration? This question is important because there are a variety of meanings that can cause an illustrator to replicate the lead as the ending. Sometimes the ending marks the passage of time in a place, as it does in *Beach*. Sometimes it shows that someone or something has gone away and come back. Sometimes the ending is about resolution. There was a problem that got worked through in the text and now things are either back to normal or changed dramatically (it can go either way) and to see the same scene communicates this powerfully.

Understanding the meaning behind the replication also depends on looking closely at how the two illustrations are different. Look with children and figure out what's different in the matching illustrations. Talk about what happened in the book that brought about the changes. Reread the words that accompany each illustration. Often, but not always, exact language will also be repeated when a picture has been replicated. And by the way, be sure to use the words *lead* and *ending* as you talk about the illustrations; this is useful language for children to use when they talk about writing as well.

The key, really, is to unpack why it made sense for the illustrator to replicate the opening picture as an ending. Understanding the sense of replication will help children when they consider trying this out in their own illustrations. And when they want to try it out, talk a bit about what the process should be for replicating. Remind them that they'll need to check between the two pictures often for accuracy.

In a Teacher's Voice: An Idea for Trying It Out

If I were making a book about going to my grandma's house for lunch on Sundays, maybe the first illustration could show me coming through the door and seeing the big table covered with dishes that hold all the wonderful food. In the last illustration, I'll do the same picture, but the door will be closed and the table will be completely clear with just the tablecloth on top.

A Writing Connection

When crafting an ending, writers of all sorts of fiction and nonfiction will often return to an opening image, scene, or idea from the lead. The technique is really quite common and often referred to as a *circular ending*. While I could give hundreds of examples of this sort of ending in written texts, I'm going to go back to the opening paragraph from Barbara Kingsolver's *The Poisonwood Bible*, a paragraph cited earlier in this book as an example of using nature to inform detail. I take some risk in using this example because the book is so complex that if you haven't read it, you won't fully appreciate the craft of it. But then it's just so darn brilliant I have to use it. To save you the effort of finding the paragraph, here it is again:

> *Imagine a ruin so strange it must have never happened.*
>
> *First, picture the forest. I want you to be its conscience, the eyes in the trees. The trees are columns of slick, brindled bark like muscular animals over-grown beyond all reason. Every space is filled with life: delicate, poisonous frogs war-painted like skeletons, clutched in copulation, secreting their precious eggs onto dripping leaves. Vines strangling their own kin in the ever-lasting wrestle for sunlight. The breathing of monkeys. A glide of snake belly on branch. A single-file army of ants biting a mammoth tree into uniform grains and hauling it down to the dark for their ravenous queen. And, in reply, a choir of seedlings arching their necks out of rotted tree stumps, suck-ing life out of death. This forest eats itself and lives forever. (1998, 5)*

The book has five different narrators. A mother and her four daughters take turns in alternating chapters telling the story of their time in Africa as missionaries. The mother is the narrator in the opening chapter and the one responsible for this incredibly lush description of the setting.

Five hundred and thirty-two pages later in the closing chapter, the daughter who has died in Africa becomes "the forest's conscience" and "the eyes in the trees." Her voice narrates the ending, and she speaks back to her mother, all the way back, to the very first page:

> *Mother, be still, listen. I can see you leading your children to the water, and you call it a story of ruin. Here is what I see: First, the forest. Trees like muscular animals overgrown beyond all reason. Vines strangling their kin in the wrestle for sunlight. The glide of snake belly on branch. A choir of seedlings arching their necks out of rotted tree stumps, sucking life out of death. I am the forest's conscience, but remember the forest eats itself and lives forever.* (537)

Part of the brilliance of this return to the beginning is the fact that the words are close but not exactly the same. The order of the words has changed some, and not all of the details from the lead are in the ending. But then the narrator is different, and several decades have past between those first words and these last. And part of the brilliance is that the replicated ending is, in some ways, a metaphor for the meaning it's expressing. *The forest eats itself and lives forever.* In the end, the words repeat themselves and live forever.

Crafting Artful Repetition

Something to Notice

The composition of an illustration may be repeated as a way to show change.

An Illustration Example

Kathy Henderson's book *And the Good Brown Earth* (2003) is the story of a grandmother and her grandson preparing and planting a garden. Gram's sensible approach to the finer points of gardening are in contrast to Joe's wonderfully reckless, childlike approach, but they enjoy their time together. The text has a line that is repeated four times across the book: *And the good brown earth got on with doing what the good brown earth does best.* Each time the line is repeated, the illustration shows the same scene looking through some bushes toward the garden and beyond. The seasons change the scene each time, from the brown of winter to the new green of spring to the deep green of summer, but the reader is aware he's looking out at the garden from the same vantage point in each illustration.

In *School Bus* (1984), Donald Crews shows the same traffic intersection in two different illustrations. In the first, the empty school buses are crossing the intersection, and a Brooklyn city bus is there as well. In the second illustration later in the book, the buses are filled with children and are once again crossing the same intersection, this time with a trash truck and a small brown car.

An Understanding for Young Writers and Illustrators

Repeating the composition of an illustration—a landscape, a location, an object, or even a person—is a good way to show that a change has taken place. The most common use of this technique is probably the repetition of a landscape picture that shows a change of seasons, like the one in *And the Good Brown Earth*. But by repeating the composition of a picture later in a book, an illustrator might show any sort of change. A room that is messy in one illustration becomes clean in another. A tree standing in the midst of a storm in one illustration is pictured in sunlight with dripping leaves in another. A child's lost doll is shown when it's first left behind on the playground in one illustration, and then later it's shown again, all ragged and weathered.

When you see an illustration composition that's been repeated, you'll first want to help children understand the repetition. Lots of people, places, and objects will be drawn into illustrations more than once in a book, and

often they will change in the course of the book, but that's not the same as this illustration decision. With this technique, the illustrator decides to draw the same picture from the same vantage point. Everything about the composition of the picture is exactly the same; only the details are changed. Start, then, by helping children see how the two illustrations are alike in terms of composition. What elements have been repeated? Be sure to use the words *repetition* and *composition* as you talk with children; these are words that will serve them well as writers too.

Next you'll want to help children understand the change that has taken place. Talk about what's different and what happened to bring about the change. Think about the illustrator's decision making. Why does it make sense to compose a picture in the same way more than once in a book? How does the repetition add to the sense of wholeness in the text?

In a Teacher's Voice: An Idea for Trying It Out

If I were making a book about how we decorate outside our house for the holidays every year, I might have one page early in the book where my dad and I are standing facing the house and no decorations are up and it's daylight. The boxes that hold everything are on the grass. A few pages later, I could show us again in the same spot, but the house will be all decorated and sparkling, and it will be night in this picture. Then after that I'll show how so many people like to drive by the house and see the lights.

A Writing Connection

Both the last illustration possibility and this one are about repetition. With the last possibility, we looked at an example of repetition in a lead and an ending from *The Poisonwood Bible* (Kingsolver 1998). Here I'd simply like to consider repetition itself, and the fact that when it is used artfully by writers, it is a powerful tool not only for making a text seem whole, but also for making it memorable. Poets, memoirists, playwrights, journalists, essayist, novelists, and speech writers often employ repetition to great effect in all sorts of texts. Who will soon forget United States President Barack Obama's artful repetition of the phrase, "Yes, we can," in his 2008 campaign speeches? Or that of Dr. Martin Luther King, Jr., who helped pave the way for Obama and so many others by leaving an echo in the ears of a nation: "I have a dream. . . ."

Readers and listeners are satisfied by artful repetition because it matches our deepest understanding of life itself. Kim Addonizio and Dorianne Laux wrote this about the quality of repetition in their book *The Poet's Companion: A Guide to the Pleasures of Writing Poetry*:

> *Everything repeats. The seasons, the patterns of day and night, babies being born and parents dying, two people discovering each other's bodies: every-thing, large and small, has happened before—or almost. Nothing repeats it-*

self in exactly the same way. Every moment is new: this day, this child, these pairs of hands and arms and legs.

In our lives we need both the comforts of repetition and the delights of change, and they need to be in balance. Too much repetition means a routine of dull habit, of closing out the world. Too much change, and we lose our center. The same principal applies to poems that use repetition. (1997, 151)

Actually, the same principle applies to any kind of writing that uses repetition—not just poems—this is the *artful* part of artful repetition. Repetition is common in the written texts of children's picture books, written as they are for an audience still so close to a love of play with language. As you read books to children, draw their attention to repetition in the text and compare this with what children are learning about repetition in illustrations. Simply making children cognizant of the role repetition often plays in good writing will serve them well into their futures as writers.

Crafting an Ending
That Pulls Multiple
Text Elements Together

Something to Notice

An ending illustration may pull visual elements together from across the text.

An Illustration Example

David Ezra Stein's book *The Nice Book* (2008) is a delightful advice book about how to be nice—something that can, of course, be a challenge for some folks. Throughout the book, all kinds of animals—magnanimous monkeys, lovable lemurs, and amiable alligators, to name just a few—are pictured enacting all sorts of niceties upon one another: scratching each others' backs, singing, sharing. The last illustrated spread reminds readers, "And don't forget, BE NICE!" and then the pictures remind readers of some of the kind animals they saw inside the book. Ten pairs of animals circle the edges of the page, each pair engaged in some nice behavior.

An Understanding for Young Writers and Illustrators

Using different examples, this particular illustration possibility is examined at length in Chapter Five of this book, so only a few ideas need to be added here.

An ending such as this one satisfies because it gives the reader a chance to revisit the text visually. The feeling is similar to the one you experience when you see game or movie or vacation highlights, or those wonderful visual montages at the end of the Olympics or the end of a year. You experienced the images once as they unfolded in real time; now you get to revisit them all at the same time, and this brings a sense of wholeness and completion to your experience.

Because of the cumulative nature of an ending like this, you'll notice that the technique works best as an ending in a book where a lot happens or a lot of characters are involved in the book. Think with children about this quality of density in the books that have endings like this, and about how the ending brings so many elements together. Also think with children about books they know that wouldn't be well suited to an ending like this. *At Night* (2007) by Jonathan Bean, for example, is a wonderful book but it isn't well suited to this sort of ending because the story is very focused and

contained. By making this distinction you'll be deepening children's understanding of the purpose behind an ending like this.

In a Teacher's Voice: An Idea for Trying It Out

In a book about how I made new friends at my new school, on different pages I could show how I became friends with Kara and Tyrese and Marney that first week of school. On the last page, I could show all four of us playing together on the playground.

A Writing Connection

An ending that pulls together elements from across a text is quite common in good writing. In addition to the three examples of this kind of ending in Chapter Five, here's one more. It's from the brilliantly crafted *Stargirl* by Jerry Spinelli. The last chapter is only two pages long, but it's perhaps my favorite chapter of all because it contains one of these very satisfying kinds of endings. The references to a variety of plot details are spread across the chapter as readers get to revisit some of the stops on the wonderful journey that was *Stargirl*. Here are three of those stops. The narrator is Leo, a main character in the book, a teenager, who is now a grown man looking back.

> *The high school has a new club called the Sunflowers. To join, you have to sign an agreement promising to do "one nice thing per day for someone other than myself."*
>
> *Today's Electron marching band is probably the only one in Arizona with a ukulele.*
>
> *On the basketball court, the Electrons have never come close to the success they enjoyed when I was a junior. But something from that season has resurfaced in recent years that baffles fans from other schools. At every game, when the opposing team scores its first basket, a small group of Electrons fans jumps to its feet and cheers. (2000, 185)*

You see in this passage the listing quality so common in this type of ending. You also see how an ending like this doesn't mean much to people who haven't read the book because they have no idea how these seemingly disparate ideas are connected. The connections are there for readers, however, and it's the connections in an ending like this that bring a satisfying sense of wholeness to the text.

Technique *29*

Repeating Details of Landscape

Something to Notice

A character or object may pass by a landscape going in one direction, and then pass by it again going back in the other direction.

An Illustration Example

With an opening invitation to his readers, "Let's go for a walk, along the block, and see what we can see, before it's time for bed," Elisha Cooper takes readers on a late-afternoon walk down a busy residential block in his book *A Good Night Walk* (2005). As you pass by homes and trees and fences, you see people and animals going about their everyday lives. The people are delivering mail, mowing the grass, fixing a bicycle, and baking pies, for instance, and the squirrels chase one another through the trees. When you get to the end of the street and see the bay, the text reads, "Let's turn and walk back the way that we came." And that's just what happens. Cooper's illustrations take the reader back past each of the homes and trees and fences passed on the walk out, in reverse order, of course, because you are going the other way.

Cooper cleverly connected the illustrations from page to page so the reader would actually feel the movement of a walk. On the walk out, whatever structure is pictured partially on the edge of the right page is pictured in its entirety when the page is turned, as if you've moved on past it just a bit. On the walk back, the movement is reversed. Whatever is pictured partially on the edge of the left page is pictured in its entirety when the page is turned.

Being about a simple evening walk, *A Good Night Walk* is a book *entirely* about passing a landscape going in one direction and then passing back in the other. More commonly, however, illustrators use the technique in a "bookend" sort of way—the going out and returning wrap around some interesting action in the middle. This is how Donald Crews used the technique in his book *Sail Away* (1995). On the way out of the harbor, the sailboat passes under a bridge and past a lighthouse. The boat then sails around a bit and gets caught in a bad storm. Then it returns to the harbor, passing back by the lighthouse and under the bridge, in the opposite direction, of course.

An Understanding for Young Writers and Illustrators

With this technique readers experience the illusion of movement through a place, a venturing out, and returning sort of movement. The returning is what gives the text a satisfying sense of wholeness, and keeping the text in mind as a whole is essential to its success.

When you see illustrations that pass by landscapes, first help children understand that the meaning must be suited to this technique. The book must be about someone or something *going somewhere*. A tractor leaves the barn and goes out to plow the fields for a day, and then returns to the barn. A child rides the bus to school, and then rides it home again after school. Friends hike up a mountain to their favorite waterfall, and then hike back. Because the technique is so specifically tied to context, a child would likely plan ahead to illustrate in this way, knowing from the start that the technique makes sense for the book she wants to write. Brainstorm kinds of topics children might write about where this illustration technique would make sense.

Next, help children understand what's essential when using the technique. The illustrations show the same places on the return trip, but in reverse order. An illustrator must check for consistency and make sure things are reappearing in just the right reverse order. Also, if someone or something is shown in relation to the passing landscape, as the sailboat is in Crews' book, for example, its orientation must also be reversed: The sailboat that is headed toward the right side of the page on the trip out is headed for the left side of the page on the trip back. By moving objects across the landscape as the pages are turned, Cooper actually used a very sophisticated orientation technique that may be beyond many children's developmental approximations. But studying how he does it will no doubt deepen their understandings of making pictures work together in compelling ways.

Look closely at what has changed in each illustration. Usually something has changed because time changes things. A squirrel is in a tree, but later it's not. A fence stands bare in front of a house; later it has someone's bicycle leaning against it. Clothes dry on a line; later they are gone. Illustrators must think carefully about how a picture would be changed by time when it reappears.

In a Teacher's Voice: An Idea for Trying It Out

If Derrick wanted to make a book about how he rides his bike and takes groceries to his grandmother every Saturday, he might use this technique. Maybe early in the book he could show himself riding his bike past the Starbucks on one spread and past the park on the next spread. Later in the book, after he's visited her and given her the groceries, he could show himself riding back past the park and then the Starbucks, in that order because he's going the other way.

A Writing Connection   Even if this technique was something writers never did with words, what it shows children about making parts of a text work together is invaluable and will serve them well as writers. That being said, sometimes writers do use this technique when it makes sense in context—when writing about a journey, for example.

A classic example is from a familiar picture book, *The Relatives Came* (1985), written by Cynthia Rylant and illustrated by Stephen Gammell. Near the opening of the book, Rylant wrote about the journey the relatives take:

> *They left at four in the morning when it was still dark, before even the birds were awake. They drove all day long and into the night, and while they traveled along they looked at the strange houses and different mountains and they thought about their almost purple grapes back home. They thought about Virginia—but they thought about us, too. Waiting for them.*

At the end of the book, after the relatives have had a good visit doing all sorts of family things together, they head back home. Rylant used words to take them back the same way they came:

> *And they drove on, all day long and into the night, and while they traveled along they looked at the strange houses and different mountains and they thought about their dark purple grapes waiting at home in Virginia. But they thought about us, too. Missing them. And they missed us.*

Interestingly, Stephen Gammell chose not to show the relatives' car passing by the same landscapes in the illustrations, though he does turn the car in the opposite direction, heading left across the spread instead of right as it did on its trip out. But Rylant chose to use the exact same words on the trip out and the trip back, capturing that same satisfying sense of passing back by and returning. And just as illustrators do with pictures, she also shows with words that things have changed while the relatives have been gone. The grapes are now dark purple, and the relatives are no longer waiting. They're missing.

Using Details of Light to Show the Passage of Time

Something to Notice   Light detail can show the passage of time across a book.

An Illustration Example   In *The Paperboy* (1996) by Dav Pilkey a young boy and his dog get up before dawn, eat breakfast, gather and fold a bunch of newspapers, and head out on a route to deliver them in the neighborhood. Over the course of the book, as night turns into day, the sky in the background changes from black to deep blue to purple and finally to the bright yellow of full-morning sun. As time passes in the book, homes that are in the beginning completely darkened, change to having lights on in the upstairs rooms, where people usually wake up first. The changing light of stars and moons, bedside lamps and bicycle lights, and even reflections on water also show that time is passing across the book.

An Understanding for Young Writers and Illustrators   When you see that illustrators have used light purposefully in the background of pictures, think with children about what the changing light shows the reader. How is the light changing from picture to picture? How does the light in one picture help the illustrator determine what the light should be in the next? Is the light changing because it's moving toward morning or toward night? Or are the skies lightening or darkening because of a change in the weather? The key is to help children see the pictures working together and the cumulative effect that changing light has on a text. Also notice how light detail changes not just in the sky, but also in the artificial lights made by people and in different ways that light reflects.

Studying the use of light to indicate time can help children become more purposeful in their composition, because so often it's always daytime and the sun is shining no matter what's happening in children's books. Explain to children how many of the topics they write about, especially the ones that come from their personal experiences, happen across time and often span from night into day or day into night. Imagine with children the kinds of topics they might write about where the changing light would make a difference: going to a baseball game in the late afternoon, for example, and leaving after dark. In this case, not only would the skies darken, the lights in the stadium would have to come on in the course of the illustrations.

As you confer with children, ask them about the time of day that should be pictured in their drawings. An entry point for many children will simply be to attend to light details in individual drawings. Making light change from picture to picture in a meaningful way will become more possible as children develop this understanding over time.

In a Teacher's Voice: An Idea for Trying It Out
I know that if Roni were to write a book about soccer practice, she could certainly show it getting darker in her book. Practice doesn't start until 6:30 and it's always dark when she finishes, so showing this across pages would be easy for her to do.

A Writing Connection
Writers often use details of light to indicate time in texts: The shadows that gather in the woods as night approaches and the lost hiker becomes anxious. The first ray of light over a tall building in a city that is waking. The midday sun scorching an already dry patch of ground.

Sometimes, writers will use details of light across a text to indicate that time is passing, just as illustrators do in the backgrounds of pictures. For example, in a wonderful piece of writing that I saved from an *Atlantic Southeast Magazine* (September/October 2006), Holden Parrish moves the entire sun across the sky as he showcases a day in the life of Corpus Christie, Texas. The piece is titled, "A Day in the Good Life," and the opening line reads:

> *It's early morning and the sun is rising over the Gulf of Mexico. A brilliant red disc peeks above the eastern horizon, silhouetting rows of gentle whitecaps. (17)*

Parrish used a sort of video camera approach to writing to capture people—some of them locals and some of them tourists—going about life in the town. He revisits the same people to see what they are doing at different times in the day, and light detail is the framing device that lets the reader know that time is passing. About midway through the piece, Parrish wrote, "The disc, now a blinding white-yellow, arcs through the Texas sky" (17), and the reader knows that the sun has begun its journey. A few paragraphs later, "The sun burns furiously from its afternoon perch" (18). And finally near the end, "The smoldering orb sinks toward its western cradle. Waning sunlight sets the bay's diamond-tipped waves in a golden surf" (19). Light details of campfires and flashlights on the beach further enhance the feeling of night in the ending.

Technique 31

Using Details of Weather to Show the Passage of Time

Something to Notice   Details of landscapes changed by weather can show the passage of time across a book.

An Illustration Example   In Cynthia Rylant's book *Scarecrow* (1998), illustrator Lauren Stringer shows the reader that time is passing by transforming the landscape in illustrations across the book. In the beginning, the scarecrow stands in a brown, empty garden with leafless trees in the landscape around him. As you move through the book and learn about what life is like for the scarecrow, however, everything changes around him. The trees take on the new green of spring, vegetables begin peeking up out of the garden soil, and a blue morning glory winds itself tightly around the scarecrow's legs. The garden continues to grow until corn and sunflowers stand as tall as the scarecrow, and other vegetables are ripe and ready for harvest. Near the end of the book, leaves and fields turn orange and brown, and on the very last page the scarecrow stands once again in an empty garden as a light snow swirls around him.

Interestingly, if you were to read only the words in *Scarecrow*, you would not sense that there is any movement through time because the text is non-narrative and is not ordered by time. However, the illustrations in *Scarecrow* capture the movement through three distinct seasons.

An Understanding for Young Writers and Illustrators   To really use this illustration technique successfully, children must build on several important understandings embedded in other techniques. First, children must make a content decision about how much landscape detail (exterior or interior) to include in their pictures. If landscape is to be included, then children must ask, *What season makes sense for the content of my book?* Once the answer to this question is established, then it's important for children to attend to the details in their illustrated scenes. *What does summer look like? How should the place I'm drawing look if it is summer?* While it's easy to think about how exterior landscapes are changed by weather, be sure children think about how interior landscapes are changed as well. For example, the snow boots pictured by a door in deep winter probably don't need to be there in the middle of summer. Finally, children must learn to keep landscape details

consistent across a book—if it's summer, for instance, it should look like summer in every picture.

Changing landscape details subtly across a book to show the passage of time builds on all these other understandings. Through your study, help children understand that this illustration technique only makes sense in books that cover enough time for a landscape to be changed by weather. Often, they'll see that lots of time—whole seasons—pass by in a book. But sometimes the time will be short, as when a storm approaches and passes through, changing the landscape in its passing.

Finally, be sure to help children understand that they don't have to be telling a *story* that goes through lots of time to use this technique. Instead, they might simply be writing *about* something—just as Cynthia Rylant was writing about a scarecrow—and show the passage of time in the illustrations. Help children imagine different kinds of topics they might write about that would be changed by changes in weather: for example, a book about playing on the playground at school or a book about the street on which a child lives. Either of these non-narrative books might show movement through time in the illustrations by showing how the landscape changes with the weather. As you imagine different possibilities, think specifically about what kinds of changes would make sense to include in the illustrations.

While it's possible this sort of landscape detail could be added to a series of pictures in revision, without a doubt, it's best to plan ahead for a text to work in this way. Your best opportunity to help a child use the technique will likely come when you are conferring and the child is thinking about a book that's not yet under way. If the topic lends itself to this sort of illustration work, help the child think about how the pictures might change across the pages of the book to show movement through time.

In a Teacher's Voice: An Idea for Trying It Out

If we were to make a book about our classroom and what it's like to spend time here during the school year, we might show the seasons changing outside the big picture window in the back. Not every page would have to include the window, but those that did might show the move from summer to fall to winter to spring. We could also repeat an illustration and show the coat rack empty in August and filled in January.

A Writing Connection

Writers often include the changing details of landscapes to show the passage of time. Patricia MacLachlan used such details to great effect in *Sarah, Plain and Tall* (1985), where the passage of time is critical because the more time that passes and the longer Sarah stays, the more likely it is she will become Papa's wife.

While the details are scattered throughout the text, what's particularly interesting is the way they start so many of the chapters. In the first chapter,

it's an interior landscape detail that hints at the time of year as the story commences:

> *"Did Mama sing every day?" asked Caleb. "Every single day?" He sat close to the fire, his chin in his hand. It was dusk, and the dogs lay beside him on the warm hearthstones.* (3)

The fire detail lets us know it is winter. The first sentence in the second chapter establishes time with landscape once again:

> *Caleb and Papa and I wrote letters to Sarah, and before the ice and snow had melted the fields, we all received answers.* (11)

The opening of the third chapter moves the story forward:

> *Sarah came in the spring. She came through green grass fields that bloomed with Indian paintbrush, red and orange, and blue-eyed grass* (16).

By the fifth chapter, we know summer has come because in the opening paragraph we learn the baby sheep have been born and Sarah sings to them, "her voice drifting over the meadow grasses" (30). In the lead to the sixth chapter, time marches on:

> *The days grew longer. The cows moved close to the pond, where the water was cool and there were trees.* (33)

And marches on in the lead to the seventh chapter:

> *The dandelions in the fields had gone by, their heads soft as feathers. The summer roses were opening.* (38)

In the eighth and ninth chapters, the landscape is changed by a weather event—a violent storm. Its impending arrival is foretold in the opening paragraph of the eighth chapter:

> *The rain came and passed, but strange clouds hung in the northwest, low and black and green. And the air grew still.* (44)

Then, at the end of the eighth chapter and the beginning of the ninth, MacLachlan paints a picture with words so clear you really can almost see *and* hear it:

> *And when it was over we opened the barn door and walked out into the early-morning light. The hail crunched and melted beneath our feet. It was white and gleaming for as far as we looked, like sun on glass. Like the sea.*
>
> *It was very quiet. The dogs leaned down to eat the hailstones. Seal stepped around them and leaped up on the fence to groom herself. A tree had blown over near the cow pond. And the wild roses were scattered on the ground, as if a wedding had come and gone there.* (50–51)

CHAPTER

10

Tone, In Pictures and In Words

FIRST, I SHOULD BE CLEAR about choosing the word *tone* for this section of illustration techniques. Words get murky, especially when we try to name intangibles, and this quality of writing can certainly be hard to pin down. Words like *mood*, *style*, and even *voice* have indistinct edges to their meanings that come close to what I mean by *tone*, but they are not the right words for my case. Tone is the word I need.

In purely artistic terms, of course, tone refers to the overall blend and intensity of color, light, and shade in a picture, all of which evoke an emotional response in the viewer. As a teacher of writing engaged in illustration study, however, I want to consider tone more broadly and include all the ways (in addition to color) artists purposefully draft and revise pictures based on the emotion they are trying to convey, just as writers craft words with tone in mind.

One dictionary definition of tone says it is "the general quality or character of something as an indicator of the attitude or view of the person who produced it." In other words, the *way* a writer or an illustrator presents something reveals his or her take on the subject. This definition best captures the sense of purposefulness shared by writers and illustrators when it comes to tone, and it is the operational definition of the word I'll be using here. With the possibilities in this section, children will learn to think about their own attitudes or views toward their topics, and then how to communicate their views effectively to readers with specific illustration decisions. But first, some thoughts about tone in writing and illustrating.

SECTION TWO Fifty Illustration Techniques

Tone in Writing

One of my mother's favorite things to say to me when I was a growing girl was, "Don't you use that tone of voice with me young lady." Usually I would reply with, "Whaaaat, I only said that. . . ." But of course it wasn't *what* I said; it was *how* I said it that was the problem. Without me realizing it, my mother was schooling me in the fine art of delivery, teaching me that how I say something can be just as important as what I'm saying. It's a lesson I utilize dozens of times a day as a writer in everything from emails to essays.

In *Writing Fiction: A Guide to Narrative Craft*, Janet Burroway wrote this about tone:

> When we speak of a "tone of voice" we mean that an attitude is conveyed, and this attitude is determined by the situation and by the relation of the persons involved in the situation. Tone can match, emphasize, alter, or contradict the meaning of the words. (2003, 292)

When I was girl, it wasn't really my tone of voice that my momma didn't like; it was my attitude when I spoke to her in certain ways. (By the way, notice the difference in tone conveyed by *momma* instead of *mother*. And think about how even a different spelling would convey a different tone, *mama*. The ways we express attitude can be very subtle.)

When I write in my notebook, I don't worry about tone because no one reads my notebook but me. But if I am expecting someone to read what I'm writing, I think a lot about my attitude and how I want my audience to respond to what I'm saying. Lee Gutkind wrote the following in her book *Keep It Real: Everything You Need to Know About Researching and Writing Creative Nonfiction*:

> Most writers have a pretty good idea of how they want their readers to respond to their work emotionally and intellectually, whether the work is a memoir about an abusive ex-spouse, a carefully researched essay about an art heist, or a tale of a fishing boat at sea. Getting the reader to follow along is the real key. (2008, 88)

What a huge writing issue this is, one that, again, influences every bit of written communication I generate. How do I want my reader to respond to this *emotionally* and intellectually? As a writer I know that the content of my message will evoke an intellectual response, but it's the tone of my writing that will evoke an emotional response. I also know that emotion trumps intellect for many readers. My mother taught me that. If my reader doesn't like my tone, he may not care about the content of my message.

Think if you will, for example, about the difference between the three following statements. The first is from an actual email I wrote to someone

explaining that I couldn't accept an invitation to speak at a conference. The two that follow are other ways I might have said the same thing.

> *I so appreciate you thinking of me again, but my schedule for the next school year already has as many trips in it as I am willing to make. I am actually now only accepting invitations for the 2011 calendar year.*

> *Sorry but I'm booked until 2011. And you need to plan now if you want me to come then.*

> *Oh, aren't you just the sweetest thing for inviting me back. I so wish I could come as you guys are the greatest, but my little old schedule is just all filled up until 2011. Maybe you could see if I could come then instead?*

The meaning of the three statements is exactly the same, but the tone of each one is very different and evokes a clearly different emotional response. The first makes me think, "Business like, but personable. I think she really is sorry she can't help us out." The second one leaves me cold and feeling like I didn't do my homework—"you need to plan now." And the last one leaves me feeling a little nauseated it's so over the top. The reader thinks, "I don't even really know her, so why is she being so familiar with me?" It's sweet, but very off-putting.

Readers don't easily separate the content of a message from its delivery, and nonfiction writers must keep this in mind. Because they narrate their own texts, nonfiction writers have a very different relationship with readers than writers of fiction. If a *fictional* narrator annoys readers with a sickeningly sweet tone of voice, there's nothing personal in that for the writer. (Unless that's not how the writer wanted the character to seem, in which case it can be very personal because the writer has failed to achieve the intended effect.)

When speaking, people use the tools of volume, pitch, gesture, and intonation to set the tone in a conversation. Even where people stand in relation to each other as they speak communicates a certain attitude. Writers don't have these physical, relational tools at their disposal. Instead, writers choose their words carefully, order them precisely, punctuate them accurately, and sometimes manipulate the font to set the right tone in writing. And the smallest decisions can make the biggest difference in tone. As an example, let's take one of my email statements and make some very small revisions.

> *Sorry but I'm booked until 2011. And you need to plan now if you want me to come then.*

> *I'm booked until 2011. And you need to plan now if you want me to come then.*

> *I'm booked until 2011. You need to plan now if you want me to come then.*

As I whittle away words in each message, the tone sharpens. The message loses all remorse with the first revision, and packs more of a punch when the *and* is removed. Somehow the conjunctive nature of the *and* softens the relationship between the two sentences. If I get rid of just a few more words, the reader will feel I am in a very big hurry and perhaps a little irritated I even had to respond: "Booked until 2011. Plan now if you want me to come then."

Tone and the Emotional Response to Pictures

Most children are naturally sensitive to changes in tone in conversation. Over time, they've come to understand what happy, angry, frightened, excited, bossy, and many other emotions *sound* like when people are speaking. And those with mothers like mine might have even heard the expression "tone of voice" and have some understanding about what it means.

The intellectual jump from understanding tone of voice in speaking to understanding tone of voice in writing is a healthy jump. I speak from experience when I say that it takes years for writers to deeply understand the impact of tone on readers, and to hone their ability to moderate tone in writing as efficiently as they do in speaking. But in the context of illustration study, young writers can get started understanding tone and can begin to draft pictures with tone in mind. The key is to first help children understand that pictures evoke emotional responses in readers, just as words do, and then to explore the tools illustrators use to moderate the tone of a picture.

Perhaps the simplest way to understand how pictures evoke different emotional responses just as words do is to compare pictures in terms of tone as we did with email messages. In my library, I found three different books with pictures of star-nosed moles in them. Now, there's not a lot an illustrator can do to pretty-up a star-nosed mole, but looking at these three illustrations, you realize there is a real continuum of just how creepy the creature can be made to seem to readers. The three pictures are quite different and evoke different emotional responses, and the titles of the books suggest the different picture tones before you even see them:

Do They Scare You? Creepy Creatures (1992) by Sneed B. Collard, illustrated by Kristin Kest.

Bubble Homes and Fish Farts (2009) by Fiona Bayrock, illustrated by Carolyn Conahan.

What Do You Do with a Tail Like This? (2003) by Steve Jenkins and Robin Page.

Take just a moment and think about what tone you would expect to see in each picture based on these titles.

If you predicted scary and creepy in the first book, you're right on target. Kristin Kest deliberately drew her mole to evoke that response. First, it appears as if the mole has sort of exploded up out of the dirt and chomped down on a very long, writhing earthworm. You can even see one tiny, sharp tooth about to pierce the earthworm's body. The reader is positioned face-to-face with the mole, but its head is tilted back and slightly to the side so you can't see its eyes. Instead, the fleshy "fingers" and the wide round nostrils of the mole's nose seem to look out at you, and the whole body part looks shiny moist, as if it should be some sort of guts on the inside of the mole instead of its nose. The claws on the feet are very pointed, like daggers, and the brown hues are dark and bold in contrast to the sickly pink color of the nose. Every decision Krist made seems designed to make this mole look like a mole you'd not like to meet.

In contrast, Carolyn Conahan's mole is much friendlier, the kind of mole you'd expect to meet in a book called *Bubble Homes and Fish Farts*. Conahan's mole is pictured swimming underwater, so right away that lends a softness to it that was absent in the other mole. Instead of violently chomping down on its prey, this mole is blowing bubbles out its nose. (Star-nosed moles breath the bubbles back in, smell them, and find food this way in water.) Conahan positions the reader face-to-face with the mole too, but its eyes are visible and, while just small slits, they almost seem playful, as if blowing bubbles is really quite fun. The brown of the body and pink of the nose have the softness rendered by watercolor, and the nose fingers look more like the petals of a lovely flower than some alien appendage. And yes, even the claws are more rounded and less sharp than the more menacing mole.

Steve Jenkins and Robin Page's star-nosed mole is very different from Krist's or Conahan's. Their mole is part of a montage of different animals with remarkable noses on a single illustrated spread, so it has no background around it, only white space. The reader is positioned above the mole, as if looking down on it, instead of face-to-face, and it's amazing what a different response this positioning evokes. The mole seems much less threatening when you look down on it than when you stare it in the face. While you can see all four feet, a tail, an eye, and the pink fingered nose, the paper collage art is far less detailed than either of the paintings. The lack of detail results in a much more detached response because there aren't many tactile sensations evoked by the picture and it's harder to respond to it as a *real* creature. This is purposeful, of course, because the lack of detail also forces attention on the main color contrast you see: the pink nose at the end of the brown body. Readers respond more to the nose than the mole.

Menacing, playful, detached and scientific. Three very different star-nosed moles rendered purposefully by four skilled illustrators.

The possibilities in this section are all about helping children think about tone in the context of illustrations, thinking that will serve them well

as writers in the future. Having been in conversations about the teaching of writing for a long time now, I'm not sure we've talked about tone enough with young writers, at least not in ways that help them understand the tremendous responsibility the writer has to get the tone right. We talk about audience, but often we talk about readers only as if they are to be considered at the very end of the process. "Now you're finished. See what your reader thinks of it." But the proficient writer has been thinking about what the reader thinks of it from word one. Your conversations about tone in illustrations will lead children to think about how readers respond emotionally to pictures, and how illustrators influence these responses with purposeful decision making.

Technique 32

Crafting Tone with Color

**Something
to Notice**   Color choices impact the tone of a book.

**An Illustration
Example**   I recently purchased three new picture books, and the use
of color in each one is dramatically different. Marla
Frazee's illustrations in *All the World* (2009) by Liz Garton Scanlon were
done in pencil and watercolor. The translucent softness of these materials
sets the perfect tone for the warm look at how families and friends are
connected as communities within the larger world. The last line reads, "All
the world is all of us."

Leslie Patricelli uses bright acrylic paints in *Higher! Higher!* (2009) and
outlines the images in the pictures with heavy black lines, intensifying the
colors even more. The rich, vibrant colors set the perfect tone here as well,
capturing the exuberant spirit of a little girl begging to go higher and higher
on her swing—all the way to outer space where she high-fives an alien—
before returning safely to her father's arms.

Just four colors—black, white, yellow, and blue—are used in the
illustrations for Cynthia Rylant's book *All in a Day* (2009). Paper artist Nikki
McClure drew all the images for the book on black paper, then cut them out
with an X-Acto knife, deciding which parts would be black and which would
be white as she cut. The cut paper was then scanned, and background color
of yellow and blue (on alternating pages) was added by a computer. The
illustrations are startlingly beautiful in the intricacy of the shapes and design,
but the minimal color does leave a bit of an emotional vacuum for at least
some readers (I'm one of them). Words like these in the text seem to suggest
color: "Every bird and every tree and every living thing loves the promise in a
day, loves what it can bring," but the finely detailed cutouts force the reader
to respond to these words visually through shape rather than color. The
emotional void likely comes from the feeling that the world is *supposed* to
have color, so its absence can be unsettling for some readers, affecting the
tone of the work dramatically.

**An Understanding
for Young Writers
and Illustrators**   An entire body of science is dedicated to the study of
the human response to color. In your classroom, you'll
simply be introducing children to the idea that people
respond to different colors in different ways, and you'll be helping them
become more purposeful in their selection of color as they illustrate their
books.

You might start the inquiry into color by talking with children about color as they know it in their lives. Ask questions such as, "If you were to walk into a room meant for children to play in, what colors might that room be painted? Why? What about a room where adults do serious business? What color would that room be?" You might talk about what colors they have in their rooms at home and why. Perhaps you could imagine someone walking into your classroom dressed all in pink, then in purple, then in red or black or green. How would you respond to these different outfits? Really any line of thinking you can imagine that will get children thinking about how they respond to color will be helpful as a starting point.

As you move to thinking about color in illustrations, you might show students the illustrations in some unfamiliar picture books and talk about what the colors in those books suggest to them. Do the colors suggest playfulness and fun or sweetness and love? Do the colors look scary or anxious or perhaps very serious? Lots of adjectives could be used to express the emotions readers feel as they look at colors, so invite children to use their own words for how the colors make them feel. It will be a bit of a challenge to respond only to color, as images will evoke powerful responses as well, but nudge children to talk just about what the colors suggest.

Then, as you read new books or revisit old ones, talk about why the illustrator chose the color scheme for the book. How do the colors match the feeling of the text? How would the text be different if the colors were very different? You might even show children another book with very different colors to help them really think about how much a dramatic color change would change the book. Be sure that children understand the idea of a color *scheme* and that color is used consistently across a book.

To talk about color, you'll need words like *soft*, *intense*, *light*, *bold*, *vivid*, *dark*, *bright*, *rich*, and a host of others that describe the qualities of color you see. You will no doubt become interested in the different materials illustrators use to produce different color effects. Watercolors create soft, translucent color. Gouache is a lot like watercolor but because it's opaque, it tends to be a bit more intense. Acrylic paintings, of course, give the deepest, richest colors. And then there are pencils, pens, charcoals, pastels, paper collage, and a variety of others. In a day-to-day writing workshop, children will probably be choosing between pencils, crayons, and colored markers for their illustrations, so you'll want to help them think about the color potentials of these materials, as well as ways to make color more or less intense with different materials.

You will probably notice that some illustrators clearly have used color to try and match as closely as possible the true colors found in nature. When this is the case, color is generally modulated, meaning different shades of a single color are used to make, say, the green leaves of a tree seem more natural than they would if just one shade of green was used. The idea that

some colors seem very natural and realistic, and others less so, is another important line of thinking about an illustrator's purposefulness. Certainly in terms of tone, on a continuum from more serious to more playful, the more natural the color looks the more serious the tone.

As children illustrate, they tend to choose the colors they need for different people and objects. A more sophisticated understanding of color would be for children to become purposeful as they choose colors for a whole book, based on the tone or feeling they want the book to have. In many ways, this connects to children's sense of the wholeness of text—the idea that the color scheme should work across the whole book to keep the tone consistent (unless there is a reason to shift it, as you will see in the next illustration possibility).

In a Teacher's Voice: An Idea for Trying It Out   If I were making a book about my nana and how sweet and kind she always is to me, I would probably choose softer, lighter colors for the pictures. I wouldn't want my illustrations to be all big and bright and bold, because that's just not the way she is. She's quieter than all that. But if I were making a book about my papa and how he takes me to the dirt track races sometimes on Friday nights, I would probably need to use lots and lots of brown in my pictures because it's always so dirty and dusty. If that were the main color, my reader would get that feeling.

A Writing Connection   In *Spunk & Bite: A Writer's Guide to Bold, Cotemporary Style*, Arthur Plotnik wrote about the power of color:

> [But] both for the writer and the reader, color is memory, color is mood, color is meaning. With color, we can strike the mind's eye dead center . . . Color need be no more than a brushstroke to evoke a mood. . . . (2007, 30)

I couldn't help but think of this recently when I came across this beautiful passage in Kathryn Stockett's novel *The Help*:

> I listened wide-eyed, stupid. Glowing by her voice in the dim light. If chocolate was a sound, it would've been Constantine's voice singing. If singing was a color, it would've been the color of chocolate. (2009, 67)

The passage is so sensual—it has sound and texture and taste and, of course, color. Readers do respond powerfully to color, and writers and illustrators alike can use this response to great effect when crafting words or crafting pictures. As Plotnik said:

> [But] color is ours—ours to use in ways that capture experiences and stir readers. With all the associations it triggers, one color can be worth a yard of paragraphs. (31)

Shifting Tone by Shifting Color

Something to Notice   A dramatic change in the use of color can represent a shift in tone.

An Illustration Example   Suzy Lee's book *The Zoo* (2004) is about a little girl's trip to the zoo with her parents. In the first four page spreads of the book as the family arrives at the zoo and begins exploring, the detailed illustrations have very limited color: everything is in blue, black, gray, and white. The one exception to this is the brightly colored peacock that can be seen somewhere in each illustration, and a tiny smudge of pink on the little girl's cheek—a bit of foreshadowing with color, as it turns out.

When the little girl follows the peacock and becomes separated from her parents, color is used to capture the very different experiences the adults and the child are having. Pages that picture the little girl happily exploring the zoo on her own include bright, vivid colors that capture her exuberate sense of freedom. Pages that picture the worried parents searching for their little girl are absent of any color but the blues, black, grays, and white that opened the book. The dramatic difference in color from one page to the next perfectly captures the very different feelings in the pictures.

Bob Graham used a very similar technique on a single spread in *"The Trouble with Dogs . . ." Said Dad* (2007). When the big, no-nonsense dog trainer comes to work with the unruly but sweetheart of a dog named Dave, he is first pictured in color as are all the other illustrations. But on the page where he teaches Dave's family to use the dreaded slip chain, Graham colored the dog trainer completely gray, matching the feeling of the whole scene. In the last of a series of seven separate scenes on the page spread, each showing members of the family trying to use the slip chain on Dave, the family is pictured in gray as well. The text reads, "But no one had a heart for the 'short, sharp jerk' on that chain." The absence of color in the dog trainer and eventually in Dave's family seems to match the feeling of an absence of heart.

Set in 1972, Eve Bunting's book *So Far from the Sea* (1998) tells the story of a family who visits the site of the Manzanar War Relocation Center in California where the father, his parents, and 10,000 other Japanese were interned during World War II. Illustrator Chris Soentpiet painted the scenes to show the father's thirty-year-old memoires of the camp in black and white,

and the scenes of the family visiting in bright, vivid color. The dramatic change in color suggests not only a different emotional tone, but also the feeling of time and distance and the fading of memories.

An Understanding for Young Writers and Illustrators

Generally, moving from color illustrations to tonal black-and-white illustrations shifts the tone from positive to negative. Humans associate color with life and vitality—a positive association—and when this changes in the midst of a picture book, the emotional response to the illustration changes with it. If an entire book is done in black and white, a reader may not be as drawn to the illustrations as he or she might be to color, but this emotion will be consistent across the text, it won't shift.

When you see books where illustrators have changed the use of color in some dramatic way, think very specifically about why this change was made. What emotional response do you think the illustrator is trying to convey with the change? It may be the worry of the parents in *The Zoo*, the seeming meanness of the dog trainer and his slip chain in *"The Trouble with Dogs . . ." Said Dad*, or the lifelessness of captivity in *So Far from the Sea*. A full range of emotions are possible, and you'll need to consider the context of the book very carefully with children to understand the illustrator's particular use of the technique.

In some books, you'll see that dramatic color changes occur consistently across the book, usually representing two different experiences (as in *The Zoo*) or two different time periods (as in *So Far from the Sea*). But sometimes a color shift is used very sparingly, even on a single page, to capture just a moment of feeling that has a different emotional tone (as in *"The Trouble with Dogs . . ." Said Dad*). Be sure children understand both uses of the technique as this will open more possibilities for them to compose with this technique in their own illustrating.

As you help children imagine composing in this way, talk about what tools they might use to dramatically shift the use of color in a book. Certainly, a pencil could be used if the shift is going to be from black and white to color, but there are other possibilities as well. Drawing with just two or three colors, say blue and black and gray, and then shifting to a much broader spectrum of color is one possibility; changing from crayons to darker, more vivid markers is another. If a child thinks this technique is something he would like to try, be sure to talk about why it makes sense in the context of the book he is making.

In a Teacher's Voice: An Idea for Trying It Out

In the book Kayla wrote about her trip to Santa's Land with her brother, she had alternating pages of text and illustrations that showed how she and her brother experienced most everything differently. "I thought the roller coaster was awesome. My brother thought it was scary. I thought the Ferris wheel was

cool. My brother thought was too high." She did all the illustrations in pencil, but what if she went back and added color to the pages that tell how much she liked the rides? The color contrast would add a whole other layer of really cool meaning to her book.

A Writing Connection   Suzanne Collins' futuristic novel *The Hunger Games* is set in the ruins of a place once known as North America. The only place not in ruins is the colorful capital of Panem. The capital rulers keep the outlying districts in line by forcing them to send one teenage girl and one boy to participate in the annual Hunger Games, a fight to the death on live TV. Notice the dramatic shift in the imagery of color as the two main characters ride a train toward the capital to participate in the games. In this case, bright, garish colors are associated with the more negative place, the capital, Collins toying expertly with her readers' expected emotional response to color.

> *Peeta Mellark and I stand in silence as the train speeds along. The tunnel goes on and on and I think of the tons of rock separating me from the sky, and my chest tightens. I hate being encased in stone this way. It reminds me of the mines and my father, trapped, unable to reach sunlight, buried forever in darkness.*
>
> *The train finally begins to slow and suddenly bright light floods the compartment. We can't help it. Both Peeta and I run to the window to see what we've only seen on television, the Capitol, the ruling city of Panem. The cameras haven't lied about its grandeur. If anything, they have not quite captured the magnificence of the glistening buildings in a rainbow of hues that tower into the air, the shiny cars that roll down the wide paved streets, the oddly dressed people with bizarre hair and painted faces who have never missed a meal. All the colors seem artificial, the pinks too deep, the greens too bright, the yellows painful to the eyes, like the flat round disks of hard candy we can never afford to buy at the tiny sweet shop in District 12. (2008, 59)*

Technique 34

Crafting Tone with Background Color

**Something
to Notice**

Background color may impact the tone of an illustration.

**An Illustration
Example**

Just saying the word *vulture* is likely to elicit a strong, negative response in some people, but April Pulley Sayre's book *Vulture View* (2007) casts these creatures in a mostly positive light. Sure, they are looking for the deadest, stinkiest thing they can find to eat, but they also ride the warm air through the sky as they "tilt, soar, scan to find the food that vultures can eat." Illustrator Steve Jenkins' cut-paper collages of the vultures aren't too menacing, but a single illustration decision near the end of the book affects the tone dramatically. As night approaches and the vultures have eaten their fill, you turn the page and the text reads, "The vultures gather in vulture trees, settle and sleep, like families." Sounds nice enough, except that Jenkins put a solid red background behind a black tree filled with black vultures, their features completely indistinct; only their outlines are clear. An orange sun sinks behind the tree and off the bottom of the page. There is no tonal difference in the red on the page that would suggest a pleasant, setting-sun sort of feeling. It's just bright, deep red across the entire spread. Blue has been the predominant background color throughout the book, so the sudden change to red is dramatic and carries a very different feeling than the other illustrations. The vultures pictured against this backdrop of red, the color of blood, seem much scarier than in any of the other pictures.

**An Understanding
for Young Writers
and Illustrators**

Lots of illustrations will have background that is filled with detail and, as a result, filled with a variety of color. But some illustrations have more solid backgrounds, and the choice of color in these backgrounds has a big impact on the tone of the picture. In *Picture This: How Pictures Work* (2000), illustrator Molly Bang explained it this way:

> White or light backgrounds feel safer to us than dark backgrounds because we can see well during the day and only poorly at night. As a result of our inability to see in the dark, black often symbolizes the unknown, and all our fears associated with the unknown, while white signifies brightness and hope. (68)

As you study illustrations with children, more than likely you'll be most interested in backgrounds *other than white* as white tends to be the background color of choice by default in children's illustrations. You'll also be more interested in backgrounds that aren't natural sky colors (if the picture is an outside picture), as sky colors are sort of a given in outdoor scenes and they change with the weather and the time of day.

When you see an interesting background color in an illustration, talk with children about your response to that color. How does it affect the way you view what's pictured against it? Imagine what the picture might look like with a very different background color. How would it change your response to the picture?

If children want to experiment with background color, you'll want to help them think of workable ways to do this. Illustrators usually use watercolors or paints to make a background, and children can do this too if these tools are available. If children are using markers and crayons, however, the smaller marking surface makes filling a background and keeping it consistent a challenge. One solution is to have children draw and color the picture for an illustration on white paper, carefully cut around it, and then paste it to a piece of construction paper of the color they'd like to use for the background. Make sure, of course, that children can articulate a reason and a purpose for wanting a background to be a particular color. Nurturing the decisiveness behind this and all decisions about illustration composition is critical.

In a Teacher's Voice: An Idea for Trying It Out

If Laurel were making a book all about her big sister, she might introduce the reader to Angelica on the first page by just drawing her and putting her on a bright pink background, because everyone knows pink is Angelica's absolute favorite color in the world. The color would also set a happy, upbeat tone for the book that would match Angelica's sparkling personality. The other pages might have a much lighter pink background, so the details in them would show up more, or they could just be plain white.

A Writing Connection

Color as a tone-setting backdrop is often found in writing just as it is in illustrating. For example, consider the opening paragraph of Cynthia Rylant's novel *I Had Seen Castles*, set in Pittsburgh just before the start of World War II:

> *Pittsburgh was darkness. The taste of smoke in one's throat and heavy smog and black soot. That was Pittsburgh. (1993, 1)*

By placing this color-specific backdrop in the very first paragraph, Rylant skillfully cast a dark tone over everything that unfolds after it.

In *The Book Thief* (2006), Markus Zusak experimented with a range of backdrop color, which adds to the chilling tone of the narrator's voice. The narrator is none other than Death himself, and as he so matter-of-factly asks the reader, "What color will everything be at that moment when I come for you? What will the sky be saying?" (4). The voice of Death holds fast to the idea that color speaks, that every moment is colored in some way. When he sees the main character, Liesel, just after a bombing in the town square, Death describes the scene with a backdrop of red:

> The last time I saw her was red. The sky was like soup, boiling and stirring. In some places, it was burned. There were black crumbs, and pepper, streaked across the redness.

> Earlier, kids had been playing hopscotch there, on the street that looked like oil-stained pages. When I arrived, I could still hear the echoes. The feet tapping the road. The children-voices laughing, and the smiles like salt, but decaying fast.

> Then, bombs.

> This time, everything was too late. The sirens. The cuckoo shrieks in the radio. All too late.

> Within minutes, mounds of concrete and earth were stacked and piled. The streets were ruptured veins. Blood streamed till it was dried on the road, and the bodies were stuck there, like driftwood after the flood. . . .

> Yes, the sky was now a devastating, home-cooked red. The small German town had been flung apart one more time. Snowflakes of ash fell so lovelily you were tempted to stretch out your tongue to catch them, taste them. Only, they would have scorched your lips. They would have cooked your mouth. (12–13)

The choice of light imagery in that last paragraph—the "snowflakes of ash" and the "lily" in the made-up word "lovelily"—stand out with such stark contrast, they are much scarier than they would be if they weren't against that angry red backdrop.

Crafting Tone with Size

Something to Notice   The size of objects in a picture impacts tone.

An Illustration Example   Kate and Jim McMullan's picture book *I'm Mighty* (2003) is about a tugboat and the work it does towing ships in and out of a harbor. The tug is personified and speaks in its own voice as it tells about its work. In the illustrations, the size of the ships in contrast to the size of the tugboat is simply breathtaking. The sight of two of the ships in particular—the *Carla*, a six-decker container ship, and the *Queen Justine*, a cruise ship—cause many children to audibly gasp when they see them and try to imagine the tiny tugboat moving them along. The McMullan's skillfully stretched the enormous ships across almost the entire page spread, both vertically and horizontally, and readers can't help but respond first to the sheer, imposing size of them as they fill the frame.

An Understanding for Young Writers and Illustrators   Size matters. When illustrators are planning an illustration, the size of the objects in the picture, and particularly the size of them in relation to one another, is significant. Sometimes the size differences are real differences, as with the tugboat and the ships. When children's topics lend themselves to showing dramatic size differences, encourage them to think about how they can best use the space in a picture to capture the size difference so the reader really responds to it.

Illustrators may also exaggerate size differences somewhat to make an object feel stronger (if it's big) or more vulnerable (if it's small). In *Picture This: How Pictures Work*, illustrator Molly Bang included size as one of her ten principals of picture making:

> The larger an object is in a picture, the stronger it feels. We generally feel more secure physically when we are big than when we are little, because we're more capable of physically overpowering an enemy. One of the easiest ways to make a protagonist—or a threat—appear strong is to make it VERY large.
>
> The same figure appears much more vulnerable if it is made very small . . . We associate size with strength—strength of any sort. (2000, 72)

As you study illustrations, if the size of objects, people, or animals (large or small) catches your attention for some reason, think with children about

why you looked twice at the size and what sort of response you had to it. Talk about the illustrator's decision making. How do you imagine the illustrator wanted the reader to respond to the element of size in the picture?

Your goal is for students to begin thinking about the size of their drawings in the planning stages of their composing. To help them achieve this goal, you'll need to look closely with them and study how illustrators use space to capture size. So often, children begin drawing and simply plop their illustrations down in the middle of the page space and don't consider filling that space with a single object, person, or animal. They also don't consider how effective it could be to place something small in the picture in a far corner or near the very bottom or very top. Molly Bang points out that the top half of a picture is "a place of freedom, happiness and triumph; objects placed in the upper half often feel more 'spiritual'" (54). This is in contrast to the bottom half of the picture where objects "feel more threatened, heavier, sadder, or constrained" (56) and also more grounded.

In a Teacher's Voice: An Idea for Trying It Out

If I were to make a book about my trip to the state fair and how scared I was at the very tip-top of the Ferris wheel, then I could make the Ferris wheel cover almost the entire page top to bottom and show me really tiny in my seat at the very top. I could make some things on the ground tiny too to show how far away and high up I felt up there.

A Writing Connection

In verbal pictures, certainly writers can describe objects, people, and animals in ways that suggest size, and readers will have the same kind of emotional response to them as they do in actual pictures. A "wee little man" evokes a particular response, just as an "enormous, protruding earthworm" does.

Choosing words that evoke size *across* a text can impact the overall tone of the work and the reader's response to the whole of it, rather than to a single image. Author Tony Johnston said this of word choice in her book *Whale Song* (1987):

> I like to think of words as piles of beads in a wonderfully cluttered shop. When I begin to write a story, all the words are available to me—bins and barrels and basins of them to run my hands through. Then the choices come.

> For Whale Song, I chose "size words" such as wide, far, great, big, colossal, mighty, tremendous, stupendous to show the vast expanse of oceans, the vast size of whales. (1996, 257)

As children come to understand the idea that size evokes a natural, human response in readers, they can be purposeful in using size—in illustrating and in writing—to set tone in their work.

Technique 36

Crafting Tone with Physical Space

Something to Notice   The physical distance between animals, people, and objects affects tone.

An Illustration Example   Narrated in the voice of the youngest sister, Angela Johnson's book *One of Three* (1991) is a book about siblings and what it's like to be "one of three" sisters. In illustration after illustration, David Soman positions the three girls in close proximity on each wide spread as they play dress up, walk to school, ride the subway, sit outside the bakery, and enjoy all sorts of fun times together. In two places, however, the two big sisters are leaving the youngest out, and on these pages the physical distance between them in the pictures stands out in contrast to the others. In one of the two pictures, the text reads, "Sometimes Eva and Nikki say I'm not invited to go with them. Not to the park, the store, or sometimes even for a walk." Almost the entire spread is empty between the two older sisters and the younger. They stand at opposite ends of a room, and all the empty white wall space between them evokes a feeling of distance and sadness.

Similarly, in Kelly Bennett's *Not Norman: A Goldfish Story* (2005), a little boy gets a goldfish and it's not the pet he wanted, not at all. On the opening page where he receives the goldfish from his parents at his birthday party, the boy is positioned at the far right side of the spread. He sits at one end of a long table with the goldfish in its bowl in front of him. His parents are at the other end of the table, positioned at the edge of the left side of the spread, as far away from Norman as illustrator Noah Z. Jones could draw them, their distance communicating just how far away they are from really understanding the desires of their little boy who wants a very different kind of pet.

In Chris Rashka's classic *Yo? Yes!* (1993), two boys encounter each other on the street. One of the boys starts up a conversation and is a little pushy. The other boy is shy, so the conversation is very tentative at first. Rashka pictures the boys on fully opposite sides of the spreads in the early illustrations, the distance between them suggesting how far they have to go to become friends. But as the conversation warms, the distance between them lessens from page to page. By the end of the book, the boys are side by side and shaking hands.

An Understanding for Young Writers and Illustrators

Most young children already understand the feeling of being left out, and so the image of someone being left out usually registers an emotional response in them. Their eyes are always drawn to the figure that's not included with the others. "Why is he by himself?" they will sometimes ask.

When you see illustrations like the ones described above, help children understand that the illustrators are using the physical distance between figures to represent emotional distance and a feeling of not being connected. As illustrator Molly Bang said, "Space isolates a figure, makes that figure alone, free, and vulnerable" (2000, 84). When readers see illustrations like these where the interacting figures are far apart, the response is almost immediate and the distance between them is felt as emotional distance. The emotion might be fear, hurt, misunderstanding, rejection, or a whole range of distancing emotions. Depending on the context, the distance could also capture a positive feeling such as freedom or release. Of course, the opposite is true as well: A feeling of emotional closeness is best represented by placing figures closer to each other in a picture, as is a feeling of threat or intimidation.

Distance isn't used just to show interpersonal emotions; sometimes it can create a very different sort of tension in a picture. One of James Croft's illustrations in Nicola Davies' *Surprising Sharks* (2003) causes readers to hold their breath a little when they see it. A huge shark fin rises from the very bottom edge of the page, and at the very top of the page, a person's legs are shown just from the shin down, making bubbles in the water. The wide expanse of blue water that separates them in the picture is simply full of tension. Readers can't help but respond to the space because they're thinking about what will happen if the space between the shark and the person is somehow closed. The emotional worry is really created by the space. If the shark was right next to the person, or worse, biting him already, the outcome would be inevitable and there would be no *time* for worry. As Molly Bang pointed out, space and distance also imply time. "Wide space can create tension between divided objects" (2000, 88–89).

Exploring this illustration possibility will be very helpful for children who haven't given much thought to proximity and the meanings it suggests when positioning figures on the page. Think with children about how they have the entire expanse of two blank pages in every spread of a picture book in which to make meaning, and how much work they can do if they use that space wisely. Remind them that space between figures can be achieved horizontally across that space, but also vertically and diagonally. Remind them that most of the time, when showing interactions between and among animals, people, and objects, illustrators will picture the figures close together in the spread. A decision to put distance between interacting figures is purposeful and represents some emotion tied to the distance.

In a Teacher's Voice: An Idea for Trying It Out

Let's say I was making a book about a shy puppy I adopted at the shelter. I might have a scene where several other dogs, including my puppy, are out in the fenced-in area. I could draw the fence running across the whole top of my spread to make it seem like a wide open space, and then have several dogs playing just as hard as they can play on the bottom right side. Way up in the left corner, just in front of the fence, I could put the shy puppy, looking on as if he wants to play but is afraid to join in.

A Writing Connection

Writers also use the physical distance between characters to convey emotion. Consider this scene in Jerry Spinelli's book *Loser* (2002) as Donald Zinkoff experiences his first day at school:

> Like the other neighborhood mothers of first-day, first-grade children, Mrs. Zinkoff intends to walk her son to school. First day is a big day, and mothers know how scary it can be to a six-year-old.
>
> Zinkoff stands at the front window, looking at all the kids walking to school. It reminds him of a parade.
>
> His mother is upstairs getting dressed. She calls down, "Donald, you wait!" Her voice is firm, for she knows how much her son hates to wait.
>
> By the time she comes downstairs, he's gone.
>
> She yanks open the door. People are streaming by. Mothers hold the hands of younger kids while fourth- and fifth-graders yell and run and rule the sidewalks.
>
> Mrs. Zinkoff looks up the street. In the distance she sees the long neck of a giraffe poking above the crowd, hurrying along with the others. It's him. Must be him. He loves his giraffe hat. His dad bought it for him at the zoo. If she has told him once, she has told him fifty times: Do not wear it to school.
>
> The school is only three blocks away. He will be there before she can catch him. With a sigh of surrender she goes back into the house. (8–9)

The physical distance Spinelli crafted into this scene actually works on two emotional levels: It captures Donald's sense of freedom and his mother's sense of surrender at the same time. Consider the contrast in tone from this passage with the tone on the next page where the physical distance between two characters, Donald and his teacher, has tightened dramatically:

> When the bell rings, the teacher, Miss Meeks, shuts the door and stands before the desk of the unusually hatted student. The other students are openly

giggling. She wonders if this boy is going to be a problem. This is Miss Meeks's year to retire, and the last thing she needs is a troublesome first-grader. (9–10)

Whether you are painting pictures with paints or painting them with words, the physical distance between characters, objects, and animals impacts the tone of the interactions.

Technique 37

Crafting Tone with Shape and Texture

Something to Notice   Pictures drawn with sharp, pointed lines, edges, and angles evoke a different response than those drawn with softer, more rounded lines and edges.

An Illustration Example   In Emily Gravett's book *Wolves* (2005), a rabbit checks out a book about wolves from the library. As the rabbit reads the straightforward, factual information about wolves, his mind creates sensational images of wolves that capture his sincere and *well-founded* (as we find out in the end) fear of them. In the illustration showing the rabbit reading the first page of the book, the reader sees both the rabbit and the picture of the wolves he's imagining inside the book. The rabbit is drawn with all soft and rounded edges; his ears, eyes, paws, and even the texture of his fur all give a feeling of gentleness. In sharp contrast, the seven wolves he imagines are drawn with sharp, angular lines; their ears, eyes, noses, tails, claws, teeth, and fur are all menacingly pointed.

Illustrator James Marshall used contrasting sharper and rounder lines to evoke different responses to the "two" teachers in Harry G. Allard Jr.'s wonderful Miss Nelson series. The kindly Miss Nelson oozes pleasantness, her softly rounded face, hair, and body in stark contrast to the narrow, wart-plagued chin and pointedly protruding nose of the mean Miss Viola Swamp. Even Miss Swamp's lips and eyebrows are pointy, and her "smile" is a firm, sharp smirk.

An Understanding for Young Writers and Illustrators   From a very young age, children understand that sharp objects are, if not downright scary, at least a matter of concern. Wariness is a natural human response to sharpness (those with knife fetishes excepted), and when something is drawn with sharp lines, edges, and angles, the reader will bring at least some of this cautious emotion to the picture. Animals, objects, and even people can be cast in a more negative tone by sharpening the edges with which they are drawn. Softly rounded edges, in contrast, evoke a softer tone.

The contrast between angular and circular suggests other tonal differences as well, as Gunther Kress and Theo van Leeuwen point out in *Reading Images: The Grammar of Visual Design*:

In contemporary Western society, squares and rectangles are the elements of the mechanical, technological order, of the world of human construction. They dominate the shapes of our cities, our buildings, our roads. . . . In nature, squareness does not exist. . . . Circles and curved forms are the elements we associate with an organic and natural order, with the world of organic nature—and such mystical meanings as may be associated with them derive from this. (2006, 54–55)

When you notice something purposefully portrayed with particularly sharp edges, something that doesn't have to be thought of as sharply edged, consider why the illustrator chose to portray it in this way. What purpose does it serve in the particular context? Sometimes the sharp–round contrast is used to evoke different responses to animals, objects, or characters in a single book, as in the two examples above. Sometimes, however, an illustrator will use softer or sharper edges to portray something in a particular way to fit the tone of a particular text. Wendell Minor's wolves in Jean Craighead George's *The Wolves Are Back* (2008) are drawn with soft and rounded edges and are beautiful creatures against the backdrop of Yellowstone National Park. There is nothing scary about them, as Emily Gravett's wolves were scary, even on the page where they are doing what wolves do—*being scary*: "They scared the elk away. They scattered the bison. They frightened the sheep up into the cliffs." Clearly, the tone of Minor's illustrations capturing the wolves' natural beauty matches the feeling George wanted her reader to experience.

As with most illustration decisions that impact tone, you can help children deepen their understandings of these decisions significantly by showing them books that portray the same animals, objects, or people in very different ways. Study these contrasting illustrations closely, and if possible, study them before reading the words so you can focus solely on the feeling you get from the picture. Just in the way something is drawn or painted, how does one illustrator make something seem one way while another portrays it so differently? Spend time imagining how an illustrator might portray things in different ways. What would a tree outside a child's window look like if the child loves the dark and the sounds of night? What would the same tree look like if the child were afraid of the dark and the sounds of night?

Consider with children the way certain tools impact how sharply or roundly something is drawn. Help them see that they won't get a lot of sharp out of watercolor, for example. Pencils and pens, without a doubt, create the sharpest lines, and the finer the point, the sharper they are. When using markers or crayons, a smaller tip will create much sharper lines than a fat tip.

In a Teacher's Voice: An Idea for Trying It Out

If I were writing a memoir about the first time I caught a catfish and how afraid I was to touch it, I could use very sharp lines to draw it. The whiskers, specifically, are what scared me, so I'd need to make sure they look very pointy and scary just as they did to me when I saw them. I can also draw the fins, eyes, and mouth with extra sharpness for even more impact.

A Writing Connection

When writers paint a visual picture with words, they know—just as artists do—the difference that sharp, pointed details make in contrast to softly rounded ones. A cat with "green eyes like daggers" is much scarier than a cat with "green eyes like deep pools of still water." I'd like to suggest, however, that the idea of sharp and pointed in contrast to soft and rounded goes a bit further than this in helping children understand tone because these visual metaphors have verbal equivalents. Words, too, can be more or less sharp, more or less soft. Even sentences can have a sharply pointed feel to them if they are written short and with little variation, or they can be longer and more meandering and feel more softly rounded.

As an example, consider the passage from Jerry Spinelli's book *Loser* cited in the previous illustration possibility. In terms of word choice, the verb *yanks* in the sentence "She yanks open the door" is a sharp, pointed word. She could have just opened the door, or pulled open the door, or tugged open the door, or even wrenched open the door, but none of these verbs packs the exact same punch that *yanks* does.

In the last two paragraphs of the passage, the structure of the sentences and the phrases inside the sentences feel sharp as well, capturing the feeling of the mother's somewhat angry surrender to her son. If you want to really hear the sharpness in tone, read them aloud:

Mrs. Zinkoff looks up the street. In the distance she sees the long neck of a giraffe poking above the crowd, hurrying along with the others. It's him. Must be him. He loves his giraffe hat. His dad bought it for him at the zoo. If she has told him once, she has told him fifty times: Do not wear it to school.

The school is only three blocks away. He will be there before she can catch him. With a sigh of surrender she goes back into the house. (2002, 8–9)

Contrast the tone of these sentences to that of the opening paragraphs of the chapter just before it, its title suggesting a softer, gentler tone, "The Bright Wide World":

He is one of the new litter of boys tossed up by this brick-and-hoagie town ten miles by trolley from a city of one million. For the first several years they

have been home babies—Zinkoff and the others—fenced in by walls and backyard chain-link and, mostly, the sound of Mother's voice.

Then comes the day when they stand alone on their front steps, blinking and warming in the sun like pups of a new creation. (3)

Again, sentence structure and length do their work to set a softer tone, as does specific word choice: *tossed* is much softer than *thrown* or *hurled* or *flung* or *pitched*.

Technique 38

Accentuating or Exaggerating Features to Impact Tone

Something to Notice   Accentuating or exaggerating a particular feature of an animal, person, or object can affect the tone of the picture.

An Illustration Example   Returning to the wolves discussed in the last illustration possibility, the illustrators made another interesting decision that affects the tone of the pictures. In her book *Wolves*, Emily Gravett chose to emphasize the wolves' sharp teeth in every single picture. Their mouths are always open, the teeth are prominently visible, and in one close-up, you can also see a hungry, dripping tongue sticking out of the open mouth. In *The Wolves Are Back* (George 2008), however, Wendell Minor painted most of the wolves with their mouths closed, and in the pictures where their mouths are open, their teeth are far from menacing. One shows an open mouth that's howling and singing, and just two softly rounded teeth are visible. In the other pictures where you can see teeth, they appear simply as a white edge around the open mouth.

An Understanding for Young Writers and Illustrators   In her book *Picture This: How Pictures Work* (2000), illustrator Molly Bang wrote:

> *When we want a picture to feel scary, it is more effective to graphically exaggerate the scary aspects of the threat and of its environment than to represent them as close to photographic reality as possible, because this is the way we feel things look. (29)*

Emily Gravett decided first to draw the wolves' teeth much more sharply jagged than they are in reality, and then she decided to feature them prominently in every picture of the wolves—another departure from photographic reality because wolves usually don't have their mouths open in such a way that most of their teeth are visible. In deciding to draw the wolves this way, Gravett set the tone for the picture and captured the feeling the rabbit has toward the wolves.

When you see illustrations where certain features of an animal, object, or person are clearly exaggerated, think with children about what the exaggeration suggests. Really any strong emotion could be substituted for *scary* in Molly Bang's advice to illustrators. For example, in *Walk On! A Guide*

for Babies of All Ages (2006) Marla Frazee gave the baby who's learning to walk a particularly oversized diaper. The sheer bulk of it emphasizes the skinny, unsteady legs of the baby, making the reader a little nervous about his prospects of actually walking on them. But the diaper also suggests safety and security—there's plenty of padding if he falls. In Amy Krouse Rosenthal's *One of Those Days* (2006), illustrator Rebecca Doughty drew an exaggeratedly huge, open mouth on the little girl representing the "Nobody's listening to you day," capturing the desperate feeling of trying so hard and not being heard.

Help children understand that the illustrator is exaggerating a feature to evoke an emotional response, so the reader experiences something either as a character is experiencing it (as with the rabbit and wolves) or simply as the illustrator wants it to be experienced. In general, you will see this sort of illustration work more in fiction than nonfiction, as illustrators of nonfiction books have some responsibility to represent animals, objects, and humans as they actually exist, not as people may perceive them based on emotion. This being said, illustrators still make decisions about what to include—and to what degree—in all illustrations, knowing that these decisions affect how readers view the picture. Minor's decision, for example, to paint so many wolves with so many mouths closed certainly affects the way readers view these beautiful creatures.

Deciding which features to accentuate to capture different emotions will be the challenge for young writers and illustrators. In many ways, accentuated features work a lot like metaphor—they *represent* something that sparks an emotional response in the reader. They are figurative images rather than literal ones, and many children will still be growing into their ability to understand the figurative/literal dichotomy in the world of representation. As you confer with children, you might look for context-specific opportunities to suggest this sort of illustration work. Explaining why an accentuated or even exaggerated feature would make sense in a particular context will help children come to understand its use.

In a Teacher's Voice: An Idea for Trying It Out

Let's say I were making a book about the time I went to a restaurant and ordered a steak and it was so big I knew I could never eat even half of it. To help my reader feel how absolutely overwhelmed I was by the size of this steak, I could draw it so it looks enormous, hanging off the sides of my plate like a prehistoric dinosaur steak. I would make the napkins and silverware and everything around it much smaller in comparison to the size of this piece of meat. This would be a bit of an exaggeration, but that is how it *looked* to me when I saw it and realized what a mistake I'd made in ordering it. By exaggerating it, my reader would feel that same emotion.

A Writing Connection   Just like illustrators, writers sometimes accentuate or exaggerate in order to set a particular tone in writing. Janet Burroway wrote:

> As author, you manipulate intensity and value in your choice of language, sometimes matching meaning, sometimes contradicting, sometimes over-stating, sometimes understating, to indicate your attitude to the reader. (2003, 293)

My favorite columnist for the *Miami Herald*, Pulitzer Prize winner Leonard Pitts, Jr., showed he is a master of intensity manipulation in a recent column about the uproar over President Obama making a back-to-school speech to the nation's school children (September 9, 2009). Here's the lead to the column:

> Well, that was close.

> Surely, we are all relieved that at least some children were protected this week from the diabolical Barack Obama. It was touch and go there for awhile after the White House announced its plan for the president to give a back-to-school address to America's kids. They might have gotten away with it, too, but for conservative pundits and politicians who spent last week raising a ruckus about this scheme to indoctrinate our youth into the president's so-cialist cult. They were able to convince an untold number of schools to pro-hibit Tuesday's speech from being shown on campus and an untold number of parents to keep their children home.

> By this decisive action, untold millions (thousands?) of our kids were saved from exposure to subversive sentiments like "pay attention," "listen to your parents" and "every single one of you has something to offer."

Pitts is not serious, he's mocking a position some took seriously, so the exaggerated seriousness of his tone effectively conveys his disdain. Whether you agree with his position or not, as a writer, you have to admire his ability to "manipulate intensity and value" through his skillful control of language. By imagining how an illustrator might draw a picture of President Obama speaking to school children if he or she wanted to convey the same sardonic tone as Pitts, you can easily see how the issue of tone is critical to both writing and illustrating. As a matter of fact, political cartoonists use exaggeration to set tone in images all the time.

Technique **39**

Using Whimsical Detail to Lighten the Tone

Something to Notice   Whimsical detail lightens the tone in illustrations.

An Illustration Example   Illustrator James Croft used a heady combination of illustration techniques to keep the tone of Nicola Davies' *Surprising Sharks* (2003) lighthearted, a tone that matches the engagingly playful text. One way Croft achieves this tone is through the use of whimsical detail. On page 10, for example, four colorful fish swim beneath a Blackberry Lantern Shark, and they are all wearing sunglasses and happy smiles on their faces as they bask in the shark's light. The factual information in the background of the illustration explains that the Lantern Shark "has light-making organs on its tummy. They help it to blend in with the silvery surface of the sea and avoid ending up as dinner for bigger fish" (10). The text achieves its purpose of engaging and informing, and Croft used illustrative license to personify the fish to good humorous effect.

Illustrator Michelle Barbera filled the pages of Ashley MacEachern's book *Lance in France* (2008) with whimsical details. Written as if the reader is following Lance Armstrong in a single race, the book is actually a composite of some of the many hardships the cyclist faced through the years as he competed in the Tour de France. With an inspirational letter from Armstrong at the end of the book, as well as more factual information about him and the race, the illustrations could strike a much more serious tone than they do and still match MacEachern's text—but they don't. Barbera had something very playful in mind as she designed the illustrations. To take just one example, on the spread where the cyclists are racing by the sea through an unusually high tide, there are lots of cheering people in the water and on land. In the water amongst them you see a yellow submarine, a Loch Ness monster, three men in a tub, and an old woman sitting on a jet ski that reads "Grand Mer 5000."

An Understanding for Young Writers and Illustrators   If an illustrator wants a book to feel lighthearted and fun when the topic doesn't necessarily lend itself to that tone, then adding whimsical details is one way to achieve that. Readers respond immediately to the feeling of details like this. *Fish in sunglasses? How fun is that! Grand Mer 5000? Makes me smile every*

time. (If you don't know, *mer* is the French word for *sea*, and *mère* is the French word for *mother*.) Often, the lighthearted tone is achieved through illustration personification—animals or objects sport human features, apparel, or props. Such whimsical detail is almost always present in animal fantasy fiction where animals act as if they are human—the red ball cap worn by Doreen Cronin's worm in *Diary of a Worm* (2003), for example.

When you see details like this in books that are not animal fantasy fiction, however, books like *Surprising Sharks* and *Lance in France*, then you have a much more interesting illustration decision to talk about with children. Why would the illustrator decide to have fish wear sunglasses in a book like this? In making this decision, what does the illustrator give up—in terms of credibility—in an informative book? What does he gain? Is there a point at which too much whimsy might defeat the purpose of the book? Can the illustrator trust readers to understand that fish don't really wear sunglasses? That it's all just for fun? Questions like these should lead children to think about the importance of audience when making an illustration decision like this. Often, in literary nonfiction for children, the use of whimsical detail softens a topic that some children might find frightening—sharks being a perfect example.

Studying the use of this technique can be tricky because one of the challenges you will face is helping children be very purposeful in their use of this illustration possibility. Many children already add whimsical detail to their illustrations without even thinking about why they are doing it. A butterfly wearing a hair bow. A bright yellow sun sporting a wide smile. A hamster with glamorous earrings dangling from its ears. While it is certainly true that illustrators add details like these in some books, they are always purposeful in doing so; the details fit the tone of the book, and they happen across the pages, not just on a whim in a single illustration. Purposefulness is key. Nudge children to have very good reasons for putting sunglasses on fish— as James Croft did.

Finally, you will also see that in books where the topic clearly lends itself to whimsy, illustrators still must pay careful attention to setting that tone in the illustrations. The red, high-top Converse sneakers and colorful boxers worn by Santa in Marla Frazee's *Santa Claus: The World's Number One Toy Expert* (2005) are good examples of details that help set a playful tone, as are the fresh little puddles of pee left on the sidewalk after a very excited dog has chased a motorcycle in David Shannon's *Good Boy, Fergus!* (2006).

In a Teacher's Voice: An Idea for Trying It Out

If you were making a book to give to your little brother about what it's like to go to the dentist, you might add some whimsical detail in the illustrations to make it seem less scary for him. You could put funny outfits on the person who cleans your teeth and on the dentist, some funny pictures on the wall, and

maybe a crazy print on the cover they put over your clothes. Or, if you wanted to go at it another way, you could actually add smiling human faces to some of the tools they use to clean your teeth.

A Writing Connection   Like so many other decisions that impact the tone in illustrations, when writers want to take a lighter, more whimsical approach to a topic, they have the tool of word choice at their disposal. As an example, consider the word *tummy* in the caption for James Croft's illustration of a Blackberry Lantern Shark cited earlier. In terms of tone, the difference between *stomach* and *tummy* is significant. *Tummy* is just a funny word—a childhood word—and in its lightness it completely neutralizes the weird and potentially scary idea of a shark emitting light from its midsection. Writers wield a great deal of power when they realize the impact of word choice on tone.

CHAPTER

11

Layout and Design, In Pictures and In Words

Y<small>OU NEVER REALIZE HOW MUCH YOU MISS</small> a single red line until it's gone.

When I picked up the May 25, 2009, edition of *Newsweek* magazine from my mailbox, I began to thumb through it as I always do, skimming to see what I might want to read. I sensed the change almost immediately, though I couldn't say what it was exactly at the moment I sensed it. "Something is different about this magazine. They've *changed Newsweek*," I thought, the very idea of it somehow unsettling.

In my hands I held what editor Jon Meacham called "the first issue of a reinvented and rethought *Newsweek*." In his weekly message to readers in the issue, Meacham explained:

> *This first issue of the reinvented* Newsweek *is, we hope, a model of the form. We have rethought the structure of the magazine, and there are now only four sections: SCOPE (for short-form pieces, including Conventional Wisdom and the rechristened Indignity Index); THE TAKE (our columnists); FEATURES (longer-form narratives and essays); and CULTURE. The magazine will close with a graphic feature titled Back Story, a visual dissection or explanation of an important issue or phenomenon that will satisfy one's curiosity or pique one's interest. (2009, 9)*

The structural changes to content were all well and good, but it was the new design features that I found disconcerting. Why did they have to get rid of the red line that for

years and years in my life as a *Newsweek* reader has run along the top of every page with text? Meacham gave no explanation for this design change, perhaps thinking—wrongly, at least in my case—that no one would notice, or if they did, they wouldn't care.

A group of young children I was working with once had a very similar response to a picture book as I had to *Newsweek*. The book, *Surprising Sharks* by Nicola Davies (2003), was new to the children, but the "Read and Wonder" series of books from Candlewick Press was very familiar to them. They knew and loved other books in the series, books such as *Walk with a Wolf* by Janni Howker (1997), *The Emperor's Egg* by Martin Jenkins (1999), and *Gentle Giant Octopus* by Karen Wallace (1998). The children were insiders and knew that books in this series are usually designed with two kinds of text, one regular and one in undulating italics giving factual information to support the regular text. They knew that on the back page of these books, readers are reminded: "Don't forget to look at both kinds of words—this kind and *this kind*." But to the children's surprise and momentary dismay, *Surprising Sharks* didn't follow this familiar design format and the friendly reminder was not there as they expected it to be. In the end, they liked the new book and saw that it did the same kind of work to engage and inform them as the other books in the series, even though it didn't have the same familiar design feature they knew and loved.

Whether they are conscious of it or not, readers respond to the layout and design of texts. Everything about how the words are placed on the page in relation to the illustrations (and anything else that might be on the page), registers in the mind's eye of the reader and can be more or less pleasing. If a reader stays with a text over time, as I have stayed with *Newsweek* and the children had stayed with Candlewick Press, features of layout and design become familiar and are an integral part of the total reading experience.

To think about how readers respond to layout and design, take for example the simple issue of how much text is packed onto a page. The denser the text—small margins, small font, tight line spacing—the harder it feels and the challenge of wading through it all seems bigger. The words and ideas may not be hard at all, but they feel that way because too many of them are packed together in the space of the page. Wider margins, bigger fonts, and looser line spacing are friendlier and more inviting to readers. As my own books have been designed through the years, I have always requested the friendliness of wide margins.

Of course, wider margins, bigger fonts, and looser line spacing are all very simple text features easily manipulated. The world in which texts are

designed today involves so much more than simply choosing pleasing text features. In *Reading Images: The Grammar of Visual Design*, Kress and van Leeuwen explain the need to teach a new sort of literacy that would encompass a much more complex understanding of the way texts are designed:

> *Whether in the print or electronic media, whether in newspapers, magazines, CD-ROMs or websites, whether as public relations materials, advertisements or as informational materials of all kinds, most texts now involve a complex interplay of written text, images and other graphic or sound elements, designed as coherent (often at first level visual rather than verbal) entities by means of layout. (2006, 17)*

What a critical understanding that texts are "designed as coherent entities by means of layout" and that this design is *often at first level visual rather than verbal*. The way a text *looks* significantly impacts how its message is received, and teachers of young writers and illustrators have a golden opportunity to help children begin to understand this important idea.

As an experienced writer, I know how much having a visual sense of how my text might look matters to my process of composing. For example, in several of the books I have written, I have wanted to include a sort of "textual interlude" between chapters, and the design of these has been very important to me. I've asked, "How can we make them *look* different so readers understand they are different from the running chapters?" The lightly shaded pages containing "Craft Pauses" in my book *Study Driven* (2006) are a design feature of this kind. Similarly, because I include examples of children's writing in most of my books, I think a lot about where the figures should be in relation to the running text. I sometimes have to ask, "How important is it that the reader see this on the same page as the text that talks about it? Should it be above the discussion or below it? To the side?" As a writer designing my text, I shift from thinking verbally about it to thinking visually, and I move fluidly between the verbal and the visual as I compose, imagining how the text I'm generating might be laid out in effective ways.

Teachers of young writers who nurture thinking about illustration work can do so much to help children understand the importance of layout and design in this richly multimodal context. With an emphasis on the visual as well as the verbal, children can become thoughtful, purposeful designers of texts. The cover, the end pages, the title page, the layout of pictures in relation to text, the back page and author's note—everything about a picture book asks that design decisions be made.

Most professionally made picture books have an author, an illustrator (sometimes the same person), and a designer. The designer makes sure all

the parts of the book work together in a cohesive way. Harcourt editor Allyn Johnson said this about picture books:

> As an editor, I take the form of the picture book very seriously. I think of it as a piece of theatre that takes place within a thirty-two page structure. Every part is important—what's happening on the title page, on the end pages, and on the back of the book. (Johnson and Giorgis 2007, 11)

The goal of studying the illustration techniques in this section is to help young writers and illustrators understand that every part of a picture book they make is important, as is every decision about how the parts will be "laid on the page." By looking closely at the layout and design of picture books, children will come to realize how many decisions are in their control as they play the roles of writer, illustrator, *and* designer with more purposeful intention.

Unlike the previous four chapters, you will find some techniques in this chapter that actually have to do with written text. These possibilities are a part of illustration study because they are all about the way written text is visually designed in picture books. Writers decide what the words will say, but how the text will *look* in the book is a matter of visual design. With some of the techniques in this section, you'll be studying how words are placed on the page in relation to the pictures, how words are sized and colored differently to make meaning, and even how print itself can become a sort of picture. You may wonder, "So what about writers who aren't yet using conventional print in their writing? Do these possibilities even make sense for them?" They do, actually. As long as children are making some distinction between print (scribble or letterlike symbols) and pictures, they can design the layout of these two elements in interesting ways in their books.

Note that the techniques in this chapter don't include writing connections, namely because thinking about layout and design is really the same for writers and illustrators—it's where the two truly intersect. In the previous four chapters, I've tried to show how writers and illustrators use different tools, but they compose with many of the same understandings guiding them. With layout and design, however, writers and illustrators not only compose with the same understandings, they compose with basically the same *tools* at their disposal. For example, a writer of a very important business letter may decide to include a nice border around his text, or perhaps a single accent line running horizontally across the top of the page. Illustrators, of course, sometimes use borders in their design too.

Related to this, a few of the techniques in this section don't include suggestions for trying them out. When this is the case, it's because the

technique is a way to make the book more visually interesting, but it doesn't have a meaning-based purpose beyond this. The first technique in this chapter, for instance, explains that words can be placed anywhere on a page in relation to a picture. I don't have to help children imagine this technique in a *particular* illustration context because it's true of *any* illustration context.

Technique 40

Designing the Placement of Words and Pictures

Something to Notice

Words can be placed anywhere on a page in relation to the illustration.

An Illustration Example

On different pages of Charlotte Voake's picture book *Hello Twins* (2006), readers will find the text positioned in a variety of places around the wonderful illustrations of the twins, Simon and Charlotte. Almost every spread has text on both the left and right pages, but sometimes the words are positioned at the top and other times at the bottom; sometimes they are more toward the edge of the page and other times more toward the center. On some pages, the lines of the text are left justified, but on other pages they are centered. Because the simple, pleasing lines and colors of the pictures are drawn without background detail, the words can really go anywhere on the creamy white space around them, and their different placements add visual variety to the book.

An Understanding for Young Writers and Illustrators

Text placement is one of the simplest design elements for children to understand, but it is also one of the most important because it impacts every single page of a book. As designers of their books, children must decide where they will put their words in relation to their pictures with each turn of the page. As they study the different ways that books are designed in terms of text placement, children will quickly see that there is no need to be locked into the de facto positioning of the words at the bottom and the pictures at the top. The words can go anywhere, and making good decisions about text placement can make a book much more visually interesting.

One of the first considerations for the design of text placement is the presence or absence of detail in the background of the illustration. If there is a lot of background detail, then the words need to be positioned so that they don't compete with this detail and so they are visible against the colors of the background. Often, the text will be placed in the lightest part of the picture, or a light spot will serve as a sort of frame for the words with color all around. Sometimes, if the colors are very dark in a background, the text will be white against it. If there is very little or no background detail (as in *Hello Twins*), the pictures and the words can go anywhere on the space of the spread.

As you study text placement, a little directional language will be necessary. Children should learn to think of an illustrated spread as a design space with four corners and both horizontal and vertical possibilities. Words such as *left*, *right*, *above*, *below*, *inside*, and *outside* will no doubt be critical to your conversations. I would also suggest introducing children to the design concepts of left justified, centered, and right justified because they are such critical concepts in the design of all kinds of written texts, not just picture books.

Using plain white paper, you'll need to demonstrate thinking about different possibilities for text and picture placement, and how the planning for this design is best when it happens *before* children begin writing or illustrating the next page in their books. While some text placement carries meaning in its very design (as we'll see with the next possibility), often the decision is simply one of what pleases the eye. The designer simply thinks, "It looks good this way," and this is the kind of thinking you'll demonstrate to children. No doubt you'll also find many opportunities to work with children in writing conferences and help them think purposefully about the placement of text and pictures in their individual books.

For children who have the fine motor control to use lines to make their text more readable, you might consider taking some plain white paper and marking heavy, dark horizontal lines (wide enough for text) on it. You can then laminate the paper so it's sturdy, and then show students how to place it underneath a piece of white paper and use the lines that show through to guide them. This way, they can have the stability of lines but also the flexibility to design in interesting ways. I would advise, however, that you make this tool one that children are free to use or not to use. In doing so, children who care about the look of clean lines will have a handy tool at their disposal, and those who aren't so concerned about the look won't feel they *should be* concerned about it.

Technique 41

Using Word Layout to Convey Meaning

Something to Notice   Sometimes the placement of words in relation to the picture matches a specific meaning in a book.

An Illustration Example   Elisha Cooper's picture book *Ice Cream* (2002) explains the entire process of making this wonderful treat— from cows in the field all the way to grocery store freezers. In most of the book, the text is written in neat, horizontal lines above, below, or in between the pictures in the illustrations. On a few pages, however, the text placement seems to match the meaning of the words. For example, consider these lines of text:

> *The milk truck pulls up to the milk co-op. Milk goes through pipes into storage tanks, through a separator that parts the milk from the cream, through a machine where some of the milk is condensed, then back through pipes to separate trucks. The milk goes through a lot.*

On a single spread, these sentences snake down and then up and then back down again in very pipelike fashion, *ᗗ* their visual design matching the meaning of the text itself. Small pictures of the different tanks and machines that do the work are placed in the wider areas between the curves of text.

On a different page, the text makes a circle around pictures of various ingredients such as nuts and chocolate chips, causing the reader to turn the book upside down to read it. The circular design of the text matches the motion of stirring, which is explained in the words:

> *They stir ingredients teaspoon by teaspoon—tasting, adding, tasting—and decide to add more chocolate, or a lot more chocolate. One scientist wipes her hands on her coat when she finds the perfect formula.*

The satisfying roundness of a circle also matches the feeling of satisfaction in a *perfect* formula.

An Understanding for Young Writers and Illustrators   In general, readers of English expect text to be horizontally linear on a page and to be read from left to right. If text is designed in some other way, usually it's because the design itself is meant to make meaning as much as the words do. When you see text that is designed to match its meaning (in a

metaphorical sense, of course), help children make the important connection between what the words say and the shape of their design. Also, look closely at how pictures are positioned around text that is shaped in an interesting way.

Sometimes text that is not horizontally linear is difficult to read and can detract from the reading experience even though it might be visually interesting. Knowing how much is *too* much will be a challenge for some children who are just beginning to experiment with this design possibility, overuse being a natural consequence of learning. Talk with children about the possibility of overdoing it and how this sort of design could be distracting for readers when it is overdone. Help children see that in most picture books, this sort of text placement is the exception rather than the rule, and the exceptionality of the design is a big part of what makes it more visually interesting rather than distracting.

In a Teacher's Voice: An Idea for Trying It Out

If I were writing a book about how incredibly rainy it is today, I might design a page where the words fall like raindrops from the top to the bottom. Against a backdrop of thick, gray sky, I'd position the words from left to right and sort of staggered, just like the rain looks as it falls outside my window. The words might say, "All day long the rain fell in big, sad drops outside my window."

Technique **42**

Using Size and Color to Convey Meaning

Something to Notice   The size and color of print can convey meaning.

An Illustration Example   Books don't really have sound, but Betsy Franco and Steve Jenkins' book *Birdsongs* (2007) seems filled with the sounds of birds. Using both size and color to design the print for the various bird calls, Jenkins captures the loud, shrill squawk of a crow's caw with huge letters and the small, high voice of a hummingbird—tzik—with tiny ones. The volume is modulated on single pages, and the seven calls of the sea gull—eeyah—are spread about the page in variously sized print, projecting louder and softer. Also, the color of the print spelling out the bird calls is different from the color of the print of the running text on each page, making the sound words even more distinctive.

Color does lots of work in Eileen Spinelli's *Heat Wave* (2007), illustrated by Betsy Lewin. The print is black throughout the text, except for the sentences that say something about how hot it was. They're all printed in red—sentences such as *Thursday was hotter still* and *Night fell, but not the temperature.*

An Understanding for Young Writers and Illustrators   Changing the size or color of print in some meaningful way is another simple design possibility common in many picture books. Children will notice size and color changes in print easily, and when they do, the key is to help them understand the purpose behind the change. What meaning does the size or color suggest that is connected to the meaning of the text? Why did it make sense for the designer to do this? Often, you'll see that the size and color of print (when purposefully changed in a text) is very sensory: Sound, size, temperature, texture, smell, taste, and even certain emotions might be suggested. Sometimes the change is purely for emphasis, just as writers emphasize words by making them bold or italicized, for example.

In picture books, size and color changes in print are almost always related to some meaning in the text. In other texts, magazines and newspapers for instance, size and color changes in print are most commonly used as design features that label different parts of a text or indicate some hierarchy of information. As children become more and more aware that print

is manipulated purposefully to make meaning, they will bring this understanding to all sorts of new texts they encounter as they grow as readers and writers.

Your goal, as with every single illustration possibility, is for children to use changes in size and color of print purposefully. As you confer, help children make smart decisions about how they might try this possibility if it makes sense in the context of their work. When children do make smart decisions about this and any other possibilities, be sure to share those with other children and highlight the purposefulness.

In a Teacher's Voice: An Idea for Trying It Out

Let's say I was making a book about helping my grandma plant a garden this spring. Maybe when I write the names of the different vegetables we plant, I could print them in the color of the vegetable. Corn could be in yellow, peas in green, tomatoes in red. And when I write "pumpkin," I could make it orange, but I could also make it big since the pumpkins grow so big!

Technique 43

Designing Print to Convey Meaning

Something to Notice
Print may be designed in particular ways for visually meaningful effect.

An Illustration Example
In Cynthia Rylant's ode to the twelve full moons of the calendar year, *Long Night Moon* (2004), illustrator Mark Siegel drew a subtle "moon glow" around each of the Native American names for the full moons—names such as Stormy Moon and Sprouting Grass Moon and Thunder Moon. A thin, shaded gray simply wraps itself gently around the letters that make up each of the names, as if the letters themselves are glowing with the light of the full moon.

Debbie S. Miller's book *Big Alaska: Journey Across America's Most Amazing State* (2006) takes the reader on a visual and verbal flight with a majestic bald eagle through the wildly beautiful state of Alaska. With each turn of a page, you are at a different location in the state, and title lines on each page announce the locations in some superlative sense. For example, "Kenai River: Biggest King Salmon" and "Matanuska River Valley: Heaviest Vegetables on Earth." A particularly interesting design feature, illustrator Jon Van Zyle framed the first letter of the first word in each title and drew a tiny background picture inside the frame. There is a fishing fly (to catch the salmon) in the frame behind the *K* in Kenai River, and a red barn and fields (to grow and house the vegetables) in the frame behind the *M* in Matanuska River Valley.

Pictures don't smell, of course, but if they did, the title of Kate and Jim McMullan's book *I Stink!* (2002) would reek. The edges of the wide block letters seem to ripple in that familiar way smell is so often represented in a picture, as if the odor is spreading out from all around it. The *I* in *I Stink!* is a garbage truck, and in his own voice, he tells what a day doing his stinky work is all about. The McMullans use the odiferous lettering very sparingly, employing it only on the title page and again later when the words *I Stink!* are repeated in the text.

An Understanding for Young Writers and Illustrators
As these examples show, print can be designed in such a way that it carries meaning in its design. Because beginning writers are in the midst of figuring out how print works and how to make letters in the first place, they are likely to be very interested in this illustration possibility. When you see that

illustrators have designed print in purposeful ways, help children first see that the basic shapes of the letters are embedded in the design. Explain that this is critical as the letter shapes are what make the symbols universally recognized (by those who use the same alphabet). If children want to experiment with designing print in interesting ways, they need to remember that the basic shape of the letter has to be in their design. This is assuming, of course, that children are using conventional letter formations fairly consistently. If they are not to that stage of development yet, then let them design away with the concepts of print they do have. No doubt, paying purposeful attention to how they are designing print will help them become more cognizant of print in general, which may nudge their development more quickly to convention.

Also talk about why an illustrator might have decided to make certain letters appear in a particular way. How does the design of the print match important meanings in the text? Emphasize the meaning connection. Help children see that this possibility is not about making an *o* in the shape of a heart or an *m* look like two rainbows stuck together just because they like the way it looks. The design needs to be purposeful and match the meanings in the book. Also, help children see that, as a general rule, illustrators use unusual print design sparingly in a book, as too much would become a distraction for the reader.

In a Teacher's Voice: An Idea for Trying It Out

Let's say I was making my same book (that I imagined in the last possibility) about helping my grandma plant a garden. Instead of matching the color of the print in the vegetable names to the color of the vegetables, maybe I could make one letter in each vegetable name look like a vegetable. For corn, I could make the straight line in the *r* look like an ear of corn, and for peas, maybe I could use little green peas strung together to make the shape of the *s*.

Designing a Cover

Something to Notice

Picture book covers are designed in a variety of ways.

An Illustration Example

The illustrators of *Fabulous Fishes* (Stockdale 2008), *Feel the Summer* (Thomson 2006), and *Baby Whale's Journey* (London 1999) each replicated an illustration from inside the book as the cover illustration. Because the illustration of the children running to the beach in *Feel the Summer* only covers the left page of the spread inside the book, the picture is exactly the same (including its size) on the cover as it is inside the book. The whales and fish on the other two book covers are the same illustration, but they've each been cropped more closely to fit the smaller space of the cover.

The illustrators of *All the World* (Scanlon 2009), *The Dot* (Reynolds 2003), and *An Island Grows* (Schaefer 2006) each made a completely new illustration for the covers of their books. The covers of *All the World* and *The Dot* each feature their book's main characters, but the characters are engaged in different actions than you see inside the books. The picture of an island with new vegetation growing on it picks up on the main idea of *An Island Grows*, but it doesn't replicate any of the inside illustrations.

The illustrators of *At Night* (Bean 2007), *The Zoo* (Lee 2004), and *A Good Night Walk* (Cooper 2005) each use the front and back covers as one continuous spread. If you open the books as wide as they will go, you will see the cover illustration in its entirety. While the covers of *At Night* and *A Good Night's Walk* simply capture a familiar landscape from inside the book, the cover of *The Zoo* actually has a story element embedded in it that extends the story inside the book. The gorilla inside his cage on the cover is holding a tiny pink boot, and the little girl who gets separated from her parents inside the book just happens to be wearing a pair of tiny pink boots.

An Understanding for Young Writers and Illustrators

Covers matter. So often the difference between having lots of readers and having just a few depends on having the perfectly eye-catching cover. The cover needs not only to catch readers' attention, it needs to capture the spirit of the book too. Helping young children become purposeful in the design of their cover illustrations is very important to them as writers and illustrators. You might start this whole line of inquiry into cover illustrations by talking with children about what they find appealing on a book cover when they are searching for books to read.

While children won't learn this just from studying cover illustrations, you should inform them that decisions about cover illustrations are usually made near the end of the writing and illustrating process, not at the beginning. In the publishing world, marketing folks often play a big role in deciding what the cover illustration will show. This makes sense because the cover is the first point of contact for most readers and getting it right matters enormously. Waiting until the end of the process to make cover illustrations will be a stretch for lots of children who have habitually always started with the cover. You want to nudge them to wait, however, because they can do much more purposeful thinking about their covers once their books are finished.

The three possibilities found in the examples mentioned previously represent three of the most common approaches to cover design: replicate a key illustration from inside the book, create a new illustration using visual elements from inside the book, or use both the front and back covers to make one continuous cover illustration—a wraparound cover (which may or may not be replicated inside the book). As you study the covers of picture books, be sure to name the decision the illustrator has made so that it's clear to children.

You'll want to think about the decision making of the illustrator. If the cover is a replicate, why, of all the pictures in the book did he or she decide to use this one on the cover? Do you think any of the others might have served just as well? If the cover is different from any of the illustrations in the book, what does it have in common with them? Usually such covers will picture the characters or setting, of course, but be sure this is clear to children. And if the front and back covers are used as a continuous space, wonder together about why the illustrator decided to make it this way. Often you'll see that such covers feature wide panoramic spaces and that spaces like this are some sort of theme in the book.

You'll need to help children think about the logistics of trying these different sorts of covers on their books. If they want to replicate an illustration from inside the book, how might they do that? If a color copier is available, a copy could be made and cropped to fit. If not, show children how to place an illustration alongside a blank piece of paper and recreate it as closely as possible.

If children want to use the front and back of a book cover as one continuous illustration, you might find large paper that could be folded to fit the inside pages after it's been illustrated. You could also simply place the front and back papers side by side, tape them, turn them over to illustrate them, and then fold them at the taped edge. If children are trying this, be sure to help them understand that the writing needs to go on the right side of the illustration so it will be in the right place when the illustration is folded to make a cover.

While doing a new illustration for the cover is logistically the easiest option, deciding what the cover illustration should show is likely the most challenging thinking children will do about covers. Probably the best way to demonstrate the thinking behind cover decision making is to look at some of the books children are making and imagine cover possibilities together, discussing the pros and cons of each.

In a Teacher's Voice: An Idea for Trying It Out

In my book about planting a garden with my grandma, I could use the front and back covers to make one long picture stretching across a row of vegetables. I could do rows of corn as they grow so tall and would look nice and bold on my cover.

Designing End Pages to Convey Meaning

Something to Notice   End pages may be designed to enhance the meaning of the book.

An Illustration Example   The end pages of Giles Andreae's *Giraffes Can't Dance* (1999) show Gerald the giraffe doing all sorts of funky dance moves. Against a light orange background, three horizontal rows of eight pictures each show the gangly guy in various poses. As your eyes move across the pictures from left to right, it's almost as if Gerald comes to life and really *is* dancing—and quite well, I might add.

The front end pages of *The Zoo* (2007) by Suzy Lee show a gorilla escaping through a break in his cage on the far left side of the spread. On the far right side, you see a small monkey looking at the gorilla and just the trunk of an elephant sticking into the illustration above his head. On the back end pages, on the far right side of the spread, the monkey is pictured with his hands on the gorilla's behind as he pushes him back through the break in the cage. This little story contained in the end pages matches an important meaning in the book, as none of the zoo animals are actually seen inside cages or fences inside the book. The gorilla who has sprung himself free of his cage suggests that, perhaps, all the animals have done the same.

The front end pages of Cynthia Rylant's book *Snow* (2008) are painted the blue-black color of a dark winter's night. A single white snowflake falls from near the top of the spread. The back end pages have the same blue-black background, but the dark night sky is now filled with snowflakes of all shapes and sizes.

An Understanding for Young Writers and Illustrators   The "end pages" of a picture book are the spreads including the hard backs of the book covers and the backs of the first and last pages. In many picture books, the end pages are simply a solid color and contain no illustrations. When illustrators choose to include the end pages in the overall design of the book, they do so with purpose.

Often you will see that end pages are designed to simply repeat visual elements found in the text, as the dance moves do in *Giraffes Can't Dance*. Sometimes, however, more sophisticated meanings are made. When this is the case, the front end pages and the back end pages will likely be different

and will show some change that matches a meaning in the text, as with the escaped gorilla and the snowflakes in the examples above. When you see end pages designed in some purposeful way, be sure to help children understand how the design matches or extends the meaning of the book.

Until you study end pages as part of the overall design of a picture book, most children will not have thought to include them in their books. Of course, the books children make don't actually have hard covers to create end pages, so it makes sense that they haven't been thinking of this design space. Once you do study end pages, however, children will begin to have ideas for how they might use these pages in interesting ways in their books. If a child wants to design end pages for a book, a hard cover isn't necessary. Simply add pages so this extra design space is there in the book.

In a Teacher's Voice: An Idea for Trying It Out

I could do end pages for my book about helping my grandma plant her garden. I could draw rows in the dirt showing the little seed packet signs sticking up on the front end pages. On the back end pages, I could show the same rows but with vegetables sticking up in them. I would need to make sure I have the vegetables showing in the same rows where their seed packets were on the front end pages so it really matches.

Using Borders

Something to Notice

Boxes and borders may be used in the design of a picture book.

An Illustration Example

In his book *Leaves* (2007) about a bear experiencing his first winter, David Ezra Stein drew a simple border of black lines against a white background around most of his illustrations. The lines are sort of free-form—not quite straight, of varying thickness and intensity, and a tiny bit of color from the picture inside spills across them into the white space. The effect is one of framing, but with a casual rather than rigid feel to it, sort of like framing a picture with your hands. Most of the pictures with borders are the same size, but there is some variation in size early in the book. Most spreads have separate boxed-in pictures on both the left and right pages, but a few of them are a single box across both sides of the spread. And interestingly enough, just four of the pictures do not have black borders around them. All of them appear early in the book.

Mélanie Watt used boxes and borders extensively in her book *Scaredy Squirrel* (2006), but in a very different way than the framing boxes in *Leaves*. Watt's boxes and borders are used to visually separate her almost listlike illustrations. For example, on one page the text reads, "With his emergency kit in hand, Scaredy Squirrel watches. Day after day he watches, until one day . . ." The page is divided into a grid of nine boxes. The text is in the center box, and in the eight surrounding boxes Scaredy Squirrel is shown in a variety of postures watching for danger through his binoculars.

In Judy Beach's *Names for Snow* (2003), Loretta Krupinski used wide borders as an integral part of the overall design of the book. On each spread, one side contains a full-page illustration and the other page is for text. On the text pages, a wide border frames a block of white space around words, and there are illustrations inside the three-and-one-half-inch space of the border itself: A snowflake is pictured in the four corners of each border, and a family of mice (acting as humans) is pictured going about life in the season of snow.

An Understanding for Young Writers and Illustrators

The edges and corners of the pages in a book form natural illustration borders. When a border is added inside this natural border of paper, it reconstitutes the illustration space in important ways. Instead of considering a single visual space, the reader must now consider at least two visual spaces, and

sometimes more depending on the placement and use of borders. The boxes described earlier in the *Scaredy Squirrel* illustration, for example, actually create nine visual spaces on a single page.

While the natural illustration borders in picture books will almost always be square or rectangular, the borders inside them don't have to be. They can be any shape, and the more different the shape is from the natural borders of the book's pages, the more visually interesting they are. Several illustrations in April Pulley Sayre's *Trout Are Made of Trees* (2008) are contained within round or oval shapes, and one illustrated spread in Brian Karas' book *Atlantic* (2002) has pictures inside the shapes of rounded arrows. In both these books, the white space around the shape forms the border. You'll want to be sure to draw children's attention to this different way of making a border when you see it in other books.

The examples from the books above represent a range of purposeful possibilities for using boxes and borders in the design of picture books, and you will no doubt see others as you study different books and see different layouts and designs. From simple framing for subtle visual effect, all the way to borders that actually do the work of illustrating, so much will become possible for young writers and illustrators when you turn your attention to these simple design features. The thinking you do with children will also have far-reaching implications. Boxes and borders are used extensively in the layout and design of texts other than picture books. Writers and designers of everything from business letters to magazines to websites use these design tools to separate and highlight different kinds of information. With an introduction in the context of illustration study, children will be well on their way to using boxes and borders in the design of increasingly sophisticated kinds of texts.

Using the Space Implied Outside a Picture

Something to Notice Pictures may extend into the invisible space beyond the natural borders of the page.

An Illustration Example On the page featuring a fire truck in Margaret Mayo's *Dig, Dig, Digging* (2001), firefighters spray water from a truck at a building that's in flames. Only the very edge of the building and part of one window can be seen, however, leaving the reader to imagine the rest in the invisible space off the far right side of the page.

The opening page spread in Suzanne Bloom's *A Splendid Friend Indeed* (2005) shows a duck walking unsteadily down what appears to be a hairy white mountain. Rising from the bottom of the spread across both pages, the reader is not quite sure what the surface might be. A turn of the page reveals that the hairy white mountain is actually a polar bear. On this page, he's pictured only from his shoulders forward, entering from the lower half of the left side of the page and stretching horizontally across to the right, as if he's lying down reading the book he holds in his outstretched hands. The duck stands on his head as he reads. One more page turn and the bear is now shown from the waist forward, still lying down, the rest of him still somewhere in the invisible space off the far left side. Finally, with one more turn of the page we see the entire polar bear, except that now he's sitting up and filling the page space more vertically than horizontally.

In Donald Crews' *Truck* (1980), the back half of a large red truck seems to exit off the far right side of the spread. Turn the page, and the front side of the same truck emerges from the far left side of the spread. In a masterful design move, Crews managed to completely reconstitute his picture space, making the edge of the picture no longer the edge but a bridge instead—a bridge from one visual space to the next.

Until the very end of the book, every page of Giles and Alexandra Milton's *Call Me Gorgeous!* (2009) shows only a very specific part of an animal. For example, a pig's ears, a porcupine's spines, and a crocodile's mouth fill most of the illustrated spreads on which they are found; the rest of the animals exist off the edges of the picture space. In the end, all the animal parts come together to form the gorgeous creature known as the reinde-piggy-pocrcu-croco-touca-flami-roos-dalma-chameleo-bat-frog.

An Understanding for Young Writers and Illustrators

When young children first begin to illustrate, they seem to operate with two misguided understandings. First, they think that if they are to picture something, they must picture it in its entirety. Second, they believe the space of a page must contain the entire space of their pictures. With illustration study, however, they will quickly see how untrue these understandings really are.

What children need to support them is a basic understanding of the principle of framing. In film and photography, framing refers to the composition of a scene within the visual field of the camera. A photograph may show a person only from the shoulders up, but the person who views that photograph naturally assumes the rest of the person is outside the frame because the picture implies space outside itself. In picture books, each page spread is like the visual field of the camera. Just like the photographer, the illustrator decides how to frame the picture, and sometimes the most visually interesting way to frame it is to show only a part of something.

As you study illustrations, you'll notice that lots of insignificant background detail extends beyond the edges of the picture frame—the branches of a tree in the distance, part of a building in a cityscape, a portion of a cloud in the sky. When part of a central, important figure in the illustration is outside the picture frame, however, you'll want to think about the illustrator's decision making. Why did he or she decide to frame the picture in just this way?

There can be lots of reasons for framing pictures in particular ways. In the examples above, the sliver of a burning building creates tension in the picture; readers can't really determine the extent of the fire because they can't see it all. The element of surprise seems to drive the framing decision Suzanne Bloom made—surprise first at what the furry animal is, and then later at how enormous he is standing next to the duck who wants to be his friend. Donald Crews' framing of the truck across two spreads creates a sense of movement in the picture, and Alexandra Milton's framing forces a focus on the individual body parts that come together in the end.

When a central figure in the illustration enters or exits the picture frame from the top, it creates even more visual interest. Illustrator Molly Bang explained why in her book *Picture This: How Pictures Work*:

> *We see pictures as extensions of reality. When we look at a picture, we "read" it as though gravity existed inside the picture as well as outside. Most pictures are rectangular, and their horizontal and vertical edges accentuate our sense of gravity's force. (2000, 60)*

Often, a figure entering a picture from the top is grounded by gravity because the ground on which it stands is pictured. But if a figure enters a

picture from the top and is not grounded in any way, it appears to be hanging there in a way that is visually very interesting. There is a wonderful baboon doing just this in an illustration in Manya Stojic's book *Rain* (2000). Also, if a figure is exiting the picture at the top, as several birds do in Kevin Henkes' *Birds* (2009), there is a wonderful feeling of escape.

With lots of talk around how pictures are framed in different ways, children will be more likely to begin trying different ways of framing their own pictures. As you work with them in writing conferences and they plan new pictures, help them imagine possibilities for using the picture space in new and surprising ways.

In a Teacher's Voice: An Idea for Trying It Out   If I were making a book about how I like to visit at my grandma and grandpa's apartment in the city, I might draw their apartment building so it goes off the top of the page. It always seems so big to me, like I can hardly see the top, so if I show it extending beyond my picture frame, maybe my readers will understand just how big it is.

Using Visual Elements in the White Space Around Words and Pictures

Something to Notice

Small, meaningful images may be used as visual elements apart from the main illustration.

An Illustration Example

Steve Jenkins used a lot of white space in his layout and design for Mem Fox's *Hello Baby!* (2009). Using collages, Jenkins pictures a different animal on each illustrated spread, but only parts of the animals are pictured. The hippo, for example, enters the spread from the right side and is shown only from the neck forward. The pictures are large, usually covering most of one page, and the text is in the expansive white space on the opposite page—"Perhaps you're a hippo with yawning jaws." In an interesting design move, a small complete image of each animal accompanies the text on each page.

Many of the illustrated spreads in Eileen Spinelli's *Summerbath, Winterbath* (2001) have a full-page illustration on either the right or left side of the spread. The opposite page has been left white and contains just the text and a small picture that relates in some way either to the words or the full-page picture that accompanies it. For example, on one page the text reads simply, "She hung sheets across the kitchen." The full-page illustration shows the mother hanging sheets, and then on the white page with text, a pair of clothespins is pictured in the bottom right corner. With so much white space around then, the small pictures create a lot of visual interest alongside the full-page illustrations.

In Nancy Hundal's *Snow Story* (1997), illustrator Kasia Charko used the same sort of two-page division: full-page illustration on one side, white background and words on the opposite side. In her white background, she drew a small birdhouse on each page just above the block of text. It's the same birdhouse on every page, but birds and snow come and go with the season, surrounding the birdhouse in different ways across the pages of the book.

An Understanding for Young Writers and Illustrators

Anywhere there is open white space in a book, an illustrator may decide to design that space to make it more visually interesting. Using small, meaningful images that connect to the text somehow is one way to do this. For example, Lauren Stringer dropped in a few snowflakes around framed

pictures like this in Cynthia Rylant's *Snow* (2008). Sometimes the white space is created by layout, where the illustration is on one side of the spread and the text on the other. In truth, many children choose this layout when they first begin making books (or, more likely, they just adopt it without thinking much about it). Showing them different ways to make the white space around their words more interesting can help them become much more purposeful in their design.

When you see this sort of design in picture books, you'll notice that sometimes these small images surrounded by white space are different on every page as they are in *Hello Baby!* and *Summerbath, Winterbath*, and sometimes the image is repeated on every page as it is in *Snow Story*. The repeated image might change across pages to match the unfolding meaning in the book, or it might stay the same. The key is to help children understand how the small images relate to the text. What is the connection between the image and the meanings in the book? Your goal is for children to design white space purposefully, not to decorate it with flowers and rainbows that don't have anything to do with what the books are about.

As with so many others, this particular layout and design possibility will grow with children as they make all sorts of texts in their lives as writers. Designing white space around the main event of a text is something text designers think a lot about. I was so pleasantly surprised when Jenny Jensen Greenleaf designed a beautiful image of a tiny heart to sit just above each of the chapter titles in my book *What You Know by Heart* (2002). The image makes the white space so much more visually interesting, but it also sets just the right tone for the book.

In a Teacher's Voice: An Idea for Trying It Out

I think that in my book about planting a garden with my grandma (yes, that same book), I might put some different kinds of bugs and worms in the white space around my illustrations. There are always a lot of creeping, crawling things in and around the garden, but because you won't really see them in the pictures of the vegetables, this would be a good way to include them.

Technique 49

Using Paper Artifacts as Visual Elements

Something to Notice   An illustration may look as if a paper artifact has been dropped or pasted into it from the world outside the picture book.

An Illustration Example   A phone book advertisement for "Pup Breakers: We Tame Troublesome Beasts!" is included in one illustrated spread of Bob Graham's *"The Trouble with Dogs . . ." Said Dad* (2007). The main illustration covers the entire right page of the spread and a small portion of the left, and in it the family is pictured gathered around the kitchen table looking at the phone book. The advertisement on a yellow background (fresh from the yellow pages) is in the white space to the left of this illustration. The text of the advertisement is very funny, but I especially like the last line proclaiming that this service is "Especially for owners so meek and mild that they can't say 'Boo!' to a grasshopper."

The end pages of Marla Frazee's *A Couple of Boys Have the Best Week Ever* (2008) look as if they have photographs strewn about them. The "photos" are drawings of course, but they have photo paper edges and they show the boys in all kinds of active scenes at nature camp, just as you'd expect to see in a scrapbook. The photos even overlap, as if they've been dropped into the scrapbook but not yet arranged and taped in.

Emily Gravett's book *Meerkat Mail* (2006) is filled with artifacts: newspaper clippings, photographs, notepapers, luggage tags, travel documents, and actual postcards that are not just pictured, but physically attached to the book so they fold out and can be read. The postcards help tell of Sunny the meerkat's journey as he tries to escape the heat of the Kalahari desert and the somewhat crowded conditions of his extended meerkat family.

An Understanding for Young Writers and Illustrators   When readers see paper artifacts incorporated into illustrations, it's as if the outside world has broken into the world of the picture book. The artifacts feel familiar because they come from the world where readers live. Talk with children about this feeling. Help them see that paper artifacts build a sort of bridge between reality and the imaginary world of the book.

You'll probably need to help children understand what paper artifacts are exactly. Give them lots of familiar examples such as receipts, menus,

schedules, notes, baseball cards, newspaper clippings, passport covers, and gift certificates. Really, a paper artifact is anything made by humans that is a record of something and is on paper. Human artifacts extend way beyond paper artifacts, of course, but paper artifacts make sense in picture books because they're one dimensional and can be incorporated easily into the paper medium.

When you see paper artifacts incorporated into illustrations, first think about why they are there. What purpose do they serve? How do they add to the meaning of the text? Could the illustrator have captured the same meaning in a different way in the illustration? Your goal is to help children see that the artifacts are not just visually interesting, they are also very purposeful.

As you study paper artifacts, talk about how they've been incorporated into the book and how they work in conjunction with other illustrations. For example, in *"The Trouble with Dogs . . ." Said Dad*, the artifact is sort of pulled out and blown up from the larger picture of the family looking at the phone book. Both *Meerkat Mail* and *A Couple of Boys Have the Best Week Ever* use artifacts in the design of their end pages, but *Meerkat Mail* also makes the postcard artifacts a part of the illustrations inside the book. When lifted, the postcards reveal an important picture element, and of course the writing on the flip side of the card is revealed as well.

Paper artifacts are often used in the design of texts other than picture books. Think about how your eyes are drawn to a picture of a handwritten police report included in an article about a crime, a picture of an actual menu in a restaurant review, or a copy of a love note in an exposé about a love triangle. Readers are fascinated by artifacts like these because they add a sense of immediacy to the more detached world of the article, review, or exposé.

When you study this layout and design possibility, some children will no doubt want to start taping things into their illustrations right away. Work with them to make smart decisions about designing in this way. Over time, children can learn that the artifacts they include should be meaningful in some way to their texts and should work in conjunction with their other illustrations.

In a Teacher's Voice: An Idea for Trying It Out

In my book about planting a garden with my grandma, I might include a picture that looks like the receipt from the garden center where we bought all our supplies. I didn't realize how much stuff you needed just to plant a garden, and showing that receipt would be one way to show my reader how amazed I was at all we bought. I could make a picture with me holding the receipt in my hands on one side of the spread, and then a picture of the actual receipt blown up and bigger on the other side.

Technique 50

Using Graphic Features to Show Information

Something to Notice   Illustrations may include labels, diagrams, charts, maps, and other visual features designed to show information in particular ways.

An Illustration Example   Writer Simon Mugford and designers Matt Denny and Kate Dunlop incorporated a number of interesting visual features to share information in their "Smart Kids" series books *Reptiles and Amphibians* (2007) and *Sharks and Other Dangers of the Deep* (2005). For example, a small graphic on each page shows the average length and danger ratings of different animals. The average length of large animals is shown by placing an outline of the animal next to an outline of a grown man. For small animals, the outline is placed next to a human hand. The danger rating (on a scale of one to five) is represented by open shark mouths in the shark book and skulls and crossbones in the reptile book. Two open shark mouths, not so dangerous. Five open shark mouths, look out. Labels in the books do lots of informative work too. Instead of just naming body parts, these labels actually give information such as the label pointing at the plumed basilisk's tail. It reads, "Long tail adds support when running on water."

An Understanding for Young Writers and Illustrators   Informational picture books are usually filled with features designed to present information in interesting ways. As a matter of fact, I could have written about each one of these features as its own design possibility. I decided to lump them together, however, because they all really do the same sort of work— they create a visual that has been designed to present information in a particular way. Most of them use a picture in conjunction with words to do this work. But thinking of ways to make pictures and words work together to inform is what's key in understanding any of these design features. No doubt, if you engage in a genre study of nonfiction in your writing workshop, you will focus on these design possibilities as a big part of that study.

Many children are fascinated by nonfiction books to begin with, and the different kinds of informative illustrations inside them usually draw attention very quickly. Your teaching goal will be to help children understand the various information potentials of different kinds of graphics. Labels force

readers to consider different parts of a whole. Maps show the layout of places and sometimes the features of places as well. Diagrams are simple drawings that help explain something—the size of a hammerhead shark compared to the size of a man, for example.

Help children understand that these design possibilities are primarily used in informative books, and that if they want to use them, they should be writing the kind of book that teaches readers about something. In a genre study of nonfiction, of course, everyone will be writing these kinds of books at the same time, and this is when your focus on these illustration possibilities will be most needed. Labeling pictures, no doubt, will be the most natural entry point for lots of children as they learn to make their illustrations do the work of informing.

Whenever possible, use labels, diagrams, charts, maps, and the like as you explore other content areas with children. Becoming familiar with them in a variety of contexts will help children use them more purposefully in their own work as writers.

In a Teacher's Voice: An Idea for Trying It Out

I could make my book about planting a garden with my grandma an informational book about gardening. I could have a map of the garden with labels that point out where we planted the different vegetables. I might even have a diagram that shows how big the different vegetables will get. And I could do a page with all the different tools we used and label each of those with its name and what it's used for in the garden.

Bibliography

Addonizio, Kim, and Dorianne Laux. 1997. *The Poet's Companion: A Guide to the Pleasures of Writing Poetry*. New York: W. W. Norton.

Albom, Mitch. "Player's Death Both Sad and Incomplete." *Detroit Free Press*. March 8, 2009.

Bang, Molly. 2000. *Picture This: How Pictures Work*. San Francisco: Chronicle Books.

Berg, Elizabeth. 1999. *Escaping into the Open: The Art of Writing True*. New York: Harper Perennial.

Berthoff, Ann E. 1984. *Reclaiming the Imagination: Philosophical Perspectives for Writers and Teachers of Writing*. Portsmouth, NH: Boynton Cook.

Bomer, Randy. 1995. *Time for Meaning: Crafting Literate Lives in Middle and High School*. Portsmouth, NH: Heinemann.

Bunting, Eve. 1996. "The Power of Words." In *Books That Invite Talk, Wonder, and Play*, edited by Amy A. McClure and Janet V. Kristo, 224–25. Urbana, IL: National Council of Teachers of English.

Burroway, Janet. 2003. *Writing Fiction: A Guide to Narrative Craft*, 6th ed. New York: Longman.

Butler, Robert Olen. 2005. *From Where You Dream: The Process of Writing Fiction*. New York: Grove Press.

Calkins, Lucy. 2003. *The Nuts and Bolts of Teaching Writing*. Portsmouth, NH: Heinemann.

Cameron, Julia. 2001. *The Writer's Life*. New York: Penguin Putnam.

Collier, Bryan. 2007. As quoted in *The Wonder of It All*. Nancy J. Johnson and Cyndi Giorgis, 37. Portsmouth, NH: Heinemann.

Collins, Suzanne. 2008. *The Hunger Games*. New York: Scholastic.

Corgill, Ann Marie. 2008. *Of Primary Importance: What's Essential in Teaching Young Writers*. Portland, ME: Stenhouse.

Dickey, James. 1990. As quoted in *Shoptalk: Learning to Write with Writers*. Donald M. Murray, 17. Portsmouth, NH: Heinemann.

Dillard, Annie. 1987. "To Fashion a Text." In *Inventing the Truth: The Art and Craft of Memoir*, edited by William Zinsser, 55–76. Boston: Houghton Mifflin.

Fletcher, Ralph. 2007. *One O'Clock Chop*. New York: Henry Holt.

———. 1999. *Live Writing: Breathing Life into Your Words*. New York: Avon Books.

———. 1996. *Breathing In, Breathing Out: Keeping a Writer's Notebook*. Portsmouth, NH: Heinemann.

———. 1993. *What a Writer Needs*. Portsmouth, NH: Heinemann.

Fletcher, Ralph, and JoAnn Portalupi. 2004. *Teaching Qualities of Good Writing*. Portsmouth, NH: Heinemann.

French, Tom. 2007. "Sequencing: Text as Line." In *Telling True Stories: A Nonfiction Writer's Guide from the Nieman Foundation at Harvard University*, edited by Mark Kramer and Wendy Call, 140–45. New York: Penguin Plume.

Frey, James. 2005. *A Million Little Pieces*. New York: Anchor.

Fu, Danling. 2003. *An Island of English: Teaching ESL in Chinatown*. Portsmouth, NH: Heinemann.

Gardner, John. 1983. *The Art of Fiction: Notes on Craft for Young Writers*. New York: Vintage Books.

Gibbs, Nancy, and Michael Scherer. "Michelle Up Close." *Time*. 26–33. June 1, 2009.

Goldberg, Natalie. 2000. *Thunder and Lightning: Cracking Open the Writer's Craft*. New York: Bantam Books.

———. 1990. *Wild Mind: Living the Writer's Life*. New York: Bantam Books.

———. 1986. *Writing Down the Bones*. Boston: Shambhala.

Gutkind, Lee. 2008. *Keep It Real: Everything You Need to Know About Researching and Writing Creative Nonfiction*. New York: W. W. Norton.

———. 1997. *The Art of Creative Nonfiction: Writing and Selling the Literature of Reality*. New York: John Wiley & Sons.

Horn, Martha, and Mary Ellen Giacobbe. 2007. *Talking, Drawing, Writing: Lessons for Our Youngest Writers*. Portland, ME: Stenhouse.

Johnson, Nancy, and Cyndi Giorgis. 2007. *The Wonder of It All: When Literature and Literacy Intersect*. Portsmouth, NH: Heinemann.

Johnston, Tony. 1996. "On Writing *Whale Song*." In *Books That Invite Talk, Wonder and Play*, edited by Amy A. McClure and Janet V. Kristo, 257–58. Urbana, IL: National Council of Teachers of English.

Katz, Jon. 2002. *A Dog Year*. New York: Villard.

Kingsolver, Barbara. 1998. *The Poisonwood Bible*. New York: Harper Flamingo.

Korman, Gordon. 2007. *Schooled*. New York: Hyperion.

Kress, Gunther. 2000. "Design and Transformation." In *Multiliteracies*, edited by Bill Cope and Mary Kalantzis. London: Routledge.

Kress, Gunther, and Theo van Leeuwen. 2006. *Reading Images: The Grammar of Visual Design*. 2d ed. London: Routledge.

Le Guin, Ursula K. 1998. *Steering the Craft*. Portland, OR: The Eighth Mountain Press.

Levine, Gail Carson. 2006. *Writing Magic: Creating Stories That Fly*. New York: Collins.

MacLachlan, Patricia. 1985. *Sarah, Plain and Tall*. New York: HarperTrophy.

Malaguzzi, Loris. 1998. "History, Ideas, and Basic Philosophy." In *The Hundred Languages of Children*, edited by Carolyn Edwards, Lella Gandini, and George Forman, 75. Westport, CT: Ablex.

Meacham, Jon. "Top of the Week: A New Magazine for a Changing World." *Newsweek*, May 25, 2009.

Murray, Donald M. 1990. *Shoptalk: Learning to Write with Writers*. Portsmouth, NH: Boynton/Cook.

National Association for the Education of Young Children. 2009. *Position Statement: Developmentally Appropriate Practice*. Washington, DC: National Association for the Education of Young Children.

National Council of Teachers of English. 2008. *Position Statement: The NCTE Definition of 21st Century Literacies*. Urbana, IL: National Council of Teachers of English.

Newkirk, Thomas. 2002. *Misreading Masculinity: Boys, Literacy and Popular Culture*. Portsmouth, NH: Heinemann.

———. 2009. *Holding On to Good Ideas in a Time of Bad Ones*. Portsmouth, NH: Heinemann.

Nye, Naomi Shihab. 2007. *I'll Ask You Three Times, Are You OK? Tales of Driving and Being Driven*. New York: Greenwillow Books.

Oates, Joyce Carol. 2003. *The Faith of a Writer: Life, Craft, Art*. New York: HarperCollins.

Parrish, Holden. "A Day in the Good Life." *Atlantic Southeast Magazine* (17). September/October 2006.

Paulsen, Gary. 2007. *Lawn Boy*. New York: Wendy Lamb Books.

———. 1989. *The Winter Room*. New York: Dell.

Plotnik, Arthur. 2007. *Spunk & Bite: A Writer's Guide to Bold, Contemporary Style*. New York: Random House Reference.

Prose, Francine. 2006. *Reading Like a Writer: A Guide for People Who Love Books and for Those Who Want to Write Them*. New York: Harper Perennial.

Ray, Katie Wood. 2006. *Study Driven*. Portsmouth, NH: Heinemann.

———. 2002. *What You Know by Heart*. Portsmouth, NH: Heinemann.

———. 1999. *Wondrous Words: Writers and Writing in the Elementary Classroom*. Urbana, IL: National Council of Teachers of English.

Ray, Katie Wood, and Lisa Cleaveland. 2004. *About the Authors: Writing Workshop with Our Youngest Writers*. Portsmouth, NH: Heinemann.

Ray, Katie Wood, and Matt Glover. 2008. *Already Ready: Nurturing Writers in Preschool and Kindergarten*. Portsmouth, NH: Heinemann.

Rowe, Deborah Wells. 1994. *Preschoolers as Authors: Literacy Learning in the Social World of the Classroom*. Cresskill, NJ: Hampton Press.

Rylant, Cynthia. 1995. *The Van Gogh Café*. San Diego: Harcourt Brace.

———. 1993. *I Had Seen Castles*. New York: Harcourt Brace.

———. 1992. *Missing May*. New York: Orchard Books.

———. 1989. *But I'll Be Back Again*. New York: Orchard Books.

Short, Kathy G., and Carolyn Burke. 1991. *Creating Curriculum: Teachers and Students as a Community of Learners*. Portsmouth, NH: Heinemann.

Shulevitz, Uri. 1985. *Writing with Pictures: How to Write and Illustrate Picture Books*. New York: Watson-Giptill.

Smith, Frank. 1988. *Joining the Literacy Club: Further Essays Into Education*. Portsmouth, NH: Heinemann.

Spinelli, Jerry. 2002. *Loser*. New York: Joanna Cotler Books.

———. 2000. *Stargirl*. New York: Alfred A. Knopf.

———. 1990. *Maniac Magee*. New York: Little, Brown.

Stern, Jerome. 1991. *Making Shapely Fiction*. New York: Dell.

Stockett, Kathryn. 2009. *The Help*. New York: Putnam.

White, E. B. 1952. *Charlotte's Web*. New York: HarperTrophy.

Wiggins, Grant, and Jay McTighe. 1998. *Understanding by Design*. Upper Saddle River, NJ: Merrill Prentice Hall.

Zinsser, William. 2001. *On Writing Well*. 6th ed. New York: Quill.

Zusak, Markus. 2006. *The Book Thief*. New York: Alfred A. Knopf.

Picture Book Bibliography

Allard, Jr., Harry G. 1977. *Miss Nelson Is Missing*. Illus. James Marshall. New York: Houghton Mifflin.

Andreae, Giles. 1999. *Giraffes Can't Dance*. Illus. Guy Parker-Rees. New York: Orchard Books.

Appelt, Kathi. 2003. *Incredible Me!* Illus. G. Brian Karas. New York: HarperCollins.

Aston, Dianna Hutts. 2007. *An Orange in January*. Illus. Julie Maren. New York: Dial Books for Young Readers.

———. 2006. *An Egg Is Quiet*. Illus. Sylvia Long. San Francisco: Chronicle Books.

Ayers, Katherine. 2007. *Up, Down, and Around*. Illus. Nadine Bernard Westcott. Cambridge, MA: Candlewick Press.

Bayrock, Fiona. 2009. *Bubble Homes and Fish Farts*. Illus. Carolyn Conahan. Watertown, MA: Charlesbridge.

Beach, Judi K. 2003. *Names for Snow*. Illus. Loretta Krupinski. New York: Hyperion.

Bean, Jonathan. 2007. *At Night*. New York: Farrar, Straus and Giroux.

Bennett, Kelly. 2005. *Not Norman: A Goldfish Story*. Illus. Noah Z. Jones. Cambridge, MA: Candlewick Press.

Bloom, Suzanne. 2005. *A Splendid Friend, Indeed*. Honesdale, PA: Boyds Mills Press.

Bowen, Anne. 2004. *When You Visit Grandma and Grandpa*. Illus. Tomek Bogacki. Minneapolis, MN: Carolrhoda Books.

Bunting, Eve. 1998. *So Far from the Sea*. Illus. Chris Soentpiet. New York: Clarion Books.

Collard, Sneed B. 1992. *Do They Scare You? Creepy Creatures*. Illus. Kristin Kest. Watertown, MA: Charlesbridge.

Collier, Bryan. 2000. *Uptown*. New York: Henry Holt.

Cooke, Trish. 2003. *Full, Full, Full of Love*. Illus. Paul Howard. Cambridge MA: Candlewick Press.

Cooper, Elisha. 2006. *Beach*. New York: Orchard Books.

———. 2005. *A Good Night Walk*. New York: Orchard Books.

———. 2002. *Ice Cream*. New York: Greenwillow Books.

Crews, Donald. 1998. *Night at the Fair*. New York: Greenwillow Books.

———. 1995. *Sail Away*. New York: Harper Trophy.

————. 1984. *School Bus*. New York: Greenwillow Books.

————. 1980. *Truck*. New York: Mulberry.

Cronin, Doreen. 2003. *Diary of a Worm*. Illus. Harry Bliss. New York: Joanna Cotler Books.

Davies, Nicola. 2003. *Surprising Sharks*. Illus. James Croft. Cambridge, MA: Candlewick Press.

————. 2005. *Ice Bear: In the Steps of the Polar Bear*. Illus. Gary Blythe. Cambridge, MA: Candlewick Press.

Fletcher, Ralph. 2008. *The Sandman*. Illus. Richard Cowdrey. New York: Henry Holt.

Fox, Mem. 2009. *Hello Baby!* Illus. Steve Jenkins. New York: Beach Lane Books.

Franco, Betsy, and Steve Jenkins. 2007. *Birdsongs*. Illus. Steve Jenkins. New York: McElderry Books.

————. 2007. *Summer Beat*. Illus. Charlotte Middleton. New York: McElderry Books.

Frazee, Marla. 2008. *A Couple of Boys Have the Best Week Ever*. New York: Harcourt.

————. 2006. *Walk On! A Guide for Babies of All Ages*. New York: Harcourt.

————. 2005. *Santa Claus: The World's Number One Toy Expert*. New York: Harcourt.

————. 2003. *Roller Coaster*. New York: Harcourt.

George, Jean Craighead. 2008. *The Wolves Are Back*. Illus. Wendell Minor. New York: Dutton Children's Books.

Graham, Bob. 2008. *How to Heal a Broken Wing*. Cambridge, MA: Candlewick Press.

————. 2007. *"The Trouble with Dogs . . ." Said Dad*. Cambridge, MA: Candlewick Press.

————. 2001. *"Let's Get a Pup!" Said Kate*. Cambridge, MA: Candlewick Press.

Gravett, Emily. 2006. *Meerkat Mail*. New York: Simon & Schuster.

————. 2005. *Wolves*. New York: Simon & Schuster.

Grimes, Nikki. 2008. *Oh, Brother!* Illus. Mike Benny. New York: Greenwillow Books.

Henderson, Kathy. 2003. *And the Good Brown Earth*. Cambridge, MA: Candlewick Press.

Henkes, Kevin. 2009. *Birds*. Illus. Laura Dronzek. New York: Greenwillow Books.

Howker, Janni. 1997. *Walk with a Wolf*. Illus. Sarah Fox-Davies. Cambridge, MA: Candlewick Press.

Hundal, Nancy. 1997. *Snow Story*. Illus. Kasia Charko. Toronto: HarperCollins.

Jenkins, Emily. 2007. *What Happens on Wednesdays*. Illus. Lauren Castillo. New York: Frances Foster Books.

Jenkins, Martin. 1999. *The Emperor's Egg*. Illus. Jane Chapman. Cambridge, MA: Candlewick Press.

Jenkins, Steve, and Robin Page. 2003. *What Do You Do with a Tail Like This?* Boston: Houghton Mifflin.

Johnson, Angela. 1991. *One of Three*. Illus. David Soman. New York: Orchard Books.

Johnston, Tony. 1987. *Whale Song: A Celebration of Counting*. Illus. Ed Young. New York: G. P. Putnam's Sons.

Karas, Brian. 2002. *Atlantic*. New York: G. P. Putnam's Sons.

Lee, Suzy. 2004 (2007). *The Zoo*. La Jolla, CA: Kane/Miller.

London, Jonathan. 1999. *Baby Whale's Journey*. Illus. Jon Van Zyle. San Francisco: Chronicle Books.

MacEachern, Ashley. 2008. *Lance in France*. Illus. Michelle Barbera. New York: HarperCollins.

Masurel, Claire. 2001. *Two Homes*. Illus. Kady MacDonald Denton. Cambridge, MA: Candlewick Press.

Mayo, Margaret. 2001. *Dig, Dig, Digging*. Illus. Alex Ayliffe. New York: Henry Holt.

McGuirk, Leslie. 2008. *Lucky Tucker*. Cambridge, MA: Candlewick Press.

McMullan, Kate. 2008. *I'm Bad!* Illus. Jim McMullan. New York: Joanna Cotler Books.

———. 2003. *I'm Mighty*. Illus. Jim McMullan. New York: Joanna Cotler Books.

———. 2002. *I Stink!* Illus. Jim McMullan. New York: Joanna Cotler Books.

Miller, Debbie S. 2006. *Big Alaska: Journey Across America's Most Amazing State*. Illus. Jon Van Zyle. New York: Walker.

Milton, Giles. 2009. *Call Me Gorgeous!* Illus. Alexandra Milton. London: Boxer Books.

Mugford, Simon. 2007. *Reptiles and Amphibians*. Designer Kate Dunlop. New York: St. Martin's Press.

———. 2005. *Sharks and Other Dangers of the Deep*. Designer Matt Denny. New York: St. Martin's Press.

Nevius, Carol. 2008. *Baseball Hour*. Illus. Bill Thomson. Tarrytown, NY: Marshall Cavendish Children.

Patricelli, Leslie. 2009. *Higher! Higher!* Cambridge, MA: Candlewick Press.

Pham, LeUyen. 2005. *Big Sister, Little Sister*. New York: Hyperion.

Pilkey, Dav. 1996. *The Paperboy*. New York: Orchard Books.

Rashka, Chris. 1993. *Yo? Yes!* New York: Orchard Books.

Ray, Mary Lyn. 2008. *Christmas Farm*. Illus. Barry Root. New York: Harcourt.

———. 1996. *Mud*. Illus. Lauren Stringer. New York: Harcourt Brace.

Reynolds, Peter H. 2003. *The Dot*. Cambridge, MA: Candlewick Press.

Root, Phyllis. 2001. *Rattletrap Car*. Illus. Jill Barton. Cambridge, MA: Candlewick Press.

Rosenthal, Amy Krouse. 2006. *One of Those Days*. Illus. Rebecca Doughty. New York: G. P. Putnam's Sons.

Rylant, Cynthia. 2009. *All in a Day*. Illus. Nikki McClure. New York: Abrams.

———. 2008. *Snow*. Illus. Lauren Stringer. New York: Harcourt.

———. 2004. *Long Night Moon*. Illus. Mark Siegel. New York: Simon & Schuster.

———. 2002. *Christmas in the Country*. Illus. Diane Goode. New York: The Blue Sky Press.

———. 1992. *Missing May*. New York: Yearling.

———. 1998. *Scarecrow*. Illus. Lauren Stringer. New York: Harcourt Brace.

———. 1985. *The Relatives Came*. Illus. Stephen Gammell. New York: Simon & Schuster.

Sayre, April Pulley. 2008. *Trout Are Made of Trees*. Illus. Kate Endle. Watertown, MA: Charlesbridge.

———. 2007. *Vulture View*. Illus. Steve Jenkins. New York: Henry Holt.

Scanlon, Liz Garton. 2009. *All the World*. Illus. Marla Frazee. New York: Beach Lane Books.

Schaefer, Lola M. 2006. *An Island Grows*. Illus. Cathie Felstead. New York: Greenwillow Books.

Shannon, David. 2006. *Good Boy, Fergus!* New York: The Blue Sky Press.

Smith, Jr., Charles R. 2004. *Let's Play Basketball*. Illus. Terry Widener. Cambridge, MA: Candlewick Press.

———. 2001. *Loki & Alex*. New York: Dutton Children's Books.

Spinelli, Eileen. 2007. *Heat Wave*. Illus. Betsy Lewin. New York: Harcourt.

————. 2001. *In My New Yellow Shirt*. Illus. Hideko Takahashi. New York: Henry Holt.

————. 2001. *Summerbath, Winterbath*. Illus. Elsa Warnick. Grand Rapids, MI: Eerdmans.

Stein, David Ezra. 2008. *The Nice Book*. New York: G. P. Putnam's Sons.

————. 2007. *Leaves*. New York: G. P. Putnam's Sons.

Stockdale, Susan. 2008. *Fabulous Fishes*. Atlanta: Peachtree.

Stojic, Manya. 2000. *Rain*. New York: Crown.

Thomson, Sarah L. 2006. *Feel the Summer*. Illus. Kana Yamada. New York: Milk & Cookies Press.

Voake, Charlotte. 2006. *Hello Twins*. Cambridge, MA: Candlewick Press.

Wallace, Karen. 1998. *Gentle Giant Octopus*. Illus. Mike Bostock. Cambridge, MA: Candlewick Press.

Watt, Mélanie. 2008. *Scaredy Squirrel at the Beach*. Toronto: Kids Can Press.

————. 2006. *Scaredy Squirrel*. Toronto: Kids Can Press.

Weatherford, Carole Boston. 2000. *The Sound That Jazz Makes*. Illus. Eric Velasquez. New York: Walker.

Wong, Janet S. 2000. *The Trip Back Home*. Illus. Bo Jia. San Diego: Harcourt.

Yolen, Jane. 2003. *Hoptoad*. Illus. Karen Lee Schmidt. New York: Harcourt.

Zeifert, Harriet. 2001. *39 Uses for a Friend*. Illus. Rebecca Doughty. New York: G. P. Putnam's Sons.

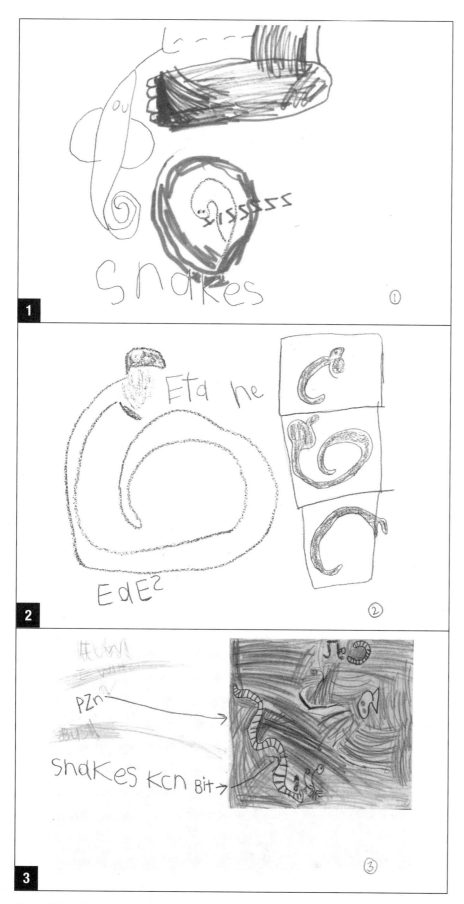

Figure 3.10   Daniel's nonfiction book about snakes. (1) Snakes. (2) Eating the eggs. (3)
Snakes can bite (label: poison).

Figure 3.10   *continued* (4) Squeeze the snake (labels: poison, antivenom). (5) Snake is leaving the egg. (6) Egg. Hatches. Two-headed snake.

- *Fine detail can convey specific characteristics in illustrations.* The two snakes on page 3 have very different coloring and markings. Daniel wisely used a small sliver of snake-wide space to make them quite distinct.

- *Details in illustrations can be labeled as a way of conveying information.* This is a feature of nonfiction and is used with directional arrows on pages 3, 4, and 5. Labels are written into the timeline boxes on page 6.

- *Illustrations can suggest meanings that aren't in the words.* Daniel explained that he drew several different biting scenarios in the illustration on page 3: the snakes biting each other, one snake biting the person in the water, and one snake biting the crab near the bottom left side.

- *An illustration can show something spatially.* The scientist on page 4 is clearly in a room (probably a lab). You can see the floor meeting the space above the floor, as well as a cabinet hanging above the floor in the back of the room.

- *One way to show motion is to use a series of broken lines.* Daniel employed this technique to show the venom coming out of the snake's mouth on page 4.

- *An illustration on a single page can be divided into a before-and-after scene, showing a change in something.* On page 5, the snake is seen sleeping inside the egg in the top drawing, and the snake is leaving the egg in the bottom drawing. A line separates the two drawings, making them distinct.

As I look at this list, I can't help but be impressed by the fullness of what this young writer has learned. Just think about how different this book is from the dinosaur book in terms of the illustration work it shows. Clearly Daniel engaged in lots of decision making as he crafted this book, and he made every one of the decisions on his own. He's not yet expert at all the techniques he's trying—expertise will come with experience—but his process is solid and it's clear his teacher has helped him expand his repertoire of possibilities for the work of composing.

You'll notice in this list that the italicized words state the operational knowledge Daniel is using to craft his illustrations. You don't see snakes mentioned in any of these italicized words, only in the examples that follow them. This is important to note because when teaching about craft, whether it's word crafting or illustration crafting, the language teachers use should not be tied to specific topics. If it is tied to a topic (like snakes), it doesn't help the writer in the future. In other words, Daniel's teacher doesn't want him to think he can only do these kinds of things when he's writing about snakes.

Figure 3.11 Daniel's airplane lifting off

For understandings about words or illustrations to become curricular understandings, they have to be untied from topics. This is what helps a writer like Daniel use a technique again in a new context, as he did in the later illustration you see in Figure 3.11. Just as he showed the process of the egg hatching in the snake book, Daniel composed a series of small illustrations to show the process of an airplane taking off.

The words I've used to articulate what Daniel knows about illustrating are not yet words he owns himself. He is certainly able to talk about his illustrations and explain why he did certain things in certain ways, but much of what he knows is implicit rather than explicit—much as a knowledge base about word crafting is for even very experienced writers. What matters is that his teachers are articulate and explicit about what Daniel knows about illustrations. His teachers need to own these words and many others like them. And when they do, they will see rich curriculum possibilities all around them, and they will be much more purposeful in helping children come to see possibilities as well.

Instructional Tips for Supporting the Composing Process in Illustration Work

- In writing conferences, ask children to talk about the decisions they've made in their illustrations. You may ask them generally, "Tell me all about what you were thinking as you illustrated this page." Or you may ask them more specifically, "Tell me about the border you've drawn around this illustration. What made you decide to use a border?" Use language that communicates your belief that everything was the result of some decision made, and over time they will come to understand process as decision making.

- When children talk about their illustrations, look for opportunities to name their thinking using the language of process. If a child says, "On the next page, I'm planning to draw a turned-over truck," you can say, "Oh, you're planning that ahead. You're prewriting it." Or if a child says, "I added more red to her face so you'd know she is hot," you can say, "That revision makes your meaning so much clearer."

- Speak often of readers when you talk to children about their decision making in the books they make. This will help children internalize a sense of audience. This kind of talk can take different forms. "What would your reader likely think if you zoomed in really close in the illustration of your dog's face on this page?" Or in a study of informational nonfiction, you might ask, "What can a reader learn from your illustration on this page?"

- Tell stories of children's process decisions during the share and reflection time at the end of writing workshop. Make smart thinking and decision making public, and just as you do in conferences, use the language of process to help children tell these stories.

- Take time sometimes just to watch and listen as children are making books. Look for evidence of interesting process decisions, and you will begin to see them unfolding all around you. Interrupt children in the midst of interesting work you see them doing and ask them about it. They are often much more articulate about their decision making when you catch them in the act.

- Demonstrate your own thinking as you make decisions about illustrations in books you're making. You may actually compose the illustration in front of children and think aloud as you do it, or you may have already composed the illustration and simply share the thinking you did with the children. Again, be sure to use the language of process as you demonstrate.

- Consider having children use a sticky note as an assessment tool and mark the page they think shows their most interesting illustration work in a finished book. Just having the expectation that there will be something to note may promote more intentional thinking about illustrations. Children may write about their decision on the note, or simply talk about it.

- Look for information about the process of composing on the websites of illustrators you and your students know and admire. Be prepared to find contradictions in what different illustrators say about process. Just as with writing, there is not just one way to go about composing an illustration. Here are a few websites where illustrators share information about process (many illustrators' websites don't have information about process). You may have to click around a bit on the different sites as some of the great process information is found in a link on the site.

Suzanne Bloom	www.suzannebloom.com
Eric Carle	www.eric-carle.com
Elisha Cooper	www.elishacooper.com
Tomie dePaola	www.tomie.com
Marla Frazee	www.marlafrazee.com
Diane Goode	www.dianegoode.com
Steve Jenkins	www.stevejenkinsbooks.com
Nikki McClure	www.nikkimcclure.com
Dav Pilkey	www.pilkey.com
Patricia Polacco	www.patriciapolacco.com
Peter Reynolds	www.peterhreynolds.com
David Ezra Stein	www.davidezra.com
Lauren Stringer	www.laurenstringer.com
Mo Willems	www.mowillems.com

- Almost all major publishers of picture books also have websites that contain valuable information about authors and illustrators. Many of them include great interviews with illustrators where the illustration process is explored in depth. The following two websites also have similar interviews and information:

  www.readingrockets.org

  www.kidsread.com

CHAPTER

4

Teaching an Essential Habit of Mind

Reading Like Writers in the Context of Illustration Study

Read widely, read enthusiastically, be guided by instinct and
not design. For if you read, you need not become a writer;
but if you hope to become a writer, you must read.

—JOYCE CAROL OATES, *The Faith of a Writer*

ON THE MORNING A STUDY OF ILLUSTRATIONS BEGAN in Lisa Cleaveland's writing workshop, we had gathered a tall stack of books filled with interesting illustrations. During workshop on this day, we were going to spend some time having the children look through these books and mark pages where they find illustrations that catch their attention. First though, I shared the book *Mud* (1996) with them. *Mud* is written by Mary Lyn Ray, a favorite author, and is illustrated by Lauren Stringer, a favorite illustrator.

As I shared this book with the children, my teaching goal was to demonstrate for them one of the most important habits of mind a writer can develop: how to read like a writer. I was demonstrating this way of reading not with the words in this book (though the words are wonderful), but with the illustrations. By teaching these children to look at the illustrations with insiders' eyes, I was teaching them the exact same habit of mind writers engage in as they read. To understand how that might happen, I first need to explain exactly what I mean when I say, "read like a writer."

What It Means to Read Like a Writer: A Metaphor

A couple of years ago, my husband and I embarked on a project to build ourselves a new home. Well, actually we had someone else build it, but Jim and I drew all the plans for it and made all the decisions from what kind of light switches we wanted to the width of the Hardieplank® siding. In the midst of all this decision making, we came to see the world of houses very differently. When we walked into someone's home, we noticed everything about the building decisions they had made. Some of them were friends' homes and we'd visited in them many times, but that year we saw them with completely new eyes. We were meticulous in our noticing, never hesitating to ask questions such as, "How high above your table does that light fixture hang?" You never know you need to think about something like that until you need to think about it.

When certain decisions were imminent, we did little studies to help us figure out what we would do. I remember going through a stack of maybe thirty home magazines once looking only at the wood trim around windows and doors in the glossy pictures of living rooms. Another time I went through the whole stack just looking at what was in that space between the top of the counters and the bottom of the kitchen cabinets. And when we needed to decide on the width of our Hardieplank®, we literally drove all over town looking at the width of siding on houses. Jim even got out of the car at one house we liked so he could measure it.

We finished our house over three years ago now, and without a doubt the experience did forever change the way I look at all houses. I can't help but notice how doors fit in their jambs and what kinds of towel rods people have in their bathrooms. But I've lightened up a lot too. I'm clearly not noticing *every little thing* the way I did when we were building our own house because I don't feel the need to notice it. The immediacy of having to make my own decisions about all the things I'm seeing in someone else's house is gone.

The habit of mind I've just described is familiar to me not just as a builder of houses, but also as a writer. It's a habit of mind I've been writing about for years now, and one that I first described in my book *Wondrous Words: Writers and Writing in the Elementary Classroom* (1999). Because I write so much myself, I can't help it, when I read other people's writing, I tend to notice how it's written. I think about what it's about too, but I am often also struck by particular decisions the writer has made about the craft of it.

Just this morning, for example, I was excited because it is Wednesday and that meant Craig Wilson's "Final Word" column would be in the Life section of *USA Today* (April 1, 2009). I love this column and read it every Wednesday morning. This morning's column I particularly enjoyed because in it Wilson is reminiscing about his father's garden, a memory I have in common with him as my parents are gardeners too. But I also admired how he wrote it, as I often do. Here's one little paragraph I especially liked:

> *But what I remember most about the garden is not the corn or the cucumbers or the crows, but a rusty tin lawn chair. Yellow faded to cream. It was one of those vintage 1950s chairs with the fan back and small holes in the seat for the rain to drain.*

I just love the way this paragraph sounds, and because I am a writer too, I understand and appreciate how he made it sound this way. As my fellow writer Leonard Pitts, Jr., says, "game knows game." It's an expression he co-opted from his teenage sons, and he uses it to describe the fact that a writer is much more likely to notice what another writer is doing than someone who doesn't write. We're all in the same game, after all.

In this short paragraph, I notice Wilson's decision to join three items in a series with only a conjunction and no punctuation. I understand that of all the things he could have named that he remembered about the garden (zucchini, plows, fertilizer, for instance), he chose three that sounded really good together—*the corn or the cucumbers or the crows*. I can easily imagine (because I've done it many times myself) that as he drafted that, he tried a number of noun options and a number of word orders until it sounded just right. Try saying *cucumber* first and listen to how badly it jars the roll off your tongue.

I love the way he lets the subject and verb of "Yellow faded to cream" be understood from the sentence before it (*The chair was* yellow faded to cream) so that it sounds more as if he is remembering this aloud in front of us, the sentence structure mirroring a very natural speech pattern.

I think how perfect it is that he settled on the words "for the rain to drain." As a reader, this rhyme works for me, I like it, but because I'm a writer too, I wonder if he struggled with the cuteness of it, thinking perhaps it would be better just to say "for the rain to run out." I imagine he might have thought about that, or maybe it came out that way the first time he drafted it and he never gave it another thought.

The point of the thinking I'm demonstrating here is this: It really doesn't matter whether my hypotheses about what Craig Wilson was thinking as he drafted his column are correct or not. What matters is that I am able to look at writing like this and think about it in this way. The level of articulation I've got about why this passage sounds good to me, and the process I imagine he might have gone through as he drafted it, are all a part of my own repertoire of techniques for writing. I can see what he's doing as he writes because I write too. Game knows game.

I often naturally do this kind of thinking in the midst of reading, and I can't help but do it. Because I write too, the immediacy of that changes the way I look at texts—just like the house I was building changed the way I looked at houses. I see writing as an insider, as someone who does it too. In her book *The Faith of a Writer: Life, Craft, Art*, Joyce Carol Oates describes the way writers read in this way:

> Because as fellow writers we realize we're not reading mere words, a "product"; we understand that we're reading the end result of another writer's effort, the sum total of his or her imaginative and editorial decisions, which may have been complex. We know, as perhaps ordinary readers, nonwriters, wouldn't care to know, that despite romantic notions of divine inspiration, no story writes itself . . . the story before us has been consciously, in some cases, painstakingly written. (2003, 110–11)

Houses don't make themselves either, so when I was building one I was acutely aware of all the decision making behind every single thing you see in a house. When I read, I am similarly aware of the fact that every word on the page is the product of someone's decision making. And I believe that much of my success as a writer has to do with me being so aware all the time of how things are written. I'm always learning from other writers.

When I went to read Craig Wilson's column on the *USA Today* website this morning, I did so because it's Wednesday and that's what I do on Wednesdays. As a reader, I like his column a lot and look forward to it each week. I didn't go there planning to study his craft; it's just that I'm always noticing things about anything I read. How long I stop to ponder something I've noticed has to do with how much it strikes me. And usually if it's just me reading for the sake of reading, I don't think about it at the technically articulate level I did with the passage above. I reread it and go on. But I am *able* to think about it at that articulate level, and that's what's important. My articulation means I own it. I could do it myself as a writer.

Reading Like a Writer, On Purpose

There is another kind of reading I do as writer that is much more intentional. I do this kind of reading precisely because I am trying to understand the craft of a particular genre. Just as I did very specific studies of parts of houses when I had very specific decisions I needed to make about my house (the width of siding, for example), I sometimes need to do specific studies as a writer. This happens any time I have to do a kind of writing that I don't have a lot of experience doing. When this is the case, I spend time reading to get a feel for the kind of writing I'm expected to do. I take former national poet laureate Ted Kooser's advice: "Before you write one poem, you need to read at least one hundred." Whether it's poems or book forwards or newsletters for the animal rescue organization my husband and I volunteer for, I try to read as many examples as I possibly can before I write one myself so I'm firmly grounded in what's expected of me.

I recently had an article published in the NCTE journal *School Talk*, and I did just this kind of reading to get ready to write. Since I don't have a subscription to *School Talk*, I wasn't familiar with what the articles are like in this journal. I scrounged around and found back issues of *School Talk*, and I read several of them cover to cover to get a feel for the writing in them. I noticed all kinds of things as I did this reading—length, content, form, organization, voice, etc. My sense of urgency and immediacy is at its highest with this kind of reading because I know I've got to write one of my own, and very soon. When I do this kind of reading, I'm not trying to understand how to write well in general, I'm trying to understand how to write well for *School Talk*.

Because I spend so much of my life writing, whenever I read, I read with the eyes of someone who will be writing again herself, and very soon. I read as an insider and, without a doubt, every act of reading deepens my understanding of the craft (or lack of craft) of writing, whether I'm conscious of it or not. I believe this ability to read as a writer and understand all texts as being the product of another writer's decision making is one of the most important habits of mind teachers can help students develop.

Once students learn to read as writers, then every act of reading has the potential to deepen their understanding of the craft of writing too. Teaching students this habit of mind also fosters independence in them as they can be learning about writing whether their teachers are there or not. And when I imagine students far, far in the future, I imagine them knowing the importance of reading before they try to write something new—as I did with my study before writing the *School Talk* article.

I and other teacher/authors have written entire books about how to read like writers and how to become articulate about the craft of written texts. The purpose of this book is not to explore that concept in depth, but instead to make the case that helping students look at illustrations in the ways I've just described—as insiders—will help them develop this habit of mind in a parallel context and, thus, come to it much more naturally as they use it to explore the decision making behind written texts. Let's go back now and think about the teaching demonstration I gave on the morning we launched the study of illustrations in Lisa Cleaveland's writing workshop.

Demonstrating an Important Habit of Mind

On the morning the illustration study was launched, it was early November and the children engaging in the study had been making picture books every day in writing workshop since school began in August. On multiple sheets of plain white paper stapled down the side to form blank books, the children used a combination of illustrations and text to compose picture books on topics of interest to them. The extent to which either the illustrations or the text were decipherable varied a lot with the natural range of development in the class, but the children had all become comfortable just doing the best they could. By this point in the year, it was clear that their teacher truly valued all their approximations, so this gave them the confidence they needed to throw themselves into the work of writing workshop.

Because they worked daily at making picture books during writing workshop, the children could not help but have that same sense of immediacy I described earlier. They illustrated *every day* at school, and they would be illustrating again later that very same day after we read and looked at *Mud* and other books. And not only did they illustrate, they used their illustrations to make the exact same kind of books as the ones they were studying. They didn't just draw a picture and write a sentence. They composed whole books just like the ones stacked up for them to study. Their teacher deliberately created a context for them to work as writers and illustrators that matched the work of Mary Lyn Ray and Lauren Stringer.

This teaching context—a workshop as a place where students make picture books—is tremendously significant because it sets children up to be insiders as they look at both illustrations and text in other picture books. Whether there was any intentional teaching around looking at picture books as insiders or not, to some extent the children would look at books as insiders anyway. They wouldn't be able to help themselves. And because the teaching context is also deeply theoretical, they would be learning all the time from what they see illustrators doing in these books.

In his groundbreaking work to understand and explain children's literacy development, Frank Smith wrote in *Joining the Literacy Club,*

> [But] the only way I can account for the enormous amounts of unwitting learning that children accomplish, much of it apparently error-free on the first trial, is that children actually learn from what other people do—provided they are the kind of people the children see themselves as being. *(1988, 8)*

The emphasis is Smith's, not mine. The teaching context is deliberately designed so that children see themselves as being the *same kinds of people* as the authors and illustrators of the picture books that surround them in their classroom. Early in the year, that's one of the reasons (there are others) the books the children are composing in don't have lines in them. Picture books don't have lines for words and boxes for pictures.

Smith goes on to say, "The teacher's role is to ensure the [literacy] club exists and that every child is in it" (12). On the morning I got ready to read *Mud* to the class, I could easily talk to the children as insiders. This is because their teacher had done her job well. She accepted all approximations and kept the children at it—making picture books every day—and so by the time I sat down to read to them, they saw themselves as illustrators. Illus-trating was something they did every day.

Noticing

After talking about the author and illustrator a little, I read the book to the children and we talked some about mud and how much fun it can be to play in it. Then I began my demonstration of thinking about how the book was illustrated. I decided to focus on one decision Lauren Stringer made several times in the book, including in the design of the front cover. She zoomed in and did very close-up illustrations of a child's feet covered in mud. On the cover, the illustration shows only from a child's knees down—the rest of the child is not pictured—and the close-up is so detailed you can actually see mud squeezing up through the toes and crusted into the toenails.

One child pointed to the air above the book and suggested that the rest of the child is there (in the air). I loved that she was thinking about where the rest of the illustration might be. We talked about how when an illustrator decides to zoom in really close on something, that means part of the whole will be missing. "You only draw the part you want the reader to focus on," I told them. "You let the rest of it run off the page."

We looked at other pages inside the book where Lauren Stringer had made this same illustration decision. We noticed that the close-ups had been drawn from different angles. In the cover illustration, you are looking straight at the child's legs and feet. Another close-up is from the back of the child and a little to the side. And in another, the child is sitting down and the bottoms of the feet are forward with the legs going back behind them, as if the reader is sitting facing the child. We also see close-ups of the child's hands covered in mud and squeezing it, and one of the feet again perched on a shovel digging into the mud.

As we talked about each illustration, I was deliberate in using the lan-guage of decision making connected to everything we saw. I said things like, "Yes, look at how Lauren Stringer showed the dirt on the bottom of the feet. She made it look so real because there's more on the heel and pad of the foot and less on this inside part, the instep." I was showing the children how I understood what we were seeing as being something the illustrator did on purpose, so I used her name often in conjunction with decisive verbs like *showed* and *made*. If I didn't do this and we simply talked in this way—"Look at that dirt on the bottom of the feet"—we'd be leaving the illustrator out and missing a very big part of what we needed to understand about what we saw. I wanted this demonstration to show the children two things: the kind of things they might notice about illustrations and that those things are the result of an illustrator's decision making.

Becoming Articulate About What We Notice

Next I showed the children how to think about why Lauren Stringer made this illustration decision. Stringer herself had shown the children how an illustrator zooms in and shows something close up, and the children were welcome to study *how* she did this even more on their own if they wanted to. As a teacher of writing, my job is to help them think about *why* she did it because purposefulness is my goal. Just as my goal is not for writers to throw in crafting moves with words just to throw them in, I don't aim for illustrators to draw things close up for no apparent reason either. If these young picture book makers were to add this illustration technique to their repertoire of techniques, they needed to understand why it would make sense to use it.

The "why" of this technique in *Mud* seemed fairly easy to articulate. In a book with mud as its focus, Lauren Stringer knew that she could make her case for the muddiness of it all if she showed it very close up. I said to the children, "If she had drawn this illustration from further away, you would be able to see the whole child and even his brown feet, but you wouldn't get the same feeling for just how muddy his feet are. I think she did these close-up illustrations so her readers would really focus on the big idea—mud."

With language like this I was showing the children how to think about the decision making behind the illustrations. But with these words, I was still talking about mud and I needed to use words that would help the children think of this as a more general illustration technique. I went a step further and said, "So to get your reader to really focus on something, you might zoom in and draw a real close-up of just a part of something. Imagine your readers leaning in close with you to look at what you are trying to show them."

Using What We've Noticed to Imagine New Possibilities

Finally, I showed the children how easily I could take something I'd noticed about an illustration and imagine doing it myself with a whole different topic. I used a couple of very specific examples, like this one:

> *Let's say I was writing a book about my brother and his girlfriend getting engaged to be married. On the part where I tell about how proud they were of the beautiful diamond ring they picked out, I might do a close-up of them holding hands so you can see everything about the shiny new ring. I'd need to look at the ring again so I could get this illustration right. Or if I were writing about Sunday dinner last week at my mom's and I couldn't believe how much good food she cooked, I might do a close-up of just the table with all the food laid out on it. Maybe I could even do it from sort of eye level, like you are looking across the table.*

Often, I'll also throw in an idea for a way a child might try this technique in one of the books I know he or she is making at that time in the classroom. On this particular day, I knew that William had been working on a book about how his dog Spot barked all the time, and so together the children and I imagined different ways William could use close-ups of Spot's head, barking of course, to get across his big idea.

The purpose of thinking aloud about possibilities in this way is simply to show children how everything they notice about illustrations can easily become something they might imagine doing themselves. Everything they see and consider becomes a possibility for future picture books they make. Later, in another day's lesson, I might show them how I (or one of them) used this illustration technique in one of my books with an actual drawing I've done. But on this day, I set out simply to demonstrate the thinking behind the habit of mind of reading like a writer, so thinking was all I did in this demonstration.

With this beginning lesson in an illustration study, I introduced these children to the same habit of mind I use as a very experienced writer when I notice how things are written. I was very explicit in demonstrating this thinking on this morning, and Lisa and I would continue to be explicit about it throughout the study. But over time, the goal is for this habit of mind to become more and more implicit, something children do but are hardly aware they are doing. Just as I often stop and reread something that I think has been particularly well crafted, our hope is that children will look twice at an illustration that's been done in an interesting way. And while we may not fully explicate what we see in writing or in illustrating (though *we could*, that's the point), we'll be learning all the time from these moments of noticing.

Instructional Tips for Supporting Children to Read Like Writers in Their Illustration Work

- Because seeing oneself as *like* another person is so critical to reading like a writer, children need to see authors and illustrators as more than just names printed on books. They need, literally, to see them. If they're not already pictured on the book flaps, find photographs of authors and illustrators online, print them, and tape them inside your books. Seeing the actual person who made all the decisions in a book helps make that connection more concrete for children.

- Always read the author and illustrator notes and dedications in books and talk about them. The information in them often makes authors and illustrators seem more like real folks to children, just as photographs do.

- Make the question, "What do you notice about the illustrations in this book?" a predictable, expected question in your discussions about books. As the question becomes routine, so will the habit of mind.

- When children point out something they notice in a book, use the authors' and illustrators' names as you discuss the decisions they've made. "Look at how Donald Crews shows the wind in the sails of that boat."

- Get comfortable with thinking imaginatively in front of children. Demonstrate how you can picture a child or someone else trying out a technique in a different book about a different topic.

- Let children know you are interested in them reading like writers on their own. Ask them to let you know if they find an interesting illustration technique in a book they are reading independently. Make time for them to share these techniques and teach other children about them.

- When you know a child has used a specific illustrator as a mentor, consider displaying pages from the child's book alongside pages from the books of the illustrator. You might add labels such as, "Look what Thomas learned from Marla Frazee! How to show many things happening at once."

- Share with children your own stories of reading like a writer. Tell them about times when you were looking at a book and noticed something the illustrator did that caused you to look again more closely. Show them how this happens both in books you're reading for the first time and books you've read many times.

CHAPTER

5

Learning Qualities of Good Writing from Illustration Techniques

Creativity should not be considered a separate mental faculty but a characteristic of our way of thinking, knowing, and making choices.

—LORIS MALAGUZZI, *"History, Ideas, and Basic Philosophy"*
in The Hundred Languages of Children

ONE MORNING, I BROUGHT A STACK OF NEW BOOKS to Lisa Cleaveland's writing workshop for Lisa and her students' study of literary nonfiction. They would be reading many of these books over the next couple of weeks, but on this morning they would just be looking through them and building enthusiasm for the study to come.

The first book they picked up, *Ice Bear: In the Steps of the Polar Bear* (2005), is by an author they already know and love, Nicola Davies, and the children were immediately struck by the beautiful, soft pastel colored illustrations Gary Blythe created for the book. The children wanted to know if they were real (photographs) or drawings. Lisa read on the inside of the front page that the illustrations were done in oil and pencil. As they looked at selected pages, they saw close-up drawings of the polar bear, as well as more distant perspectives, but all of them had been rendered with the blue and white softness and indistinct edges that snow brings to any landscape.

The next book in the stack just happened to be another Nicola Davies book, *Surprising Sharks* (2003). The book is illustrated by James Croft, and he used bright, primary colors, whimsical drawings of sharks, and all kinds of labels, close-ups, and inset pictures to illustrate Davies' engaging text about sharks. The children were particularly interested in one illustration where a shark is swimming toward a red fish in the middle of a large bull's-eye on a bright orange background. As they looked at this illustration, Lisa picked up *Ice Bear* and began to think aloud. She said:

> *It's a different kind of illustration. Look at the difference. I look at this book* [Ice Bear] *and I think, "Wow, kind of serious." And I look at this book* [Surprising Sharks] *and I think, "Kind of out there." Like the bull's-eye. Would you expect to see a bull's-eye in this* [Ice Bear] *book?*

As I listened to this conversation about very different illustrations in two books by the same author, I was struck by how much this was also a conversation about a very important *writing* issue—the issue of tone. To explain how I made this big connection from this little snippet of classroom talk, let me first explain what I mean by the quality of tone in writing.

Understanding the Quality of Tone in Writing

Tone, of course, is very connected to voice in writing. In *Live Writing*, Ralph Fletcher describes voice in this way:

> *When I talk about voice in writing, all I mean is the sense of the author's personality that comes through the words on the paper. Writing with voice sounds honest and authentic. It has conviction and integrity. It has the quirks and rhythms of human speech. Writing with voice makes us feel as if we're listening to a real person. (1999, 33–34)*

The thing is, a real person is moody and subject to all kinds of emotions that impact the sound of the voice I'm listening to as I read. That's where tone comes in, as in "tone of voice." Using careful word choices, deliberate sentence structures, and well-timed paragraph breaks, writers may strike a tone in a text that is humorous and lighthearted or somber and serious, haughtily pretentious or hauntingly eerie, breathless and out of control or measured and suspiciously neurotic, and on and on. Really, any sort of feeling a writer would like to convey can be achieved with careful word crafting.

Consider, for example, the tone in these two leads written by Pulitzer Prize winning columnist Leonard Pitts, Jr., of *The Miami Herald*. The first was written on the five-year anniversary of the war in Iraq (March 19, 2008).

> *And five years later, here we are.*

> *There were no weapons of mass destruction. We were not greeted as liberators. The war did not pay for itself. The smoking gun was not a mushroom cloud. There was no connection to 9/11. The course we stayed led over a cliff.*

Worse, Iraq has become a recruiting station for Islamic terrorists. One presidential candidate foresees a 100-year occupation. Electricity is still a sometime thing in Baghdad. The war that was supposed to pay for itself was recently projected to cost us $3 trillion—that's trillion, with a "t," that's a three followed by 12 zeroes, that's three million millions. And American forces have sustained more than 33,000 casualties, including 4,000 dead and 13,000 wounded too severely to return to action.

Whether you agree with his assessment or not, one thing is for sure, you can tell from reading this that Leonard Pitts, Jr., was *ticked off* when he reflected on the five years U.S. troops had been in Iraq. He began his column with the conjunction *and*, a sardonic reference to all that had come before, and making this short opening sentence stand on its own as a paragraph punctuates it even more. The very short, deliberately invariable sentence structures in the second paragraph sound something like the ominous ticks of a bomb about to explode. And the little tantrum over what a trillion really means in the third paragraph comes together to voice unequivocal anger right from the start in this column.

Contrast this angry tone with the lead to the column Pitts wrote just after the inauguration of Barack Obama (January 21, 2009).

It begins before the sun does.

Not yet 5 A.M. and there is at a suburban Metro station a line of people going out of the station and up the escalator and around the corner and down to the far, far end of the parking lot. In town, it's worse.

They crowd into this city, into their capital, like ants crowd atop a sugar mound, for the new president's inauguration. They have come in numbers that make it impossible, sometimes, simply to move. They have come from dining room tables where bills are stacked beneath pink slips. They have come from sick rooms where loved ones have died, literally, of poverty. They have come from a dawning realization that they were sold a war they didn't need to wipe out weapons that didn't exist. They have come from bar stools and church pews, from classrooms and factory floors and from mansions. Beyoncé is here, Denzel Washington is here, Jay-Z and Diddy are here. And Motown poet Smokey Robinson is here to see, as he puts it, "the arrival of the real meaning of the United States of America."

When I read this, I sense that Pitts was incredibly moved by the events he witnessed that day. He made the interesting choice to begin with the pronoun *it*, its antecedent unknown but hinting at something almost mythical, something "before the sun." This tone continues with his decision in the second sentence to put "there is" before the prepositional phrase "at a suburban

Metro station," instead of after it where it would sound more like everyday talk. The series of prepositions in that sentence—*out, up, around,* and *down*—combined with the repetition of *far* suggest the enormity of what he witnessed. His tone is reverent, the repetition of "they have come" and the listing of names sounding almost liturgical. And the longer sentence structure gives the lead a clear tone of reflection, the sound of someone slowing down to really savor the meaning he is making.

Again, whether you agree with his political stance or not, if you are a writer, you have to admire Pitts' ability to use written text to convey so much of himself on paper. He exhibits not only a strong voice in his writing, but if you follow his writing over time, you see he has the dexterity to help readers hear vastly different emotions in his writing voice. Rarely is there any doubt about the audible tone of voice he would use if he were to speak his columns to you in person. That is—in part, at least—what wins you Pulitzers.

Understanding the Quality of Tone in Illustrating

What does any of this, then, have to do with a group of young children and their teacher discussing illustrations in picture books? Well, a lot actually. A whole lot once you begin to recognize illustrations as works of composition just like words. Illustrations come together in particular ways because illustrators make all sorts of decisions—and revisions of decisions—just like writers make. Many of the words we use to talk about the qualities of good writing are the same words we use to talk about the qualities of illustrating, and the understandings about these qualities run parallel in writing and illustrating as well. Take this discussion of tone, for example.

When Gary Blythe chose to use softly muted pastels and James Croft decided to use bold primary colors, they made dramatically different decisions that affected the tone—the overall feeling—of each book. Without even reading the words, Lisa and her students realized they were looking at two very different kinds of books, both of them literary nonfiction, both written to engage and inform readers on a topic, but the overall feeling of each was very different.

Blythe's illustrations make *Ice Bear* just *look* like a more serious take on these magnificent creatures. The tone of the illustrations suggests the tone of the words. The paintings the children saw are so beautiful they just expected to find beautiful, perhaps even poetic words to go with them. And that's exactly what they found when they read the book through—words like these from the last page:

> *We Inuit, we watch Nanuk, as we first watched when the Earth seemed new and Polar Bear showed us how to love the Arctic—how to hide from blizzards in a house of snow, how to hunt for seals with patience and speed, how*

to live in starlit day and sunlit night. Many polar bears and Inuit have
passed since then, and still we share our world with gratitude and pride. (27)

In contrast, Croft's bright, humorous illustrations in *Surprising Sharks* looked to the children like they might lead them on a fun-filled frolic through the fascinating world of sharks. Inside, they found words like these from the lead to the book:

You're swimming in the warm blue sea. What's the one word that turns your
dream into a nightmare? What's the one word that makes you think of a
giant man-eating killer? Shaaaaarrrkk!

Shark? Yes, it's a shark! It's a dwarf lantern shark. It's the smallest kind of
shark in the world, just bigger than a chocolate bar. Not a giant, certainly no
man-eater, and a killer only if you happen to be a shrimp. (6–9)

These opening words spoken directly to the reader, written with the playful immediacy of present tense verbs, and pulling a bit of a surprise (the shark is not really a killer, after all) deliver exactly what the illustrations suggest they will deliver.

Connecting Writing and Illustrating

"Would you expect to see a bull's-eye in this book?" With this simple question and the thinking she modeled connected to it, a thoughtful teacher opened up a little idea with big potential. By nudging her students to think about how a bull's-eye would be very out of place in the middle of the *Ice Bear* book, Lisa introduced her students to a very important understanding about writing as well. The more general version of her question, "Does this sort of illustration fit well with the others in terms of overall effect?" works just as efficiently for writers who are crafting texts: "Do these words fit well with the overall effect I'm trying to create here?" For example, imagine how odd it would have been for Nicola Davies to make this sort of additive revision to the last page of *Ice Bear*.

Many polar bears and Inuit have passed since then, and still we share our
world with gratitude and pride. The Inuit say, "Polar bears rock!"

While those words are certainly one way to express the clear message of the book, the hip sounding tone of "Polar bears rock!" is just all wrong for the tone used in the rest of the book.

Writers think about consistency of tone often as they draft and revise. Sometimes when I'm working on my own writing, I'll read something I've drafted and think, "That sounds a little smartypants-ish," or maybe, "This needs to be toughened up a bit." In these instances, what I'm really considering are issues of tone. The words I've written just don't fit well with the tone I'm trying to strike. When Lisa thought aloud about the question, "Would you expect to see a bull's-eye in this book?" she was demonstrating this same important line of thinking about consistency of tone to her young students.

A Shifting Understanding

By looking closely at the decisions illustrators make in picture books, teachers can help children understand many of the most important concepts about quality writing. Illustrators make meaning with pictures, and writers make meaning with words, but they both *make meaning*, and rich curriculum lies in understanding all the ways their decisions intersect. The key is, in order to help students grow as writers, teachers need a deeply grounded understanding of the ways thinking about writing and thinking about illustrating are the same. This, however, is very new thinking for many teachers—myself included.

From working with teachers through illustration studies in writing workshops, I've known for some time that these studies hold tremendous potential for helping children become more intentional in their meaning making as they illustrate. By looking closely at a rich variety of decisions illustrators make in picture books, many new and interesting possibilities are opened up to children who make picture books too. The thing is, for a long time I only thought of what children were learning in those studies as being about illustrating. It wasn't until I had a series of "aha" moments like the one I had listening to the *Ice Bear/Surprising Sharks* conversation that I realized that the understandings informing so many illustration techniques are the same understandings writers use to craft texts with words. And I know that if I hadn't spent years of my professional life trying to understand and become articulate about the craft of writing, I probably would have missed this important connection entirely.

Realizing the connection between writing techniques and illustration techniques has brought about a huge shift for me as a teacher of writing, and particularly for me as a teacher of young writers. The NAEYC *Position Statement: Developmentally Appropriate Practice* states:

> *Learning and development are most likely to occur when new experiences build on what a child already knows and is able to do and when those learning experiences also entail the child stretching a reasonable amount in acquiring new skills, abilities or knowledge. (2009, 10)*

Build on what a child already knows and is able to do. By simply changing the way I think and talk about the decisions of illustrators in picture books, I now see enormous potential for helping children come to own so many important understandings about the craft of writing, but to know them first in the context of illustrations. I'm wearing very different teaching glasses now as I look at decisions illustrators make, illustrators like six-year-old Anna.

Seeing an Illustration Decision in a New Way

A number of years ago during a study of memoir in her first-grade writing workshop, Anna worked for days on a lovely picture book about her memories of a family trip to Disney World. Whenever I share her book with teachers, there is always an audible sigh in the room when we get to the ending (Figure 5.1). Anna used a meaningful combination of written text, "Don't worry Mom and Dad, I won't forget," with small illustration vignettes of places around Disney World. Readers are meant to look at the small illustrations and be reminded of the trip Anna wrote about earlier in the book.

This technique—bringing illustration details from throughout the book together in a single closing illustration—is often used by illustrators at the end of a picture book. Mélanie Watt, author and illustrator of the Scaredy Squirrel series of books, used this technique at the end of *Scaredy Squirrel at the Beach* (2008). The text says, "P.S. As for Scaredy's next visit

Figure 5.1 Anna's memoir ending

to the beach, it might be sooner than he thinks . . ." And then in small, boxed illustrations you see scenes from earlier in the book when Scaredy is at the beach.

I had read Eileen Spinelli's book, *In My New Yellow Shirt* (2001), several times and not even noticed that the illustrator, Hideko Takahashi, had used this technique. A group of children I was reading the book to pointed this out to me (this happens often—children notice things before I do). On the next-to-the-last-page spread of this book, the little boy's mom is undressing him for bed and there are toys scattered about the room. Savvy eyes will notice that all the things the boy has imagined himself being in his new yellow shirt are pictured as toys in this illustration: a duck, a lion, a taxi, a lazy caterpillar, a daffodil, a fancy tropical fish, a tennis ball, a trumpet, a canary, a butterfly, a golden treasure, a banana, and a yellow submarine. They are all there in this closing illustration (trust me, we checked), taking the reader on a visual journey back through the book.

What these three illustrators know, and the understanding that informed each of their closing illustrations, is that one way to craft a satisfying ending is to remind readers of the journey they've taken. Notice that the way I've phrased that understanding, *one way to craft a satisfying ending is to remind readers of the journey they've taken*, leaves open the possibility that this sort of ending might be crafted either with illustrations or words. It doesn't matter which way it's crafted, the understanding is the same.

Patricia MacLachlan used this understanding as she crafted one of the most beautiful closing paragraphs in all of fiction, the ending of *Sarah, Plain and Tall*:

> *Autumn will come, then winter, cold with a wind that blows like the wind off the sea in Maine. There will be nests of curls to look for, and dried flowers all winter long. When there are storms, Papa will stretch a rope from the door of the barn so we will not be lost when we feed the sheep and the cows and Jack and Old Bess. And Sarah's chickens, if they aren't living in the house. There will be Sarah's sea, blue and gray and green, hanging on the wall. And songs, old ones and new. And Seal with yellow eyes. And there will be Sarah, plain and tall. (1985, 58)*

If you haven't read the book, you won't really get much out of this ending because all the details are references to small details from the book. With words, MacLachlan achieved the same effect Anna and Mélanie Watt and Hideko Takahashi did with illustrations as she takes the reader on a journey back through the beautiful love story she crafted.

Twice in the closing two chapters of her memoir, *But I'll Be Back Again*, Cynthia Rylant employed this same technique, but she did it in single sentences. The first comes in the closing sentence of the next-to-the-last chapter as she explains why she keeps a plastic Paul McCartney doll from her child-hood safe in a trunk:

> *Maybe in some way, by protecting this doll, I am protecting that part of my childhood which smells like pink powdered bubble gum and Harold Treadway's mouth and Calvin Ramsey's leaf collection and the rain falling on Bobby Kennedy's face. (1989, 58)*

Rylant used the conjunction *and* to join the references to stories that she told earlier in the memoir, the effect being to run them together more than make them distinct, as they would be if she had separated them with commas. The commas or conjunctions decision (or both, or neither) is one a writer must make any time she lists a series of things, and because of the different work a comma (it separates) and a conjunction (it joins) do, the decision matters because it affects meaning. With this particular technique, the commas or conjunctions decision has an illustration parallel. Mélanie Watt chose to box in the illustrated vignettes in *Scarredy Squirrel*, making them more separate and distinct scenes, the boxes serving a purpose similar to the work of commas separating a series of words. Hideko Takahashi, on the other hand, incorporated all the illustrated details into a single illustration, connecting them more closely as the conjunction *and* connects the details in Rylant's closing sentence.

The last sentence of the last chapter of *But I'll Be Back Again* employs the technique again, but this time with a different punctuation decision:

> *But every child will have his heartaches. I just hope that along with these each child will have a hero, and music, and at least one kiss he will never forget. (1989, 64)*

Making reference to Robert Kennedy, the Beatles, and that kiss from Jimmy Williams Rylant says she'll never forget, the writer crafted a fine, fine ending using the same understanding Anna used when she came to the close of her Disney memoir: *one way to craft a satisfying ending is to remind readers of the journey they've taken*. One used words, one used pictures, but the understanding about craft was the same. And understanding *that* has fundamentally changed my teaching.

Understanding how to talk about illustrations in ways that support children's growing understandings about writing is what this book is all about. The work is far-reaching in its scope. Think of the texts I used here to make this case: newspaper commentary and chapter books set down alongside picture books. It will be a long time before five- and six-year-olds will need to think about tone in the same ways Leonard Pitts, Jr., thinks about tone, but if the teachers of these children understand how many of their decisions are really just like his, then they can more thoughtfully teach them toward that future as writers.

Instructional Tips for Supporting Illustration–Writing Connections

- The fifty possibilities for illustration study in Section Two of this book are organized by qualities of good writing, and most of them also include very specific writing connections. As you study the illustration examples and writing connections, you should begin to see many similar connections in your own reading. When you do make connections, demonstrate your thinking about them to your students.

- If you read chapter books aloud to your students, you might consider selecting excerpts and exploring illustration–writing connections. Read an excerpt (more than once if necessary) and ask students to imagine how they might picture the meaning of the words in an illustration. The thinking students do will help them see the connection between what words do to make meaning and what illustrations do to make meaning.

- Whenever you demonstrate your own thinking about composing an illustration, be sure to point out how you would write your meaning if you were using only words and not pictures. You can just do this quickly in response to your drawing, or you might consider extending the teaching demonstration over two days. On the first day you model your thinking about composing the illustration, and on the second day you show children how you made the same meaning with writing. Of course, it won't be *exactly* the same meaning because the modes have different potentials, but the subtle differences will make for good talk that should deepen children's understandings.

- As you confer with children, you might share with them the words that come to mind as suggested by their illustrations. For example, if a child has drawn a picture of a very tall building, you might say, "That building looks like it almost touches the sky. All the other buildings are so small around it. It seems like the king of the buildings." Just respond naturally with whatever words come to mind. The point is to show children how pictures suggest meanings that can be expressed by words.

CHAPTER

The Writing Workshop

Planning and Implementing a Unit of Study in Illustrations

If a curriculum is truly learning-centered, then that curriculum is based on inquiry and the search for questions that matter to us, whether we are adults or children. The function of curriculum is to support us in the inquiry process of searching for questions and ways of looking at those questions. Without inquiry, a sense of purpose and meaning in learning is lost and our natural inquisitiveness as learners is deadened.

—KATHY SHORT AND CAROLYN BURKE, *Creating Curriculum: Teachers and Students as a Community of Learners*

AT THE END OF WRITING WORKSHOP ON THE FIRST DAY of a study of illustrations, a group of children gathered for a time of sharing and reflection. They were excited because they spent most of the workshop looking closely at illustrations in books and marking pages where the illustrator had done something interesting. I had demonstrated what "something interesting" might mean in a teaching demonstration at the beginning of the workshop, showing the children a variety of close-ups of muddy feet in the book *Mud* (1996), illustrated by Lauren Stringer and written by Mary Lyn Ray.

As the children gathered in the meeting space, their teacher and I could see that their picture books had lots of sticky notes in them. This was good. It meant we had our study already laid out for us. We would spend the next couple of weeks looking at what the children had noticed in these books and turning their noticings into curriculum, working together to become more and more articulate about ways to make smart illustration decisions. Our goal for this work was twofold. First, we wanted the children to become much more intentional in how they made decisions about their own illustrations. And second, we wanted to plant seeds of understandings about qualities of good writing within the context of illustrations.

On this first morning, we decided to look at a few of the things the children found so we could build enthusiasm for the study to come. William was the first to share; he showed us an illustration in the book *Hoptoad* (2003), illustrated by Karen Lee Schmidt and written by Jane Yolen. He had picked a good illustration to share, one with lots of potential, and we were not surprised as the books we had gathered for the children to study were all rich with potential. We picked them precisely because we knew the children couldn't help but find interesting illustration decisions in them.

In the illustration William shared, Karen Lee Schmidt positions the reader in the backseat of a truck. We see the backs of the father, son, and dog in the front seat, on through the windshield of the truck, down the road to a small frog hopping by, and to the horizon beyond. The entire illustration is framed by the windshield we're looking through, and we can even see the father's concerned look reflected in the rearview mirror. Very cool. We were all very excited about what we might learn from an illustration like this and the other illustrations the children were anxious to share.

A Unit of Study Is a Unit of Study

A study of illustrations in writing workshop almost immediately raises the level of thinking and decision making children engage in as they make books, so I believe illustration study is a must on a primary curriculum calendar. And because children grow so much in the study regardless of their developmental capabilities with word making, the earlier in the year the study comes, the better. With two or three weeks of nonstop thinking about the decisions illustrators make, the entire year is transformed as children learn to notice illustrations in every book they encounter across all other studies.

I started with this classroom vignette because it highlights a very important point I'd like to make about illustration study. While it would be temptingly easy to use the illustration techniques highlighted in the second half of this book and plan a series of lessons that teaches children one of these techniques each day in a predictable minilesson format, I don't believe that's the best way to go about this teaching. Students need the opportunity to *study* the decisions of illustrators, not simply be told about them. Teachers also need the opportunity to study with their students, because adults always learn from children when a study is based on noticing. Children just notice more than we do. It's that simple.

A series of lessons about illustration techniques would make up a unit, but not a unit of *study*. In a preplanned unit, students are recipients of curriculum. In a unit of study, students are active cocreators of curriculum. And students need to be active, helping to generate curriculum around the framing question: *What does it mean to make smart illustration decisions?* For one thing, their engagement in the process of study teaches them to see illustrations as insiders, the corresponding habit of mind to reading like writers (as Chapter Four explains).

Children's engagement in study also teaches them how it is one knows the answer to such a question: *What does it mean to make smart illustration decisions?* In their wonderful book *Understanding by Design*, Grant Wiggins and Jay McTighe say, "If students are to understand what is known, they need to simulate or recreate some of the inquiry by which the knowledge was created" (1998, 33). If the study has no *study* in it, then students may very well think that the way one knows what it means to make smart illustration decisions is to be the teacher and have the book of lessons. But with *study* in the study, children learn about illustration decisions, but they also learn *how to learn* about them, an instructional gift that can serve them well throughout their lives—not just when studying illustrations.

This chapter, then, will explore how to plan and implement a unit of study in illustrations, with the guiding focus always on the decision making of the people behind the pictures. I'll work from a predictable framework for study in the writing workshop, a framework I use to plan study around any topic where the curriculum lies in texts: a study of any genre of writing or any aspect of the craft of writing (Ray 2006). The framework itself is actually more than just a set of instructional practices; it's part of the curriculum itself because the process of study teaches students how to learn about writing as much as it teaches them about writing itself.

Here is the predictable framework I use to plan any unit of study, untied from the specific context of illustration study:

- **Gather** a stack of texts that are good examples of what I want to study.

- Make sure students know what it is we're studying and that I **expect** them to write under the influence of this study.

- **Immerse** ourselves in reading and talking about the gathered texts and what we notice about how they're written.

- **Study** some of them closely until we've become articulate (and can chart) about how people write this kind of text.

- **Write** (both teacher and students) something that could go in the stack of texts we've been studying and be articulate about how our writing fits in the stack.

Generally, the work of a study as it's described in this framework will unfold over several weeks in a writing workshop. In different studies across the year, the teaching practices should be familiar and predictable. This is essential. When the teaching is predictable, students come to understand what study means and to own the process of study as learners. With predictable teaching, students learn to expect to be shown examples of the kind of writing or illustrating teachers want them to do—an expectation that gives them important agency as writers. They learn to read these examples with a critical eye, noticing and thinking deeply about the decisions the writers and illustrators made as they crafted them. They learn to imagine possibilities for their future work from what they find as they study. And once again, students learn not just about writing and illustrating from this framework for study, they learn *how to learn* about them.

Utilizing the Framework for Illustration Study

Now let's explore these predictable teaching practices as they might unfold in a study of illustrations in the writing workshop. My hope is that you will find this section explicit enough to help you get started with illustration study, but open enough to let you find your own way through the study with the students you teach. As you read this section, I also hope you can imagine doing similar teaching work in studies such as:

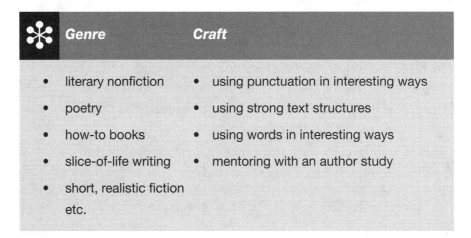

✳ *Genre*	*Craft*
• literary nonfiction	• using punctuation in interesting ways
• poetry	• using strong text structures
• how-to books	• using words in interesting ways
• slice-of-life writing	• mentoring with an author study
• short, realistic fiction etc.	

Gather

Planning for any unit of study begins with deciding which texts you'll use for the study. In primary writing workshops, the texts will almost always be picture books because children need to be able to compose with both pictures and words. As an example, Figure 6.1 is a list of books one teacher gathered for a study of illustrations in a kindergarten writing workshop.

Books Gathered for a Kindergarten Illustration Study

Beach, Elisha Cooper

Birds, Kevin Henkes, Laura Dronzek

Call Me Gorgeous!, Giles Milton, Alexandra Milton

A Couple of Boys Have the Best Week Ever, Marla Frazee

Hoptoad, Jane Yolen, Karen Lee Schmidt

I'm Bad!, Kate McMullan, Jim McMullan

Incredible Me!, Kathi Appelt, G. Brian Karas

Let's Play Basketball, Charles R. Smith, Jr., Terry Widener

Mud, Mary Lyn Ray, Lauren Stringer

Rain, Manya Stojic

Rattletrap Car, Phyllis Root, Jill Barton

Santa Clause: The World's Number One Toy Expert, Marla Frazee

Scaredy Squirrel, Mélanie Watt

Scaredy Squirrel at the Beach, Mélanie Watt

Snow, Cynthia Rylant, Lauren Stringer

Summer Beat, Betsy Franco, Charlotte Middleton

39 Uses for a Friend, Harriet Ziefert, Rebecca Doughty

Up, Down, and Around, Katherine Ayers, Nadine Bernard Westcott

Walk On! A Guide for Babies of All Ages, Marla Frazee

The Zoo, Suzy Lee

Figure 6.1 Books gathered for a kindergarten illustration study

Gathering books for an illustration study is relatively easy compared to gathering for genre or craft studies, because practically any picture book might potentially go in your stack of books for the study. Having said that, it is also true that some books are better than others. You are looking for books where you see lots of interesting illustration decisions and can imagine learning a lot from studying them closely. The books should feel full of potential and make you excited about the prospect of studying them with your students. You might look through the examples in the second section of this book to give you some good ideas about the kinds of illustrations you are looking for and to find titles of books you might use to get you started.

As you gather, you'll be thinking about both breadth and depth for your study. A good rule of thumb is to have at least enough books in your stack that you have one book for every two children. This will allow you to use partnerships as children study books independently. Ideally though, it would be great to have a book for every child; that way partners can share the two books between them. These books will give your study breadth. For depth, make sure you have two or three of these books in mind that are so rich with potential you know you'll want to study them especially closely.

You might consider selecting as many familiar books for an illustration study as you can, as long as they offer what you need in terms of interesting decision making about illustrations. If children know a book already, then as a class you can move much more quickly to studying the illustrations because it's not necessary to read the book and become familiar with it first. However, don't let this keep you from gathering books that will be new to the students as well. New books only mean you must find time to read them, either in writing workshop or at some other time of the day. And of course, with the breadth of texts you'll gather, you probably won't have time to look at them all as a whole class anyway, so whether it's an old favorite or new book really doesn't matter.

Once you've collected the books you'll be using, check to see if they include a photograph of the author and illustrator on the book jacket. If they don't, you might take time to see if you can find photographs of the illustrators on the Internet. You'll be talking so much about the illustrators' decision making and calling them all by name, and it will be very helpful for children to picture the people you are talking about. Photographs make the illustrators seem much more real to children.

Expect

On the day you launch the study, you'll want to have all the books together, perhaps in a basket or a box, so children can see them as a collection of books you've purposefully gathered. Begin by explaining what the books have in common and why you've put them together: *because they all have some really wonderful illustrations in them, and we are going to study them to get smarter about our own illustrating.*

Next, take your students on a tour of the books, opening a few of them up to peek inside and see a little of the illustration work you're excited about. Go ahead and quickly demonstrate some thinking about what you notice in the illustrations as you look through the books. An early demonstration of this thinking will get students noticing on their own very quickly. Name the illustrators of the books you look at on your tour, and show photographs of them if you have them. The goal of this tour is to get children excited about the study they'll be doing. The books should make children think as they look at them, "Hey, I would like to try making pictures like that in my books."

Finally, make sure that children know that by the end of your study, you expect that each of them will have made at least one, and maybe several, books that you could place in the basket with the others because they have really interesting illustrations in them too. As you read about in Chapter Four, the point of making this expectation very clear right from the start is to create the sense of immediacy that is so necessary for students to look at the books and study them as insiders.

If you have student books from illustration studies in previous years, you might show these to the children as you talk about the books they (this year's students) will make in the course of this study.

As with every other kind of teaching work in this predictable framework for study, over time, children will come to recognize your teaching and they will already know that you expect them to write something like what you'll be studying. Over time, you won't even have to explain this. They'll know the expectation is there the moment they see you've gathered some new stack of books for study in writing workshop.

Immerse
Students Study Books Independently

In any study, and especially in illustration study, you'll want to plan at least one day (and maybe more) when children work independently in partnerships during writing workshop and study from the breadth of books you've gathered. Getting their hands on the actual books connects children to the study in a tangible, meaningful way, so much more than if the books stay safely tucked in a basket under the teacher's care.

If children are new to study in the writing workshop, be sure you spend some time helping them understand why reading is a necessary part of a writer's work. You might share with them former national poet laureate Ted Kooser's advice mentioned earlier in Chapter Four. Kooser says, if you want to be a poet, "Before you write one poem, you need to read at least one hundred poems." I shared this advice with a group of second graders once and the room got absolutely silent as the children stared at me, wide-eyed. Finally, a little boy in the back broke the silence and said, "Oh, jeez." I guess the idea of reading so much before writing was a little overwhelming for them, but Kooser's advice is absolutely sound and is echoed by writer after writer. If you want to be a good writer, you must read. This is why purposeful reading is an essential part of study in the writing workshop.

You should have demonstrated the kinds of things you want children to notice about illustrations when you took them on a tour of the books you'd gathered for the study. This demonstration should be enough to get kids started noticing on their own, but if you feel they need another demonstration, you might wait until day two of the study to have children look at books independently. Waiting gives you an opportunity to do another teaching demonstration before you send them out with books, just as I was doing on the teaching day described at the beginning of this chapter.

As children study the books you've gathered, give each partnership three or four sticky notes so they can mark pages where they see something that interests them in the illustrations. Be sure to explain to the children that they need to save the notes for the most interesting things they see. If students are new to this sort of work with books, you might want to demonstrate how to look through a book and notice several different illustrations, and then decide which one to mark to share with the class. If it is developmentally appropriate for the students you teach, encourage them to write what they've noticed about the illustrations on the notes attached to them. As the study progresses, you'll return to many of the pages children noted in the books to develop new curriculum from what you see there.

Because they are studying the illustrations, it isn't necessary for the children to be able to read the words in the books you give them during this part of the study. As a matter of fact, the ability to read the words in books independently need not be a prerequisite in any study in a primary writing workshop. In order to write and illustrate well, beginning writers depend on teachers to give them access to much richer texts than they are able to read independently. Imagine how limited children's vision of what is possible in writing and illustrating would be if they only studied from books they could read independently.

On the day (or days) when children study books independently, you'll want to plan for an extended time of share and reflection at the end of writing workshop so children can show others what they've found while it's very fresh. Rather than sharing all the noted pages with the whole class, it makes sense to have partnerships first share with other partnerships so everyone gets a chance to show what they've found. You may also choose to follow this sharing with a few whole-class looks to build even more enthusiasm, but you won't have time to look at them all. Make sure children know you'll be studying many of their noted pages over the coming course of the study.

After a day or two of independent reading immersion, you'll begin working as a whole class for the remainder of the study, and reading immersion and the close study that accompanies it will be very intertwined. This is different from the typical genre study where you read a lot of examples first as a whole class to get a feel for the genre before moving on to close study.

You will probably find it easiest to spend time as a class studying one book closely for several days before moving on to another. Start by selecting a book you've chosen to give your study depth. A few children will have studied the book independently, so it should have some pages already marked in it. If the book is not familiar, you'll need to read it aloud first and talk a bit about it as readers. If it's a book you've read as a whole class before, you may choose not to reread it and spend just a few minutes remembering it.

After familiarizing the class with the book, you'll need to find some place inside it to get your inquiry started. There are several ways you might do this. You could simply begin working your way through the book page by page and asking children what they notice on each one. You might start by looking at the pages already noted and have the students who put the notes there explain their thinking. You might simply ask, "Who remembers a page where you thought the illustration was particularly interesting?" or you might share something you've noticed in a particular illustration. However you go about finding illustrations to talk about, you'll be building curriculum from what the children and you notice, and you will be recording what you're learning about how to illustrate well.

If the first book you choose is particularly rich with potential, you may spend several days studying it. Just work by the clock each day and spend as much time as you want to allow for whole-class instruction (say ten to fifteen minutes) developing curriculum from what students notice. When it feels like the energy for talking about one book is waning, move on and study another book for a few days. Undoubtedly, as you study subsequent books, much of what you see will be familiar and you can move quickly to talking about only what is new and different. You should also find that students are making connections to what they saw in illustrations when they studied books independently—"This is showing motion just like the picture of Santa on the pogo stick in the book we looked at!" Let the children share these connections when they make them. You won't have time as a whole class to study all the books they studied independently, so connections are a good way to bring those books into the whole-class conversation.

As with most studies in writing workshop, there is no defined scope and sequence to the curriculum generated by the study, and this is particularly true in illustration study. Your goal is for depth rather than coverage, so feel free to head in any direction that seems to capture your students' interest. You will almost certainly find rich curriculum there. Plan to learn a lot with your students for as long as there is energy for the study, or until you simply need to move on—whichever comes first.

Study

Close study is the talk around something you've noticed that leads you to explicit curriculum. In illustration study, you will be doing the work of close study right from the start, taking time to notice specific decisions illustrators have made, talking about why they made them, and guiding children to imagine making similar decisions in their own writing. You will know your talk about an illustration has led you to curriculum when you feel the need to stop and write something down—something like, *Sometimes an illustration can be pictured from very far away* or *The text can be placed anywhere on the page in relation to the picture.* For example, the talk about the illustration from *Hoptoad* that William shared with the class (mentioned earlier) led to a simple but powerful new understanding for most of the children: *people (or animals or objects) in a picture can be shown from behind instead of from the front.* Further exploration deepened this understanding to include the idea that when illustrators picture people from behind, it's often so the reader is looking past the person and seeing what he or she sees that lies ahead.

As you record what you are learning in a study, you might consider making a chart that combines words and pictures. Lisa Cleaveland makes reduced-sized copies of illustrations from books that show the possibilities listed on her chart during a study. Children who are not able to read the words on the chart use the pictures to help them remember the possibilities they have talked about.

If you haven't done a lot of study work in your teaching, this may seem challenging—this idea of talking with children about what they notice leading you to the language of explicit curriculum. I understand that challenge and have written this book in large part to help you meet it head on. As you study the fifty illustration techniques in Section Two of this book to deepen your knowledge base, you will be introduced to the language of curriculum with each technique. I also discuss each illustration technique with an eye toward the kind of talk you might have in close study with children. Reading from these sections should give you a feel for how you might lead discussions with children about what they notice in books in ways that will help them grow as writers and illustrators.

Write

In illustration study, because children don't need to make a specific kind of book as they do in genre study, they should be encouraged to start trying what they are learning in the study right away. They can make whatever kinds of books they'd like to make, but the influence of the study should begin to show in these books. As you confer with children during the study, be sure to support their decision making and help them try what makes sense for them in the context of the books they are making. Use the share and reflection time at the end of each writing workshop to showcase interesting decisions children are making about illustrations. Whenever possible, display children's books alongside professionally made picture books to show similar decision making about illustrations.

For assessment at the end of the study, ask students to choose the book they have made that shows their most interesting illustration work. Encourage them to explain the decision making in the book they have chosen. You'll also want to look for the continued influence of the study on students' writing throughout the year. Just because the study is over doesn't mean the thinking stops.

Inviting the Art Teacher in on the Study

In writing workshop, the focus of illustration study is on composition and decision making, of course, not on drawing techniques. Having said that, the study will no doubt generate wonderful possibilities for collaboration with an art teacher who might show children *how* to draw pictures in particular ways. If there is a willing art teacher in your school, share with him or her some of the more interesting illustration curriculum you've generated in your study and ask for help in showing children tips and techniques for drawing. No doubt a few basic lessons in line, perspective, framing, shading, etc., would very quickly raise the quality of children's illustrating.

Fifty Illustration Techniques and the Qualities of Good Writing They Suggest

A Predictable Framework

CHAPTER SEVEN   *Ideas and Content, In Pictures and In Words* **95**

CHAPTER EIGHT   *Precision and Detail, In Pictures and In Words* **131**

CHAPTER NINE   *Wholeness of Text, In Pictures and In Words* **165**

CHAPTER TEN   *Tone, In Pictures and In Words* **195**

CHAPTER ELEVEN   *Layout and Design, In Pictures and In Words* **226**

*W*elcome to Section Two of *In Pictures and In Words*. This section of the book is all about looking at illustrations with new eyes. These new eyes will help you and your students see more in illustrations, think about the decisions illustrators have made behind what you see, find new possibilities for your own illustration work, and also grow in your understanding of many qualities of good writing.

Fifty different illustration techniques are grouped into five clusters based on the qualities of good writing to which they correspond: ideas and content; precision and detail; wholeness of text; tone; and layout and design. Each cluster of techniques begins with an introduction explaining their connection to a general quality of good writing. These explanations are critical as they fuel the forward thinking teachers need in order to see how talking about illustration decisions can also help children understand important qualities of good writing.

A Predictable Format

You will find that the write-ups of the illustration techniques follow a predictable format designed to help you think about illustrating and writing as parallel composing processes. Each write-up contains:

- Something to notice
- An illustration example(s)
- An understanding for young writers and illustrators
- An idea for trying it out
- A writing connection

A little explanation of each of these parts of the format should be helpful in making sense of all that you will find here.

Something to Notice

Each write-up begins with "something to notice," a simple, usually one-sentence statement about a particular way illustrations may be rendered. The

purpose of these statements is to name the illustration technique in a general
way, untied from any specific illustration context. This untying is important
because, though a specific example will follow, you might find this illustration technique in any book.

An Illustration Example(s)

While the "something to notice" statements name the technique, the illustration examples show you what they mean in the context of an actual picture book. Using favorite books from my own library, I describe what's
happening in an illustration so you can see how the illustration technique
is specifically rendered. I've purposefully kept these descriptions quite focused and have not attempted to explore their deeper meanings in the context of the specific books I'm describing. I've done this because their
purpose is to help you begin thinking immediately *outside* the book I'm describing: Does the kind of illustration I'm describing seem familiar to you?
Have you seen something similar in another book? Many of the illustration techniques will seem very familiar, and the examples I use should
lead you straight to other books you know where illustrators have made
similar decisions.

I should note that while I clearly took this opportunity to introduce you
to some very fine picture books in my examples, you don't need these particular books to engage in illustration study with your students. For most
any of the books you'll read about, I could just as easily have pulled my examples from dozens of other books to show the same illustration technique.
All you really need to do this teaching is a stack of picture books you love
from your own personal library, and your "new eyes" to look and think
about what's inside those books.

That being said, you'll also see that I pull examples from some books
more than once, some even several times. I've done this purposefully because I want to demonstrate that a single picture book might be filled
with ideas and carry lots of weight in a study of illustrations. In my experience with study, it is not uncommon to spend several days talking about
the different illustrations in a single, richly crafted picture book. Books
like this also become the "go-to" books teachers use when conferring because they can so quickly find illustration examples inside them to show
children. So if you did want to purchase some new books to get started in
a study, the books that are cited several times would be a good place to
begin.

An Understanding for Young Writers and Illustrators

After each text example, you'll find a short discussion of the illustration
technique; this is meant to help you think more deeply about it if you study
it with your students. This section also includes ideas for kinds of thinking

you might do with this kind of illustration, beginning (predictably) with examining the illustrator's decision making.

In a Teacher's Voice: An Idea for Trying It Out

In this section, I demonstrate how a teacher might imagine using the illustration technique in a picture book a student or the teacher might make. You'll notice the voice in this section is a first-person teaching voice. As I've taught children and adults to study the craft of writing for many years, I've realized this last step is critical to making an understanding stick. If writers—or illustrators—can't imagine using a crafting technique (with words or pictures) they've seen in a new context, with a completely different topic, then the technique hasn't really become part of their crafting repertoire. You'll want to make this imaginative thinking a part of what you demonstrate as you study illustrations, so this section of each write-up is simply meant to give you an example of the sound and substance of this kind of thinking.

A Writing Connection

While the introduction to each of the five clusters of illustration techniques explains their connection to a quality of good writing, many of them will also have a writing connection that extends or makes more specific the general quality of good writing it supports. In these sections, you'll learn more about the composing connection between writing and illustrating.

Drawing from my own experiences as a writer and reader, and from my library of books on the craft of writing, these additional writing connections show how the decisions illustrators make are often based on the same understandings writers use to crafts texts with words—an idea you first read about in Chapter Five of this book. Finally, for reasons explained in their introduction, the techniques in the last cluster—the layout and design cluster—don't have additional writing connections.

As you read the writing connections, you may be struck by how sophisticated the understandings are and wonder how they might help you as you teach very young writers. The connections are really meant for you, to help you build a knowledge base about the craft of writing and use it as a sort of long-range, panoramic lens through which you view your work with children. Having some sense of where an understanding might be headed in your students' futures as writers can help you "steer the ship" better as you explore illustration techniques with them. It's not important or even suggested that you try to help very young children understand the specific content of the writing connections I share. What is important and suggested is for you to tuck them into your knowledge base and let them help you think of the illustrations you see in picture books in whole new ways.

The Illustrators Behind the Examples

Some of the examples in this section come from books where the author and illustrator are different people, and some come from books where one person did both. No doubt, doing the work of both writing and illustrating (as children do) is a much more integrated composition process in terms of idea and content development. The author/illustrator has the luxury of developing an idea simultaneously with words and images, and he may change one to work more efficiently with the other. On the other hand, the illustrator working independently develops ideas and content only from the suggestion of the words, and (as a general rule) she cannot change those words to better suit her meaning making.

Of course, children make decisions as both authors and illustrators when they make books, but in the study of illustrations, they can learn from books where the author and illustrator are the same person and from books where the author and illustrator are different. It really doesn't matter. While the process of composing might be quite different, the products aren't really that different. Illustrators working with another author's written text use the same techniques illustrators use when they write the words themselves. And in the end, the point of the study is to help children build a broad repertoire of illustration understandings that will greatly expand their potential for sound decision making.

How to Use This Section

As Background Knowledge in a Study of Illustrations

The fifty illustration techniques covered in this section are not intended to be taught as a series of lessons in a unit on illustrations. For one thing, there are far too many of them. For another, as I explain in Chapter Six, I believe an illustration study should be just that—a study. In the course of the study, children should be actively involved in finding illustrations that interest them and, working with their teacher, developing curricular understandings from those illustrations.

The fifty illustration techniques you'll read about in this section should help you think about illustrations in a whole new way, as parallel to qualities of good writing. The techniques I name and describe should also help you notice so much more in the illustrations you see. I know that when I first started studying illustrations with children, I realized I'd been missing a lot through the years, not really thinking about what I saw in illustrations—and especially not thinking about the decision making behind what I saw. My hope is that by naming and describing all these different techniques, you too will begin to see more as you look at illustrations.

Finally, you'll find that the write-ups of these illustration techniques will become a practical reference you can use to help you think about the curriculum generated by an illustration study in your classroom. I know for certain that if you ask your students to find illustrations that interest them, much of what they find will be accounted for in the techniques I've written about across these five clusters. The knowledge base you'll build from having read about these ideas will help you teach more responsively and intentionally into your students' discoveries, even when they discover a technique I haven't written about here.

As Background Knowledge for Conferring

As you confer with young writers, having a knowledge base about illustration techniques brings more fullness to your teaching. The more you know, the more you have to offer children in direct response to their work. And once you understand the connections between illustration decisions and the qualities of good writing, you'll feel more comfortable teaching in the context of children's illustration work as you confer. As you show children techniques for illustrating with purposeful intention, you'll be simultaneously helping them understand what it means to write well.

As Background Knowledge for Other Units of Study

Whether it's how-to books, literary nonfiction, poetry, slice-of-life writing, or another genre you might be studying in your writing workshop, if children are producing the genre in picture-book form, then a deeper knowledge base about illustration techniques will inform your teaching. Nonfiction genres in particular rely heavily on the interaction between text and image, and developing a keen eye for this is critical to helping children make quality nonfiction books. The illustration techniques you'll learn about in these write-ups will help you teach into what children notice about illustrations even when some other topic is the focus of the study. They will also help you as you model using your own writing. By simply making interesting illustration decisions as you model, and by explaining them to children, your teaching demonstrations can actually have several powerful layers of meaning to them.

7

Ideas and Content, In Pictures and In Words

ONE OF MY FAVORITE ILLUSTRATIONS in my personal library of picture books was created by Laura Dronzek for Kevin Henkes' book *Birds* (2009). The background of the two-page spread is completely white, and a single black line about a quarter inch thick cuts horizontally right through the middle of all that whiteness. That's all there is. The text, written in the bottom right-hand side of the spread reads, simply, "and they were gone." These four words are a continuation of a series of sentences that begin on the previous page and tell of seven birds on a telephone wire that didn't move for the longest time, and then, "I looked away for just a second. . . ." You turn the page and they are, quite literally, gone.

My admiration for this illustration does not lie in the fact that I look at it and think, "Hey, I could draw *that*." What I admire is just the incredibly cool decision Dronzek made to illustrate it this way. "What a great idea," I thought when I first looked at it. As a matter of fact, that single illustration was enough to make me buy the book. I couldn't wait to share this book with folks who'd never seen it, get to this page, and experience the wonderful surprise of that illustration with them. And though I've shared the book a number of times now, I still find great pleasure in the response this page brings to new readers.

"What a great *idea*," I thought. I admired Laura Dronzek's *idea* for this illustration, and as a teacher of young writers who use illustrations as they compose, it's essential that I understand the importance of seeing an illustration and thinking about the idea work behind it. Idea work is something children will need to understand to become proficient writers.

95

Illustrators, just like writers, have to have and develop good ideas for their illustrations. One of the most noted and accepted qualities of good writing is the presence of solid, well-developed ideas. Writers have to have something to write about; they must have content. In Ralph Fletcher and JoAnn Portalupi's wonderful collection of lessons, *Teaching the Qualities of Writing* (2004), they wrote of ideas, "At its most basic, writing relies on the writer's ability to generate ideas. Even before a writer thinks of shaping, ordering, or detailing those ideas, she has to gather them in her mind" (8). These words are just as true of illustrations. Imagine Ralph and JoAnn had said, instead, "At its most basic, illustrating relies on the illustrator's ability to generate ideas. Even before an illustrator thinks of shaping, ordering, or detailing those ideas, she has to gather them in her mind." *Birds* is chock-full of Dronzek's rich and plentiful ideas for illustrations, and the lone empty wire stretching across the plain white page is certainly an idea that is both engaging and surprising.

Every time you turn the page in a picture book, you see the result of an illustrator's idea work. Just as writers must have ideas for what comes next and next, what to leave in and what to leave out, how much to reveal or how little, illustrators have to decide what to show in an illustration. It's a content decision they are making, just as writers make. You may be thinking, "But the words really suggest the content to illustrators, don't they?" The words do suggest content, yes, but the illustrator still has to have and develop an idea for how she will picture that suggestion.

There are lots of ways an illustration could go, just as there are many ways a writer might go with a single idea. Dronsek might just as well have drawn the empty wire with a backdrop—say, with an empty field behind it, or a row of houses, or a busy city street. She might have shown just the very tips of the birds' feathers exiting the very top of the page. She might have shown the little girl she pictures later in the book (the antecedent for the "I" in the text) looking up from the bottom of the page at the empty wire. What the reader sees pictured on this page might have been very different had the illustrator developed a different idea for its content.

Just as illustrators have to decide what they are going to picture in the picture, writers have to decide what they are going to write about. Pulitzer Prize winning author Annie Dillard wrote in "To Fashion a Text," "The writer of any work, and particularly any nonfiction work, must decide two crucial points: what to put in and what to leave out" (1987, 55). It seems so simple, put that way, but of course it's the great challenge of all writing. For example, when I started this chapter this morning, I had an idea for it. I knew I wanted to write about how the idea work that illustrators do is really a lot like the idea work that writers do. But that idea—as I just stated it—no more tells me what to write or what my content should be than "and then they were gone" told Laura Dronzek what she should put in her illustration.

My idea for this chapter was only a *suggestion* of content. I still had to decide what to write about to best develop this idea in an engaging way. There were lots of other picture-book illustration examples I might have used, but I chose the one from *Birds*. And I didn't have to start with a picture-book illustration example at all. I thought about starting with a child's illustration and then explaining the idea work the child did to make the illustration. I also considered starting the chapter by showing how often I develop ideas as a writer in my notebook, using a specific entry I'd written about green beans as an example. If I had started the chapter this way, I would have then made the connection between my idea work (as a writer) and an illustrator's idea work. I thought about several ways it *could* go, but eventually I had to decide which way it *would* go. This decision making is at the heart of the process of developing an idea.

Writing this chapter, or writing anything else, is first and foremost a process of deciding what my content will be. To write well, writers need ideas, and then they need ideas for how to express those ideas. There's nothing to organize or find just the right words for or strike just the right tone with if a writer doesn't first decide what it is she wants to say. Similarly, before illustrators can choose just the right colors or design a page or render a very specific detail, they must first decide what it is they are going to picture in the picture.

Illustrators have lots of decisions to make when they think about what the content of an illustration will be. Here are a few examples of these kinds of content decisions:

- What, exactly, will I picture in my picture?

- Will I use a single illustration, or multiple, separate vignette illustrations?

- Will I zoom in very close or zoom out and show a wide angle?

- Will I picture my subject from the front or the back? From the side, perhaps? From above or below?

- How much background detail will I use for the central image? Lots, or none at all? If none at all, should I leave it white, or use another color?

- Will I stick close to the words, or will my illustration extend them in some significant way?

The techniques included in this section are all about the content decisions illustrators make as they compose illustrations for picture books. Understanding illustrations as the end result of someone's *idea for content* will help you talk to children about illustrations in ways that support their growing understanding of this essential quality of good writing. As you talk with children about these techniques, you'll help them see that imagining the content for an illustration is not simply a matter of "drawing what the words say." You'll show them that the words are only a suggestion of content and there are many different ways they might decide what to picture in their pictures. And in doing this work, you'll be helping them learn what it means to grow and shape an idea into engaging, even surprising content— such an important thing for a writer (or an illustrator) to understand.

Technique 1

Crafting with
Distance Perspective

**Something
to Notice**

Illustrations have distance perspective: a central image may
be pictured as far away, close up, or any distance in between.

**An Illustration
Example**

In Martin Jenkins' *The Emperor's Egg* (1999), illustrator
Jane Chapman used the perspective of distance to great
effect several times in the book. In the opening spread, we see a male
emperor penguin far off in the distance. He is very small against the snowy
landscape all around him. The text on this page (7) reads, "But wait . . .
what's that shape over there? It can't be. Yes!" The illustration supports the
idea that a reader might question what is seen because it is off at such a
distance. A turn of the page shows the emperor penguin again, but this time
he's pictured as if the reader is standing right behind him, his full height filling
most of the single page. The words on this page suggest this much closer
distance as they say in big, bold letters, "It's a penguin!" Two pages over
(12–13) and Chapman has zoomed in so close, only the bottom third of the
penguin is visible; the rest of him disappears off the top of the page spread.
The close-up allows us to see the egg safely tucked on top of his feet and
underneath his warm tummy.

**An Understanding
for Young Writers
and Illustrators**

In truth, every illustration has distance perspective.
When the perspective is striking, it's because the
image is pictured far away or very close up. Distance
perspective is something children can easily try in their own illustrating. You'll
want to help them understand that if a central image is important to the
meaning of an illustration, as the emperor penguin is in *The Emperor's Egg*,
then choosing the best distance perspective is one of the first content
decisions an illustrator will make for each turn of the page. Showing the
central image from far away makes the landscape around it more prominent
in the scene and creates a sense of distance for the reader. Zooming in close
on the central image lets readers see actions or details as the focal point,
rather than the image as a whole.

As you look at illustrations that show distance perspective, talk with
children about the illustrator's decision making. Why does a faraway picture
make sense here? Why a close-up? How do the words and meaning

suggest the distance? If you want to dig deeper into the whole concept of distance perspective, you might try reading some text from an unfamiliar book (without showing the illustration) and let children think about which distance perspective the words suggest. Ask them, "How far away do the words make you feel?" The key is to stress that the meaning of the words suggests the distance. Feel free to use words like *panorama*, *close-up*, *zoom*, and *perspective* as you talk about illustrations that show clear distance decisions.

Size, of course, is very related to distance perspective. People and objects seem smaller the further away they are. Think with children about the size of people and objects as you look at pictures that show different distance perspectives. Your goal is to help children realize that how large or small they draw something in a picture matters to how close or far away it seems to the reader. Quite likely, children haven't been thinking about this as they set out to draw their pictures. They've just been drawing things and however big they are, they are. Teach toward intention and nudge children to think about distance perspective as they plan the composition of a picture. It will take most of them a long time to grow into this decision making, but that's okay. They've got plenty of time to grow.

In a Teacher's Voice: An Idea for Trying It Out   Let's say you were making a book about your dog and how he is such a faithful friend. I can imagine an illustration that shows the school bus coming up the road and there, in the distance, is your dog waiting for you in the yard. He'll be far away in this illustration, and that will probably make your reader want to see him more closely, just like you want to see him at the end of a long day away. Perhaps then you could turn the page and picture him up very close, just his face and your face in the middle of a big, welcome-home lick!

A Writing Connection   In a lecture entitled "Cinema of the Mind," included in *From Where You Dream: The Process of Writing Fiction* (2005), Pulitzer Prize winning author Robert Olen Butler explored the idea that "fiction technique and film technique have a great deal in common" (63).

> *The narrative voice in fiction is always adjusting our view of the physical world it creates, which is equivalent to another group of film techniques on a continuum from* long shot *to extreme* close-up, *and the many stages in between . . . The narrative voice always places our reader's consciousness at a certain distance from the image it's creating. It can place us at a far away distance or bring us into a position of intimate proximity by its choice of detail, by what it lets through the camera lens. (66)*

He then used a very short passage from a short story by Ernest Hemingway, "Cat in the Rain," to illustrate distance perspective in writing.

The American Wife stood at the window looking out. Outside right under their window a cat was crouched under one of the dripping green tables. The cat was trying to make herself so compact that she would not be dripped on.

"I'm going down to get that kitty," the American Wife said. (67)

Butler pointed out that in the space of this short passage, the distance perspective shifts a number of times. In the first sentence, Hemingway "evokes the full figure of the wife standing at the window . . . kind of a medium long shot. We see her fully across the room" (68). In the next sentence, we see what she is seeing out the window, the cat under the table, a longer-range shot, but then we move in for a close-up in the next sentence as we see the cat making herself compact to avoid the rain. Finally, when the woman speaks, our attention turns back to her and we see her again, closer now, speaking.

In the development of scenes, writers create a perspective of distance with words and the images they suggest, just as illustrators create a perspective of distance in pictures. If you want to understand this concept even more thoroughly, you might try lifting scenes from your current reading and think about the distance perspective the words suggest to you. If you were to illustrate those words, how close in or how far away would you imagine picturing your picture?

Technique 2

Crafting with Positioning Perspective

Something to Notice

Illustrations have positioning perspective: a central image may be pictured from the front, the back, the side, above, or below.

An Illustration Example

The big city setting in Bob Graham's *How to Heal a Broken Wing* (2008) is the perfect landscape for the author/illustrator to use positioning perspective to its full effect. In three page spreads early in the book, we see all five positioning decisions. When the bird has just flown into a window and fallen to the ground, we see it lying on the sidewalk with tall buildings looming up behind it, as if we are looking up at them from where the bird rests. On the next page, we see only the bottom halves of pedestrians walking by the injured bird; some are pictured from behind, some from the side, and some straight on. The next page shows the boy and his mother walking up from the subway below, as if we are looking down on them.

Different positioning perspectives continue throughout the book, with perhaps my favorite being on a page with no text. The child and his parents are in the living room where they've just brought in the injured pigeon in its box. The illustration is rendered as if there is a camera in the ceiling of the room and the reader is looking down on the tender scene unfolding below.

An important early decision an illustrator must make is from what position he or she will picture the central image in the illustration.

An Understanding for Young Writers and Illustrators

Like distance perspective, positioning perspective is something children can easily try in their own illustrating. Help students understand that the illustrator is in charge of how the reader sees the scene. He or she decides what to picture in the picture, and also where the reader will be positioned to view that picture.

As you look at central images positioned in different ways, talk about what the angle (front, back, side, above, below) allows the reader to see around the image. Discuss the illustrator's decision and how the picture would be different from a different angle. Do the words and the meaning suggest a certain position for the reader to view the scene? What kinds of feelings do different positions evoke in the reader? For example, something pictured from below and looking up might suggest smallness and vulnerability. Something pictured from above looking down, might suggest loneliness or isolation. Pictured from behind, images have a bit of mystery to them because the more natural face- or front-forward position is obscured. Unpack the illustrator's decision making as much as possible so children can imagine making similar decisions about their own illustrations.

In a Teacher's Voice: An Idea for Trying It Out

If we were making a book for next year's kindergartners about coming to school for the first time and how that can be kind of scary at first, I can imagine several illustrations where we might position the reader in interesting ways. For example, what if we pictured a boy or girl from behind and sort of looking up at the big double doors where you enter the school? That would probably give the feeling of how small and frightened some children feel on that first day. And we could do at least one classroom picture from above, as if the reader were in the ceiling looking down at the child in a room full of children and tables and books and centers. This would help the reader experience how some children at first feel a little lost in all the busyness of the classroom.

A Writing Connection

Just as with distance perspective, positioning perspective is really about placing the reader's visual consciousness in a scene the writer is crafting. And scenes are essential to good writing whether it's fiction or nonfiction. In *The Art of Creative Nonfiction: Writing and Selling the Literature of Reality* (1997), Lee Gutkind wrote, "Scenes (vignettes, episodes, slices of reality, and so forth) are the building blocks of creative nonfiction" (33). Writers use words to create scenes and illustrators use pictures, but in either case readers are always positioned somehow in terms of how they view the scene.

Take this scene from Jon Katz's memoir *A Dog Year* (2002) where he wrote about picking up Devon, a troubled dog he had agreed to adopt. The scene takes place in the Newark airport as the author is kneeling down in front of the dog's crate that's just been placed on the floor of the busy airport terminal.

Inside the crate, Devon was still pinwheeling. I'd yet to glimpse his face.

"Devon," I called. "Devon, I'm going to open the door, boy. It's going to be okay." I've always talked to my dogs, not because I imagine them to understand my words, but so that they can pick up my tone or mood. It's almost a reflex.

The thumping and twirling stopped, and I saw a pair of wild, ink-dark eyes. They bespoke power and intensity, as well as terror. And no wonder. In the morning, home, in laid-back, sparsely populated Texas. Then to the airport, into a crate, onto a plane's cargo hold. Takeoffs and landings, not once but twice. Holed up in the dark. Hours in the air. Unloaded down a ramp, driven across the airport's dank runways, dragged across the floor of a tumultuous terminal, confronted with a large stranger calling his name.

In those first two paragraphs, I feel as if I am looking over Katz's shoulder as he kneels down in front of the crate and peers in at Devon. The words suggest an illustration pictured slightly from above and behind Katz, his silhouette covering part of the crate that's facing forward. In the third paragraph, I imagine a montage of scenes from different angles: "unloaded down a ramp" makes me feel as if I'm below and looking up at the ramp, and with the "tumultuous terminal," I'm repositioned above the scene so I can take in lots of detail and feel the tumultuousness. Whether the tool is words or illustrations, positioning perspective is critical in the art of crafting of scenes.

Technique 3

Crafting the Background

Something to Notice   The central image in an illustration may have lots of background behind it, just a little, or hardly any at all.

An Illustration Example   In *"The Trouble with Dogs . . ." Said Dad* (2007), author/illustrator Bob Graham approached his backgrounds with lots of variation. In just two page turns you see a whole range of background possibilities. First, in one illustration the much larger dog, Rosy, lies asleep on the floor with the smaller dog, Dave, lying across her back. The only background is a bit of the floorboards stretching out to either side. On the other side of the same spread, the mother, father, daughter, and two dogs are gathered around a blue couch. The floor is pictured again, with some shoes beside the couch and a yellow pillow. A little more background, but nothing beyond the couch—no walls, no windows, no other furniture. The room is really not there. When you turn the page, what you see is very different. There is a wide panoramic view of a park with lots of green grass and straight rows of flower beds, and trees and people all about. Dave, who has cut himself lose from the family walk, is just a tiny figure in the midst of all that background.

To some degree, the amount of background an illustrator includes is connected to the distance perspective of the picture. A close-up shot of something will often fill a page, leaving little room for background. But the decision is based on more than distance. For example, on the page just before the couch scene described above, there is another couch (this one outside on a porch) pictured from about the same distance, but with lots more background around it. Graham made a very different decision in two very similar illustrations, and the words don't give much of a clue as to why. In the park scene, on the other hand, the words demand background as the reader longs to see Dave "cut a picnic party clean in two." The background is necessary to show the distance Dave has run away from the family.

Without a doubt, some illustrators choose to use more white space and less background detail as a general matter of style. Peter H. Reynolds, for example, one of my favorite author/illustrators, tends to use a lot of white space around his images and less full-color, full-page backgrounds. But in many other books you will see illustrators making a rich variety of decisions about when to include lots of background around a central image and when not to.

An Understanding for Young Writers and Illustrators

Many children don't include a lot of background in their illustrations, so looking closely with them at backgrounds can help them think in new ways about their composing. First, you'll want to help children define *background* as everything you see around the central action or image in the scene (if there is a central action or image—sometimes there's not, as in a picture of a landscape). As you look at illustrations with varying amounts of background, discuss the illustrator's decision making. Why did a lot of background make sense in this picture? And why very little in this one? Sometimes the use of background detail is clearly connected to the meaning of the words, and without it the meaning is not nearly as fully developed. If this is the case (as in the park scene from *"The Trouble with Dogs . . ." Said Dad*) talk about it with the children. Talk about how much is lost if you see only the action and not the setting all around it. And conversely, sometimes the focus on an image is diluted when too much background is around it.

If you'd like to explore this idea more fully with children, try reading scenes from beginning chapter books and talk about how much background is included around the action in these scenes. This will help children come to understand the concept in written text as they are seeing it in illustrations.

In a Teacher's Voice: An Idea for Trying It Out

If I were making a how-to book about dog grooming, I can imagine that I wouldn't need much background in my illustration of the bathing process. I could just have the sprayer, the soap, a towel, and some sort of floor or ground underneath. But on the page where I describe taking the dog for a walk in the warm sunshine to help its hair dry (not what they do at the groomer's, but what we do at the Ray house), then it would be good to include background in order to capture the feeling of taking a walk on a sunny day.

A Writing Connection

A picture book is a collection of scenes, just as a good work of fiction or an interesting feature article includes different scenes that bring the information to life. The scenes taken together, of course, have an overall setting, but then each individual illustration or scene has a setting of its own, captured in the background detail the illustrator decides to include. When crafting a scene with words, the writer must decide how much background to include, just as the illustrator makes this decision when drawing a scene. John Gardner wrote about the importance of that decision making in his book *The Art of Fiction: Notes on the Craft for Young Writers*:

> [T]he writer pays close attention, in constructing the scene, to the relation-
> ship, in each of its elements, of emphasis and function. By emphasis we
> mean the amount of time spent on a particular detail; by function we mean

If a writer devotes too much time to background that doesn't really matter, he risks losing his reader's interest. The writer who leaves out background that would help the reader understand the scene more fully, risks writing an underdeveloped plot for a story or frame for an article. If you are in the midst of reading a novel just now, it might be interesting for you to pay attention to how much background is included as you move from scene to scene. You will probably see that the amount varies a lot, as it often does in picture books.

Writers routinely ask, "How much background is necessary to show in this scene?"; illustrators ask the same question. The picture book form, of course, has an entirely different potential in terms of what makes sense to include in a background than a text comprised only of words, but this doesn't negate the fact that the decision about background must be made.

Technique   4

Showing Two Sides of a Physical Space

Something to Notice   An illustration may show two sides of a physical space simultaneously: inside and outside; above and below.

An Illustration Example   *Up, Down, and Around* (Ayers 2007) is a lively little book about vegetables that grow above the ground, below the ground, and ones that vine around. In the book, illustrator Nadine Bernard West created several scenes where the reader can see what's happening both above the ground and below the ground. In one scene, you see a beet growing underground with a mole and a bug and several burrowing worms to keep it company, while aboveground (in the same illustration) you see a rabbit munching on the beet's leaves and the frantic gardener running toward the rabbit as if to shoo it away.

In *Snow* (Rylant 2008), illustrator Lauren Stringer used this technique multiple times to show both the inside of a building and the outside at the same time. In some scenes, the reader is positioned inside looking out, as you see on the first page where the little girl is in bed asleep and through her window you see outside into the snowy night. Turn the page and you are now positioned outside looking in where you see the little girl and other children in their classroom at school. The fat, falling snowflakes loom large in your outside view, as if you are standing there truly looking inside the school in the midst of all that snow.

The idea is this: If knowing what's happening on the other side of a physical space is important for the reader to understand, the illustrator may show both sides of that space in a single illustration.

An Understanding for Young Writers and Illustrators   As you look at illustrations like these, you'll want to help children think about why it was important for the illustrator to show both sides of a physical space. What do you learn about "the other side" that makes the whole illustration more meaningful? Be sure to discuss the illustrator's decision as to which side of the scene the reader gets positioned (i.e., outside looking in, inside looking out). How does it feel to be on that particular side of the physical space?

You'll notice that there are just a few "tools" for showing two sides of a physical space. Windows, doors, and cracks are most commonly used to show the inside and outside of a space, and a horizon line of some sort—

marking ground or water or floor, etc.—is used in an illustration showing above and below. Make sure you talk with children about these common tools for illustrating in this way.

In a Teacher's Voice: An Idea for Trying It Out

One of my most vivid memories of my grandmother is seeing her inside her kitchen window over the sink as we would run from the car into her backyard. If I were to make a book about her, I would definitely want to use this technique to capture that moment when I was outside in her lovely yard and could see her inside that window waiting for me. Seeing both sides of that scene are very important to the whole feeling of that moment in my memory.

A Writing Connection

Writers often make readers aware of what's happening outside the physical parameters of a scene too. The car horn that suddenly blares and interrupts a very important family conversation around a kitchen table. The rain that pounds on the roof of a house where a frightened child is tucked into bed. The light inside a stranger's house that the stranded traveler sees in the distance. Details like these, rendered with words, make readers feel as if they are experiencing both sides of a scene at once.

In the opening scene of Ralph Fletcher's novel *One O'Clock Chop* (2007), the author used words in just this way.

"Wise Man, Four Letters."

Mom glanced over at me; I didn't have any idea.

"'Sage.'" She wrote it down.

We were sitting side by side at the kitchen table. There was a fat wedge of morning sun warming my shoulders. I yawned, feeling too lazy to focus on the crossword puzzle. Doing the crossword felt a little too much like school, which I wanted to forget, since my summer vacation had just started. (3)

That fat wedge of sunshine breaking through brings the other side of the physical scene (taking place in the kitchen) into the image. If this scene were in a picture book, the illustrator might very well allow the reader to see both inside the kitchen and outside the window as well. Sunny summer days are important because the book is a summer romance story, much of which takes place outside, so the fact that it is sunny outside is important to the overall story that will unfold.

Sometimes writers and illustrators make readers aware of the other side of a physical space just to show life sort of going on outside a scene, but often, the detail you see on the other side matters in some way to the main scene that is unfolding.

Technique   5

Using Scenes to Show Different Actions

Something to Notice   Small, separate scenes show different actions.

An Illustration Example   In *"The Trouble with Dogs . . ." Said Dad* (2007), Bob Graham drew three separate scenes with white space around them on a page illustrating the actions in a single listing sentence. Speaking of the young puppy Dave, who's always into mischief, the text reads, "He often tied Kate in knots, left small puddles on the kitchen floor, and tore holes in the tights of her school friends." The three illustrated scenes show Dave engaged in each of these actions, and the first one actually clarifies the meaning a bit as we see Kate with Dave's leash wrapped around her legs (tied in knots). Not one of the three scenes has any background detail in it at all; only the exact action of the words is pictured so that the focus is totally on the actions. Graham's idea for the content of this illustration came straight from the words, and both the sound and feeling of *items in a series* in the words lent themselves naturally to *illustrations in a series*.

Sometimes illustrators use small separate scenes to show what one action looked like at different times. In one spread of Leslie McGuirk's *Lucky Tucker* (2008), for example, Tucker the dog has gone to the dog park. The words say, "He got to play and wrestle with all his best friends." Instead of showing just one scene of Tucker at play, three scenes show him actively playing with different dogs. There is no sequence of time in these scenes; each one is just a different little snapshot of different play action.

An Understanding for Young Writers and Illustrators   Whenever you come across multiple scenes on a page (rather than a single scene), emphasize for the children this decision that the illustrator made. Talk about why multiple scenes work well with the text, and how seeing these different, separate actions is effective because we learn so much in just a small space of text and illustration. Notice whether the words name the different pictured actions (as in the first example above) or whether the words name only a single, general action and the pictures show it in different ways (as in the second example). Both are quite common. Make the point that words and pictures, working in this way, can explain a lot quickly.

Make sure children think about the necessary absence of significant background when multiple scenes are pictured on a single spread. For scenes to be separate, they can't be connected by a single background; each scene must stand alone.

If the separate scenes match a series of actions explicitly stated in the text, you might use the grammatical term *verb phrase* for the parts of the sentence(s) that name the action. The illustrations showing the different actions will help children visualize the meaning of *verb* as action, and you might as well go ahead and introduce the concept of *verb* in a context where it will make sense.

In a Teacher's Voice: An Idea for Trying It Out

Let's say that you were writing a book about how you and your best friend enjoy being together. One page of text might say, "We like to ride on our bikes, build with Legos®, and swim at the city pool." Your illustration could then show three scenes of the two of you doing these three things. Or, you might have a page that just talks about the swimming: "We like to swim at the city pool." Then you could show different scenes of you swimming at the pool—doing handstands, racing each other, diving off the diving board.

A Writing Connection

When Bob Graham wrote the sentence that matches this illustration, he was actually employing a common word-crafting technique. Writers often use a series of active verb phrases in a single sentence, packing a lot of different meaning into just the grammatical space of a sentence. When writers craft in this way, the verb phrases work almost like an overview of a big idea: *Dave was always into something.* Similarly, when Leslie McGuirk chose to show Tucker playing in three different scenes, the result is that the separate scenes on a single page build a bigger idea about the actions over time: *Tucker had a big time at the dog park!*

Nancy Gibbs and Michael Scherer employed this technique (showing different actions) with words to great effect in a *Time* magazine cover story about First Lady Michelle Obama (June 1, 2009).

> *The White House became as much Michelle Obama's stage as her husband's even before she colored the fountains green for St. Patrick's Day, or mixed the Truman china with the World's Fair glasses at a state dinner, or installed beehives on the South Lawn, or turned the East Room into a jazz lounge for a night or sacrificed her first sock to the First Puppy. (28)*

Just as we learn a lot about Dave from Graham's sentence, the verb phrases here are meant to overview a very big idea in a compressed space of text: *Michelle Obama is a different sort of First Lady.* Imagine a picture book illustration for this sentence and your mind just naturally pictures a vignette illustration showing the First Lady engaged in these different scenes. The words do exactly the same work illustration vignettes do in a picture book.

Technique *6*

Using Scenes to Capture the Passage of Time

Something to Notice   Small, separate scenes can capture what happens over time.

An Illustration Example   Sometimes illustrators use multiple vignette illustrations to show what happens over time. A common technique in nonfiction to show how time brings about change, illustrator Sylvia Long used it to great effect in Dianna Hutts Aston's *An Egg Is Quiet* (2006). On one page spread Long shows what a hen, a salmon, and a grasshopper look like as they develop inside their eggs. For each creature she uses five drawings to show how they've changed at specific stages in their development, arranging the three timelines horizontally from top to bottom down the page.

Illustrators also use multiple vignette illustrations to show action unfolding over time. Bob Graham uses this extensively in *How to Heal a Broken Wing* (2008), beginning with the fall of the bird after it has flown into the side of a building. Three successive pictures on one page show the bird tumbling down. Some of the later uses of this technique in the book are much more intricately detailed; in fact, in true picture-book fashion, the illustrations carry significantly more of the storytelling weight in the book than the words carry. In one particularly rich spread, nine separate vignettes show the sequence of actions that begin with taking the bandage off the bird's wing, to letting him test out a short, inside flight, to picking him up after the test flight proves unsuccessful and giving him a fresh drink of water.

An Understanding for Young Writers and Illustrators   Illustrators often picture multiple scenes on a single page spread, and these scenes don't show time passing (they're there for some other reason). So when scenes do show time passing, you'll want to make sure this is very clear to students. Talk about how important the sequence is to understanding what unfolds over time. Imagine why the illustrator might have wanted the reader to see something happening *over* time instead of *frozen* in time (as most illustrations are). Notice how the illustrator arranged the scenes—usually left to right, top to bottom, just like text—so you are able to read them in order.

Once an illustrator makes the decision to show something happening over time, then he or she faces the next really important question: "What, specifically, should I show and in what order should I show it?" As you look at illustrations like this, name the actions that are actually shown and think about what has likely been left out. How much time passes between them? Why do you think the illustrator decided to picture these actions? You will find that illustrators usually choose actions that show significant change and move the scene forward.

Sometimes the passage of time is marked by words in addition to multiple illustrations. When this is the case, the illustrations almost always picture the actions that are unfolding in the words. Talk about the different potentials of these two approaches (text or no text). You might also think with students about what the words *would* say in a series of illustrations without accompanying text.

In a Teacher's Voice: An Idea for Trying It Out   If you were writing about yourself and a friend going to get ice-cream cones on a hot summer day, on a single page you might use a series of illustrations to show how you go from neat stacked cones to messy dripping half-eaten cones to no cones and messy faces. Your words might say, "Eating an ice cream cone is a joy from start to finish (well, not so much the finish)." The illustrations would then help the reader experience that joy—from start to finish.

A Writing Connection   A series of illustrations showing the passage of time requires the illustrator to think in a very linear, sequential fashion: "What do I show first, and next, and next?" The order and the choice of what to show are very important. In the case of scientific showing, as with the development of eggs, *what* to picture is not the question so much as *when* on the timeline of development should you next stop and show. But with unfolding action, the decision making is all about following a meaningful sequence of actions that add up somehow and show time unfolding.

In his classic book *On Writing Well* (2001), William Zinsser wrote this about linearity and its role in writing well:

> Learning how to organize a long article is just as important as learning how to write a clear and pleasing sentence. All your clear and pleasing sentences will fall apart if you don't keep remembering that writing is linear and sequential, that logic is the glue that holds it together, that tension must be maintained from one sentence to the next and from one paragraph to the next, and that narrative—good old-fashioned storytelling—is what should pull your readers along without a tug. (265–66)

Any illustrations like the ones in *How to Heal a Broken Wing*, so clear in how they show the passage of time, can surely help students begin to get a feel for linearity in the order of ideas—and even for the feeling of tension in the movement from one idea to the next. When the illustration technique is used effectively, one picture makes you want to look at the next picture and the next. The tension of an idea that's building and gaining momentum pulls you along through the series of illustrations, just as good writing pulls you along in the way Zinsser says is so critical.

The other concept informing an illustration like this is a kind of word crafting I sometimes call "making a long story short." In a single sentence, a writer passes through lots of time and moves a whole story quickly to its conclusion. Mitch Albom used the technique in a moving piece he wrote in the *Detroit Free Press* about the disappearance of NFL player Corey Smith (March 8, 2009):

> *Oh, you get used to that in sports. Players get traded. They get injured. But Corey Smith went fishing last weekend, on a boat off Florida's gulf coast, and he never came back. The boat tipped over, the seas were rough, hours passed, and by the time rescuers arrived, three of the four passengers—including Smith—were lost.*
>
> *Not traded. Not cut.*
>
> *He's here.*
>
> *And then he's gone.*

In terms of technique, both writers and illustrators know that in a very small space—the space of a single sentence or a single illustrated spread of a picture book—a whole story can play out by simply naming (with words) or showing (with pictures) the significant actions that move the story forward.

Technique 7

Using Scenes to Show Movement Through Different Places

Something to Notice

Small, separate scenes can show movement through different places.

An Illustration Example

Dianna Hutts Aston's book *An Orange in January* (2007) follows an orange from the moment it blossoms, through its growth and harvesting, to its place on a grocery store shelf, and finally into the hands of a little boy who shares it with his friends at school. When the orange is packed on a truck for its journey to the store, the text on one page spread says, "it followed the skyway over mountains, across deserts and plains, until. . . ." Illustrator Julie Maren followed the suggestion of these words and drew three separate scenes showing these three distinct places. Each scene is inside a rounded space against a solid green backdrop, and a ribbon of road winds around the scenes and across the page. The truck can be seen driving toward the mountains on the road in the very bottom left-hand corner of the page spread.

Sometimes writers suggest movement through place—a journey—but distinct places are not suggested in the words. On one page of Anne Bowen's *When You Visit Grandma and Grandpa* (2004), the text reads, "When you visit Grandma and Grandpa, you ask, 'Are we there yet?' 'Are we there yet?' Are we there yet?' two times, five times, a HUNDRED times, until Mama says, 'Enough!' and you say, 'But how long?' and Mama says, 'Soon now. Very soon.'" Illustrator Tomek Bogacki created three scenes on this page showing the car (from different vantage points) moving along different roads and streets. The illustration clearly shows that a journey is unfolding, but the different places are far less distinct than those in *An Orange in January*. You see only different houses and trees in each one, not entirely different geographic regions as you do in Maren's illustration.

An Understanding for Young Writers and Illustrators

In many ways, this technique—like the previous one—is about movement through time as much as it is about movement through place. Help children understand that when illustrators capture movement over great distances on a single page spread, they are also capturing the passage of time it took to travel all that distance. Think with children about this decision. Why not spread out the movement through different places across pages?

Often, when great distances are captured by an illustrator on a single page, the same distance is covered in the words in a very short space, perhaps even a single sentence, as it was in these examples. The writer decides first to move the narrative forward quickly because what happens on the journey is not important; the destination is what's important. Typically, the illustrator is following the writer's suggestion.

As you talk about illustrations like this, notice the detail in the different scene locations. How distinct are the different places pictured in the scenes? What details did the illustrator include to mark the places as distinct? Typically, you'll find that the more specific the words are about the movement through place, the more specific detail you'll find in the illustrations.

Often, the mode of transport used to move through places is represented somehow in the illustration as well. It may be a car or truck moving along a road, a plane flying through the sky, a boat, a train, a spaceship, or an oxcart, but usually the vehicle or road (e.g., tracks, path, waterway) followed is incorporated into the illustration somehow. Be sure students notice this aspect of the illustrator's decision.

If you encounter an illustrator who made a different decision when the text suggests movement through place, be sure to talk about that as it will deepen children's understanding about decision making. If you read Janet S. Wong's *The Trip Back Home* (2000), for example, you'll see such a decision. On one spread the words say, "Then in our brand new traveling clothes, we flew a day and a night and a day, wiping our faces awake with hot towels when we arrived in Korea." But illustrator Bo Jia used a single illustration across the entire open spread showing a plane flying low over a field, presumably coming in for landing in Korea. He decided to just skip the journey of the words and picture the arrival at the destination.

In a Teacher's Voice: An Idea for Trying It Out

If someone were to make a book about our class trip to the aquarium in Pigeon Forge, Tennessee, you could certainly use this technique to get us there quickly and get on with telling about all the cool fish and sharks we saw there. You might start with us loading up on the bus very early that morning before it was even light. Maybe then a scene with everyone settling in and thinking about the big day ahead. And then, with a turn of the page, you could have three scenes: the bus moving down Jonathan Creek with mountains all around, the bus coming out of the mountains and onto the big interstate with trucks and cars all around, and then the bus moving along a street in Pigeon Forge with all the shops and restaurants on each side. You could also make the background get lighter in each one to show the sun coming up. The words might say, "It was a long way and took a long time to get there. We all wondered, 'How much further?' Then, we were there."

A Writing Connection   In *Live Writing: Breathing Life into Your Words* (1999), Ralph Fletcher compares controlling time in narrative to sharing something you've taped on your camcorder with friends. Most of us fast-forward through lots of the less important parts of the tape so we get right to the highlights we want our friends to see. Good writers do the same thing. Ralph says, "It's important to realize that real time is not the same thing as writing time. Good writers don't just sit back and let the tape run" (70). Good writers cut to the chase, but many inexperienced writers don't know that.

Ralph goes on to give a classic example teachers encounter with children's writing all the time:

> *Let's say you want to write about a vacation your family took to Disney World. You begin by writing about packing, going to the airport, boarding the airplane. You use up so much energy writing about the trip to Florida that when you reach the part in the story where you're actually at Disney World, you discover that you've run out of gas. . . . Many writers waste too much time carefully describing a part of the story the reader really doesn't need to know about. (70–71)*

Thinking about illustrations that show movement through place—and, hence, time—can help children begin to understand the narrative control of time in writing.

Using Scenes as a List

Something to Notice

Small, separate scenes may work like a list, showing lots of different detail but unconnected by any background.

An Illustration Example

Twice in Elisha Cooper's book *Beach*, the author/illustrator uses small, densely packed-in images, each with a little white space around them but no background connecting them, to show a whole lot of scene or object possibilities on a single page. In one of these illustrations, more than fifty different sunbathers sit or lie in a rich variety of different postures, wearing all manner of beach attire in all shapes and sizes and in every shade of tan. In another wordless spread later in the book, all sorts of natural beach debris fills the spread from side to side and top to bottom, unconnected by a background of any kind, even though the words on the previous page suggest a background: "Nearby rocks are covered with broken crab legs, shells, mussels, ladybugs, barnacles, and seaweed that looks like lettuce." The rocks aren't pictured, just the debris. This kind of illustration gives the reader the feeling of density, of *so much stuff* all cluttered about. Sometimes you will see this same technique employed but with labels attached to the images (often in informational books).

An Understanding for Young Writers and Illustrators

This sort of illustration usually engages children's attention quite raptly as they love to look closely and see more and more in it. Because of its visual appeal, the idea of making an illustration like this might hold lots of appeal for children. Your job will be to help them think about when an illustration like this makes sense as a composing decision. Focus on the illustrator's decision to pack so much into a space but keep all the images separate. Why does the illustrator want the reader to see so much in a single space? Usually it's because the feeling of *so much* is important to the meaning in the text.

The absence of background is important to think about too. How would it have been different if there were a connecting background and the images were incorporated into a single scene? Why have them all separate even when they might occupy the same physical space? The absence of background causes the reader to consider each of them distinctly rather than as one part of a larger picture.

As you talk about illustrations like this, you might want to use the word *list* to talk about what the picture pictures. Why? Because you could use words, often nouns, to name all the different things you see "listed" in the picture. And as you'll see when you read the writing connection I've included in this section, presenting a list is exactly what writers do when creating this same visual image with words. The concept of a list is very useful when the technique is connected to similar work with words.

In a Teacher's Voice: An Idea for Trying It Out

One memory I have is of my dad's fishing tackle box. I used to love to take all the different flies and lures and plastic worms out of that box and look at them. If I were writing about that, I might make an illustration like this with lots of different tackle box "stuff" on a page. The page before it would show a closed tackle box and might say, "Daddy always had great things in his tackle box. I loved to look through it." Then a turn of the page would reveal all the wonderful contents. Using individual pictures would work better than showing all the gear in the tackle box because the gear would be all bunched together in the box, and harder to see.

A Writing Connection

Writers will sometimes catalogue a scene with a list too, especially when the purpose is to show density, just as this illustration technique suggests. One of my favorite examples of this is a classic, from a description of the barn in E. B. White's *Charlotte's Web* (1952):

> *The barn had stalls on the main floor for the work horses, tie-ups on the main floor for the cows, a sheepfold down below for the sheep, a pigpen down below for Wilbur, and it was full of all sorts of things that you find in barns: ladders, grindstones, pitchforks, monkey wrenches, scythes, lawn mowers, snow shovels, ax handles, milk pails, water buckets, empty grain sacks, and rusty rat traps. It was the kind of barn swallows like to build their nests in. It was the kind of barn children like to play in. And the whole thing was owned by Fern's uncle, Mr. Homer L. Zuckerman. (13–14)*

E. B. White achieved the same effect here with words as Elisha Cooper did with illustrations. In the opening lines Wilbur's *particular* barn seems important, and there are directional details that indicate background to the image the words suggest. But then the list starts and the background of that particular barn fades and the feeling is just one of density, of so much barn stuff inside a barn.

Technique 9

Showing, Not Telling

Something to Notice

The text tells something general; the illustrations (often a series of small, separate scenes) show something very specific.

An Illustration Example

In one spread of LeUyen Pham's book *Big Sister, Little Sister* (2005), the text reads, "The big sister usually does things first. I'm the Little Sister. I'm always catching up." With white space around them, six separate scenes show the reader exactly what "things" the big sister does as the little sister catches up: losing teeth, cleaning house, flirting with boys, riding bikes, reading, and, simply, growing taller. In this case, the word *things* operates as a pronoun, and the illustrations become the antecedents for that pronoun, showing what it stands for.

Pham used this same technique three more times in the book, the words telling and the illustrations showing. When the text reads, "The Big Sister watches out for me," three illustrated scenes show what this means. In one scene, the two sisters are holding hands and eating ice cream as they wait to cross the street. In another, the big sister is applying sun block to the little sister's nose, and in the final scene the big sister covers her little sister's eyes as a couple kisses on TV. These scenes are all on one page in response to that simple, telling line of text.

An Understanding for Young Writers and Illustrators

Young children's texts are often filled with general, telling statements such as, "My mom is nice." Learning to use an illustration to show specifically what a general statement means can make a big difference in the quality of meaning in these texts. As you come across examples of this—where illustrators chose to picture multiple scenes on a page (rather than a single scene)—emphasize this decision with children. Talk about why multiple scenes work well with the text on these pages, showing several specific examples of what the words only tell.

As you talk about illustrations like this, name the text as *telling* and the pictures as *showing*. Reread parts of the text without the illustrations so children can see how a statement that only tells is really very shallow in its meaning. Conceptually, the difference between telling and showing will be very useful for children later when the talk is focused only on the craft of writing. Showing can be achieved with words just as it is with illustrations. To help children understand this, you might consider taking a page where an illustrator has used this technique and write the scenes with words.

In a Teacher's Voice: An Idea for Trying It Out

If I were making a book about my friend Kim, I might write, "Kim is always very helpful." In my illustrations, I could show several scenes depicting ways she is helpful: handing me a recipe, pinning up my pants to hem them, bringing me fresh herbs from her garden, or walking one of my dogs so I don't have to walk more than one at once!

A Writing Connection

Probably the most heralded and oft-delivered advice in the teaching of writing is "show, don't tell." The advice is simple and easily employed, especially when it's in direct response to something a writer has told in a very nonspecific way. Imagine giving this advice to LeUyen Pham: "Don't tell us your sister watches out for you. Show her watching out for you, holding your hand and waiting to cross the street, for example." Which is exactly what she did in her illustrations, of course, because this technique is all about showing. The words tell; the illustrations show.

My favorite explanation of the show-don't-tell adage is in Natalie Goldberg's now-classic book on writing, *Writing Down the Bones* (1986):

> *Some general statements are sometimes very appropriate. Just make sure to back each one up with a concrete picture. Even if you are writing an essay, it makes the work so much more lively. Oh, if only Kant or Descartes had followed these instructions. "I think, therefore I am"—I think about bubble gum, horse racing, barbecue, and the stock market; therefore, I know I exist in America in the twentieth century. (69)*

Knowing how to back up a statement with concrete pictures is a very important skill for both writers and illustrators.

Technique 10

Crafting a "Backstory"

Something to Notice

Illustrations may have characters and/or action that are never mentioned in the words.

An Illustration Example

If you saw only the written text for Cynthia Rylant's book *Snow* (2008), you would never say that the book is, in part, about a little girl and her grandmother because these two characters are never mentioned in the words. The grandmother, who likes to knit and garden and read books with her granddaughter, and the little girl, who goes to school, has a good friend to play with in the snow, an orange kitten, and a stuffed spotted dog, are both products of illustrator Lauren Stringer's idea and content development. Speaking of the book on her website, Stringer says, "The main character in the story is *snow*, however I introduce a grandma and her grand-daughter on the title page to help carry the story of snow throughout the book" (www.laurenstringer.com). That introductory illustration shows the two, along with their cat, looking out a window expectantly—as if waiting for snow.

In this beautiful ode to snow, Rylant uses a second-person point of address throughout most of the text: "The best snow is the snow that comes softly in the night, like a shy friend afraid to knock, so she thinks she'll just wait in the yard until you see her." If the text were to stand alone without the illustrations, the likely antecedent for *you* would be the reader. It's a stance that is often used to engage readers directly in thinking about a topic. The text is transformed in its picture-book form, of course, and Lauren Stringer's decision to introduce and develop characters throughout the illustrations creates a backstory for the written words.

An Understanding for Young Writers and Illustrators

Children often notice a backstory in illustrations before adults do. Hearing a text and hearing no reference to the characters or actions featured in the illustrations, children will often ask, "Who is that woman? Who is that little girl? What are they doing in this book?" As you talk about illustrations like this, emphasize the idea of two texts, one in the pictures and one in the words, doing very different work but coming together to make a single, rich text. To deepen the idea of two texts, you might reread some of the book without showing the illustrations so children realize what a different text it is without them.

Talk about other decisions the illustrator might have made. What might be pictured in the pictures if the illustrator had decided not to include a backstory? In the example I give here, for instance, Lauren Stringer might have created various snow scenes with lots of different people in them, or with no people in them, instead of using these consistent characters. If she had, it would be a very different book.

If it makes sense in the context of your talk with children, don't shy away from using the language of grammar. Talk about how Rylant used a pronoun, *you*, but she didn't say who the *you* might be; she didn't give it an antecedent. That left room for Stringer to create the *you* in the illustrations. Using grammatical terms in context and defining them as a part of natural talk will help children come to know them over time.

In a Teacher's Voice: An Idea for Trying It Out   Let's say William was going to make a book about tractors because he knows so much about them. He could have pages that told things about them like this: *Tractors have two big wheels in back and smaller wheels in front. Tractors need gas to run. Tractors last longer when you keep them in a shed or barn.* Just a book of facts about tractors. But in his illustrations, he could show a farmer and his dog on every page doing some kind of farm work with the tractor. He would never mention them in the words—only show them in the illustrations. Then his reader would be learning about tractors but also seeing how on farms, tractors play a big part in the everyday work.

A Writing Connection   Having a story unfold "behind" the main text is actually a technique writers of nonfiction sometimes use to great effect to engage readers. For example, in the midst of an informational article about animal rescue, a writer might interject small narrative scenes from the story of a single animal that went through the system, from impoundment to foster care to permanent adoption. The story unfolding alongside the information enhances the reader's experience with the information. Talking about this illustration technique creates an opportunity for young writers to begin to understand the idea that dual texts might be combined to make a more powerful whole.

Figure 1.1 Bats are nocturnal.

Figure 1.3 There are all kinds of spiders!

Figure 1.3 What do Black Widows do?

Figure 1.4 You've never seen a grape nose.

Figure 1.5 Starr's illustration of the gym.

Figure 1.4 You've never seen an apple face.

Figure 1.4 You've never seen a banana mustache.

Figure 2.1 Daniel's book: *What Do Dinosaurs Do?*

Figure 2.2   Reilly's first book about CAT® machines.

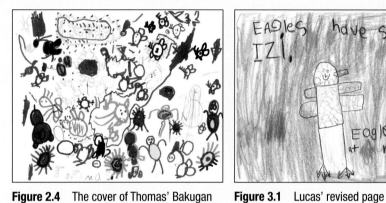

Figure 2.4   The cover of Thomas' Bakugan book.

Figure 3.1   Lucas' revised page

Figure 3.4   From Sammi's book *Seasons*

Figure 3.6   Me and Katie go to the waterfall.

Figure 3.7   Nate and Blake practice basketball.

Figure 3.8   I can paint the birds.

Figure 3.8   I can paint the world!

Figure 3.9   Ella's *Book About Dresses and Weddings*

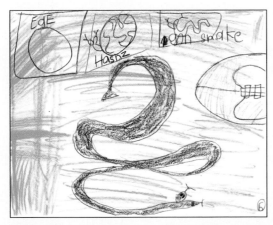

Figure 3.10   Eating the eggs.

Figure 3.10   Snakes can bite.

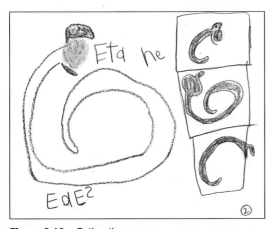

Figure 3.10   Egg. Hatches. Two-headed snake.

Figure 5.1   Anna's memoir ending

When Students Study Illustrations . . .

Here and on the following pages are illustrations from five different picture books and examples of the kinds of things students say when they study illustrations. Working from what students notice, teachers point out the decisions illustrators have made and the techniques they've used to compose a picture in a particular way.

"Let's Get a Pup!" Said Kate by Bob Graham

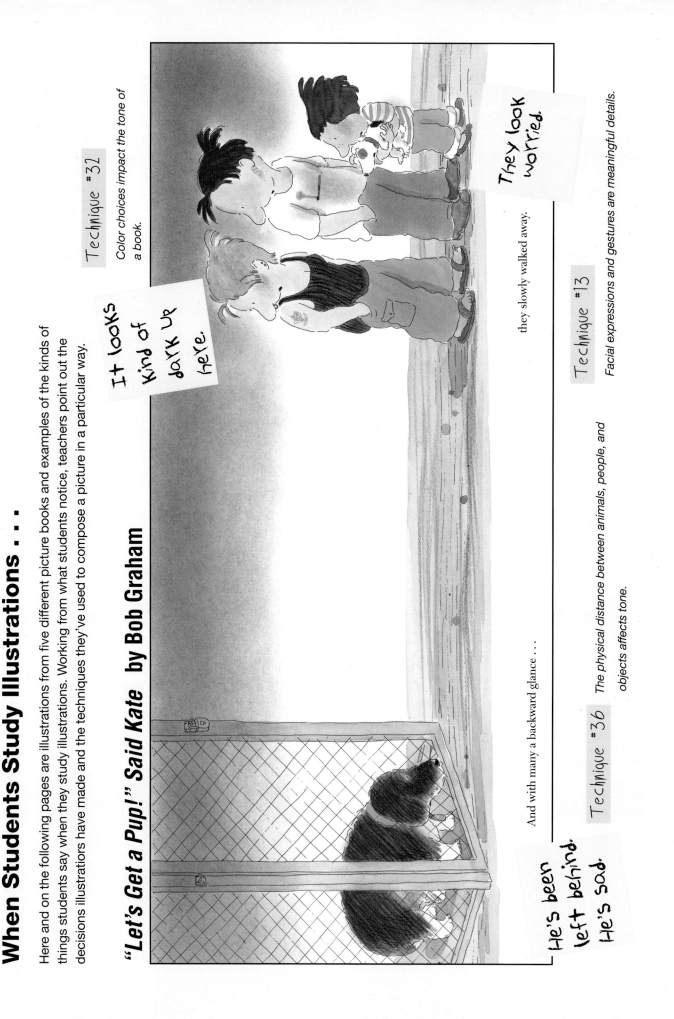

It looks kind of dark up here.

They look worried.

He's been left behind. He's sad.

And with many a backward glance . . .

they slowly walked away.

Technique #32
Color choices impact the tone of a book.

Technique #13
Facial expressions and gestures are meaningful details.

Technique #36
The physical distance between animals, people, and objects affects tone.

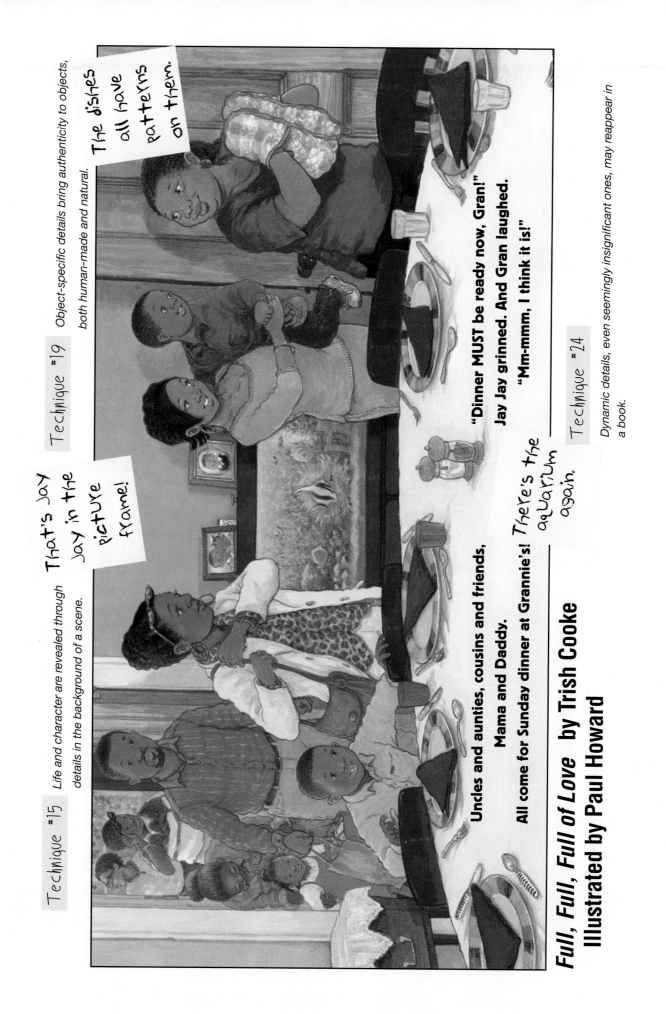

Technique #15   Life and character are revealed through details in the background of a scene.

Technique #19   Object-specific details bring authenticity to objects, both human-made and natural.

Technique #24   Dynamic details, even seemingly insignificant ones, may reappear in a book.

That's Jay Jay in the picture frame!

The dishes all have patterns on them.

There's the aquarium again.

"Dinner MUST be ready now, Gran!"

Jay Jay grinned. And Gran laughed.

"Mm-mmm, I think it is!"

Uncles and aunties, cousins and friends,
Mama and Daddy.
All come for Sunday dinner at Grannie's!

Full, Full, Full of Love by Trish Cooke
Illustrated by Paul Howard

Mural on Second Avenue and Other City Poems
by Lillian Moore Illustrated by Roma Karas

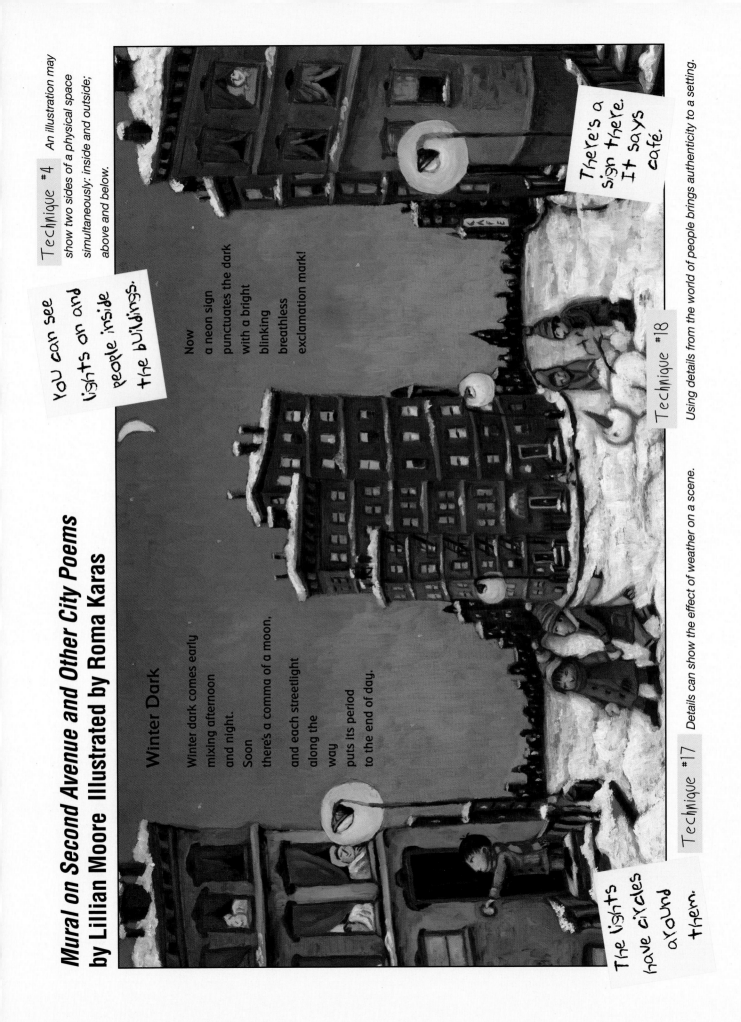

Winter Dark

Winter dark comes early
mixing afternoon
and night.
Soon
there's a comma of a moon,
and each streetlight
along the
way
puts its period
to the end of day.

Now
a neon sign
punctuates the dark
with a bright
blinking
breathless
exclamation mark!

You can see lights on and people inside the buildings.

There's a sign there. It says café.

The lights have circles around them.

Technique #4   An illustration may show two sides of a physical space simultaneously: inside and outside; above and below.

Technique #18   Using details from the world of people brings authenticity to a setting.

Technique #17   Details can show the effect of weather on a scene.

"The Trouble with Dogs..." Said Dad   by Bob Graham

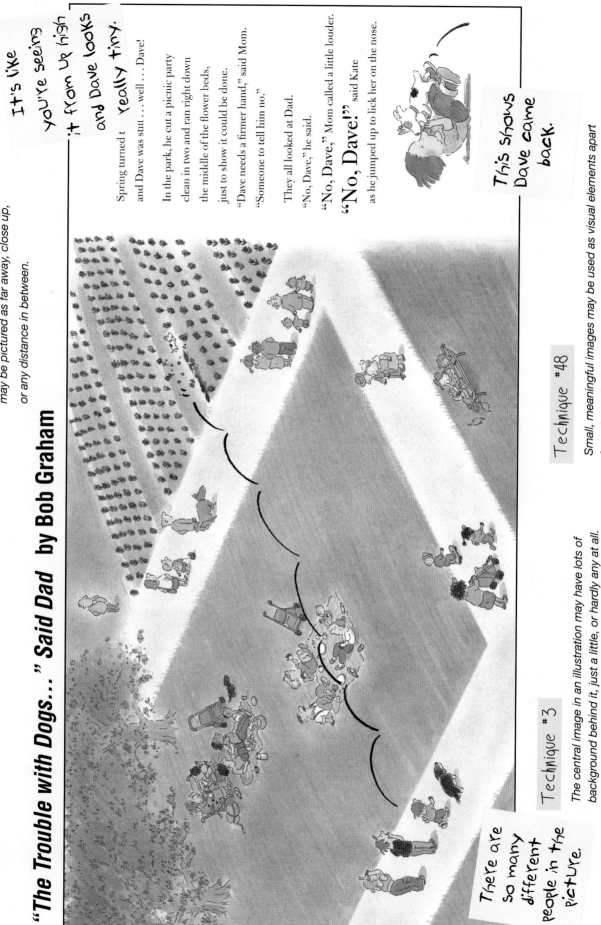

Technique #1   Illustrations have distance perspective: a central image

may be pictured as far away, close up, or any distance in between.

It's like you're seeing it from up high and Dave looks really tiny.

Spring turned t
and Dave was still ... well ... Dave!

In the park, he cut a picnic party clean in two and ran right down the middle of the flower beds, just to show it could be done.

"Dave needs a firmer hand," said Mom. "Someone to tell him no."

They all looked at Dad. "No, Dave," he said. "No, Dave," Mom called a little louder. "No, Dave!" said Kate as he jumped up to lick her on the nose.

This shows Dave came back.

Technique #48

Small, meaningful images may be used as visual elements apart from the main illustration.

Technique #3

The central image in an illustration may have lots of background behind it, just a little, or hardly any at all.

There are so many different people in the picture.

Up, Down, and Around by Katherine Ayres
Illustrated by Nadine Bernard Westcott

Technique #47
Pictures may extend into the invisible space
beyond the natural borders of the page.

You can just see their legs and feet.

The words are written curvy.

Technique #43
Sometimes the placement of words in relation to the picture
matches a specific meaning in a book.

Cucumbers climb around and around.

Technique #20   Details can create the illusion of motion.

It looks like the ants are moving.